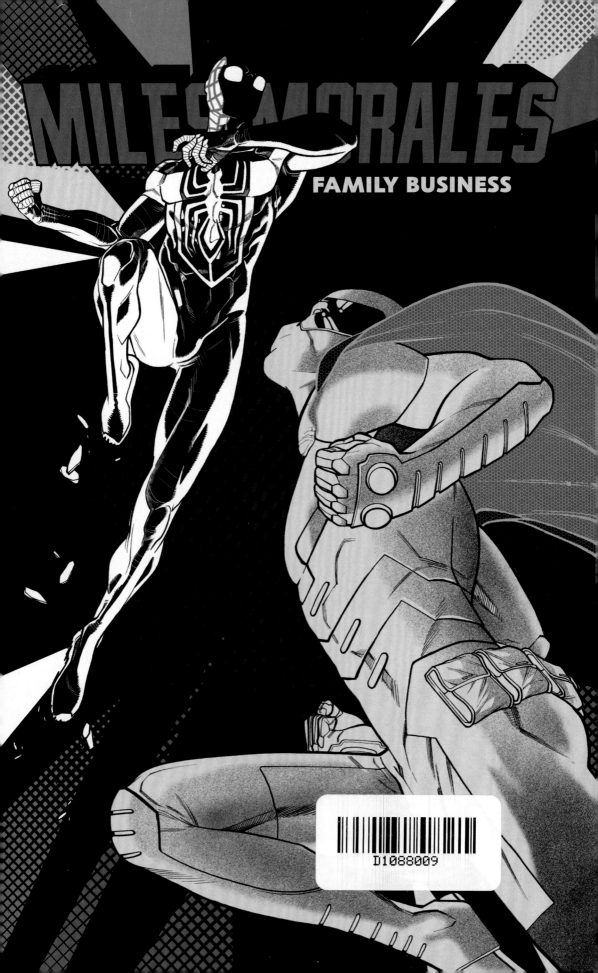

MILES MORALES

FAMILY BUSINESS

MILES MORALES

FAMILY BUSINESS

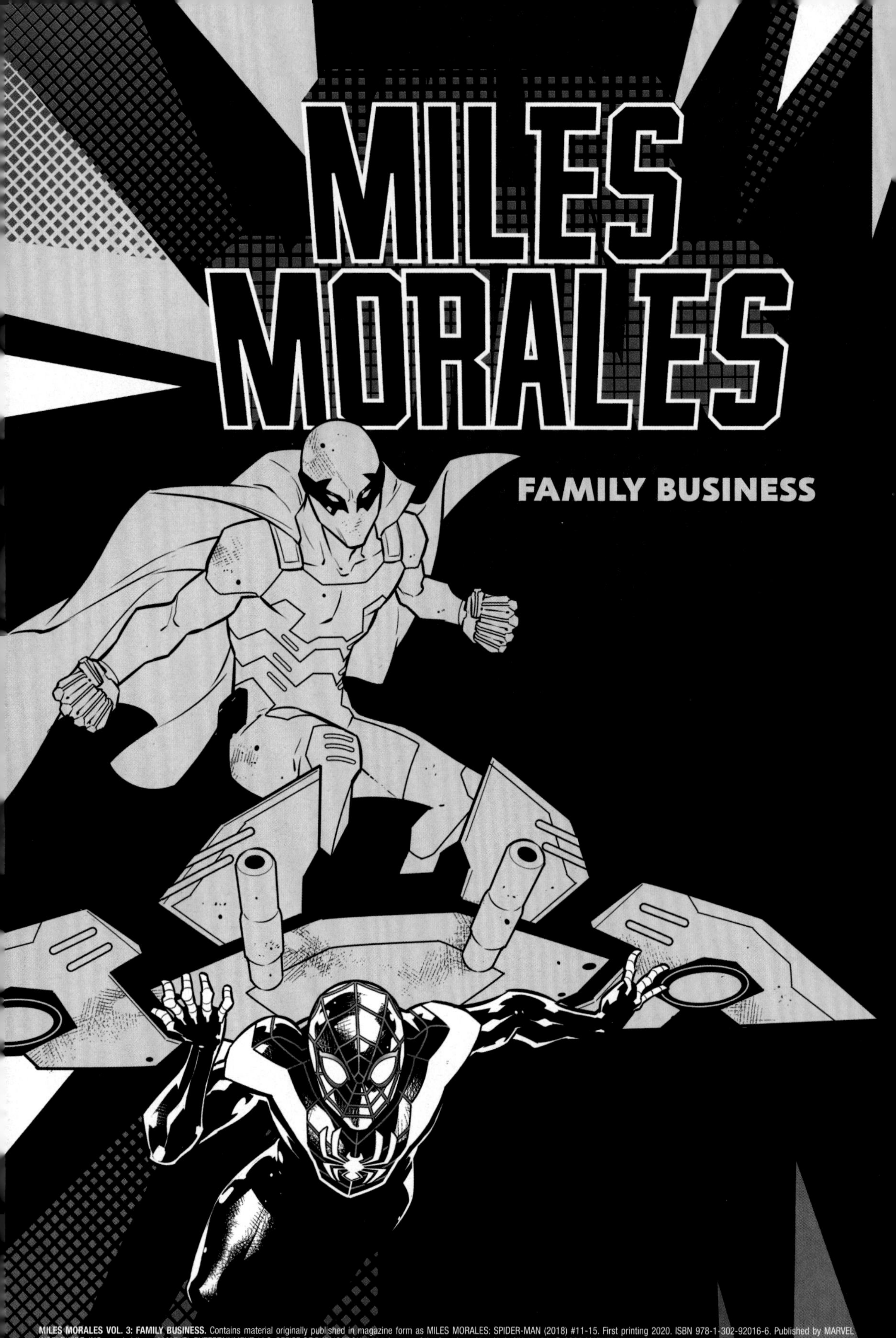

MILES MORALES VOL. 3: FAMILY BUSINESS. Contains material originally published in magazine form as MILES MORALES: SPIDER-MAN (2018) #11-15. First printing 2020. ISBN 978-1-302-92016-6. Published by MARVEL WORLDWIDE, INC., a subsidiary of MARVEL ENTERTAINMENT, LLC. OFFICE OF PUBLICATION: 1290 Avenue of the Americas, New York, NY 10104. **Printed in Canada.** KEVIN FEIGE, Chief Creative Officer; DAN BUCKLEY, President, Marvel Entertainment; JOHN NEE, Publisher; JOE QUESADA, EVP & Creative Director; TOM BREVOORT, SVP of Publishing; DAVID BOGART, Associate Publisher & SVP of Talent Affairs; Publishing & Partnership; DAVID GABRIEL, VP of Print & Digital Publishing; JEFF YOUNGQUIST, VP of Production & Special Projects; DAN CARR, Executive Director of Publishing Technology; ALEX MORALES, Director of Publishing Operations; DAN EDINGTON, Managing Editor; SUSAN CRESPI, Production Manager; STAN LEE, Chairman Emeritus. For information regarding advertising in Marvel Comics or on Marvel.com, please contact Vit DeBellis, Custom Solutions & Integrated Advertising Manager, at vdebellis@marvel.com. For Marvel subscription inquiries, please call 888-511-5480. **Manufactured between 5/29/2020 and 6/29/2020 by SOLISCO PRINTERS, SCOTT, QC, CANADA.**

Saladin Ahmed
WRITER

Zé Carlos (#11, #14), Ig Guara (#11), Javier Garrón (#12-13, #15), Kevin Libranda (#13), Alitha E. Martinez (#13), Ray-Anthony Height (#14) & Belén Ortega (#14)
ARTISTS

Dono Sánchez-Almara (#11), Protobunker (#11, #13) & David Curiel (#12-15)
COLOR ARTISTS

VC's Cory Petit
LETTERER

Mike Hawthorne & David Curiel (#11); Ken Lashley & David Curiel (#12); AND Javier Garrón & David Curiel (#13-15)
COVER ART

Lindsey Cohick
ASSISTANT EDITOR

Kathleen Wisneski
EDITOR

Nick Lowe
EXECUTIVE EDITOR

SPIDER-MAN CREATED BY **Stan Lee & Steve Ditko**

COLLECTION EDITOR **JENNIFER GRÜNWALD**
ASSISTANT MANAGING EDITOR **MAIA LOY**
ASSISTANT MANAGING EDITOR **LISA MONTALBANO**
EDITOR, SPECIAL PROJECTS **MARK D. BEAZLEY**
VP PRODUCTION & SPECIAL PROJECTS **JEFF YOUNGQUIST**
BOOK DESIGNERS **SALENA MAHINA**
WITH **JAY BOWEN** AND **MANNY MEDEROS**
SVP PRINT, SALES & MARKETING **DAVID GABRIEL**
EDITOR IN CHIEF **C.B. CEBULSKI**

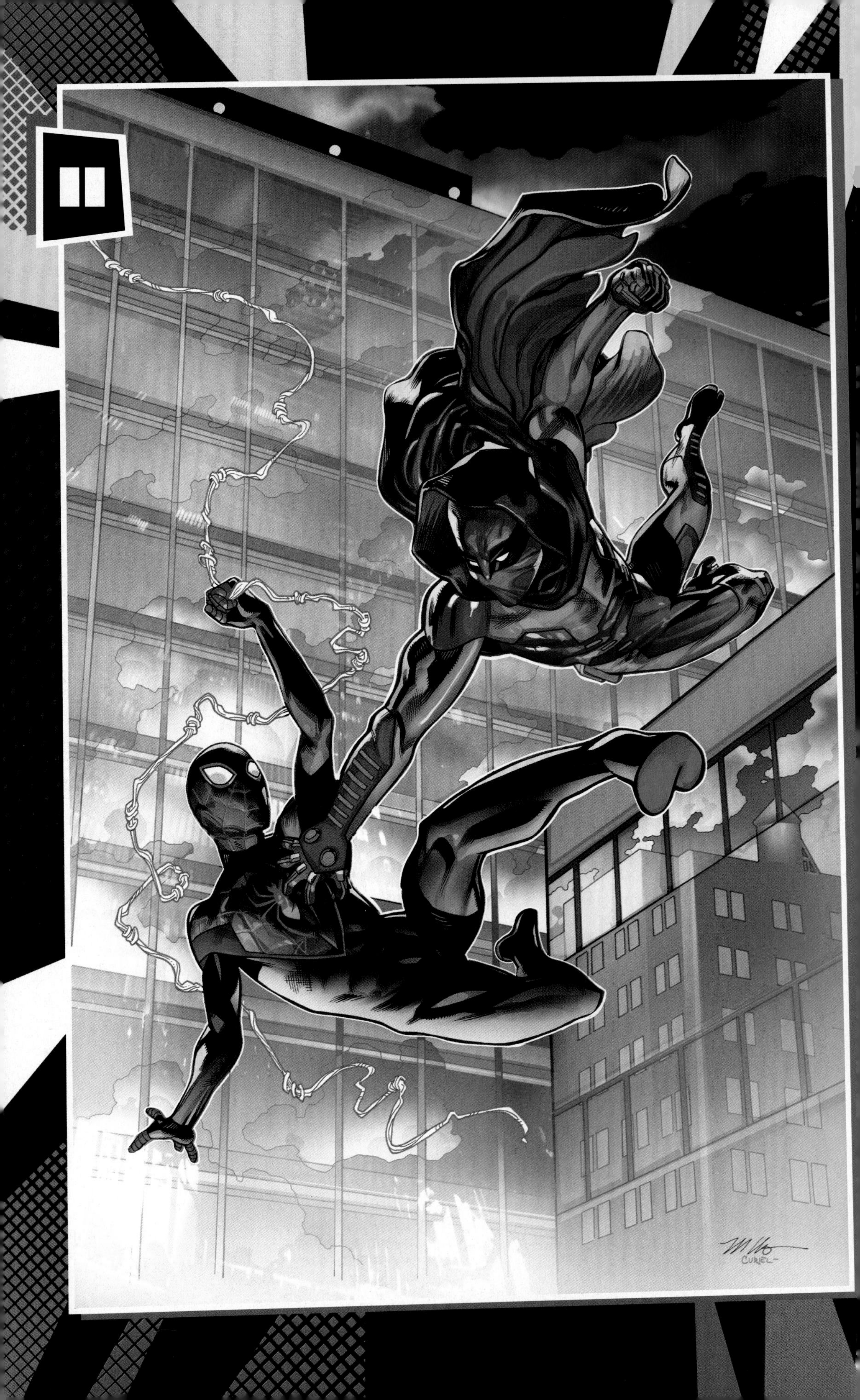

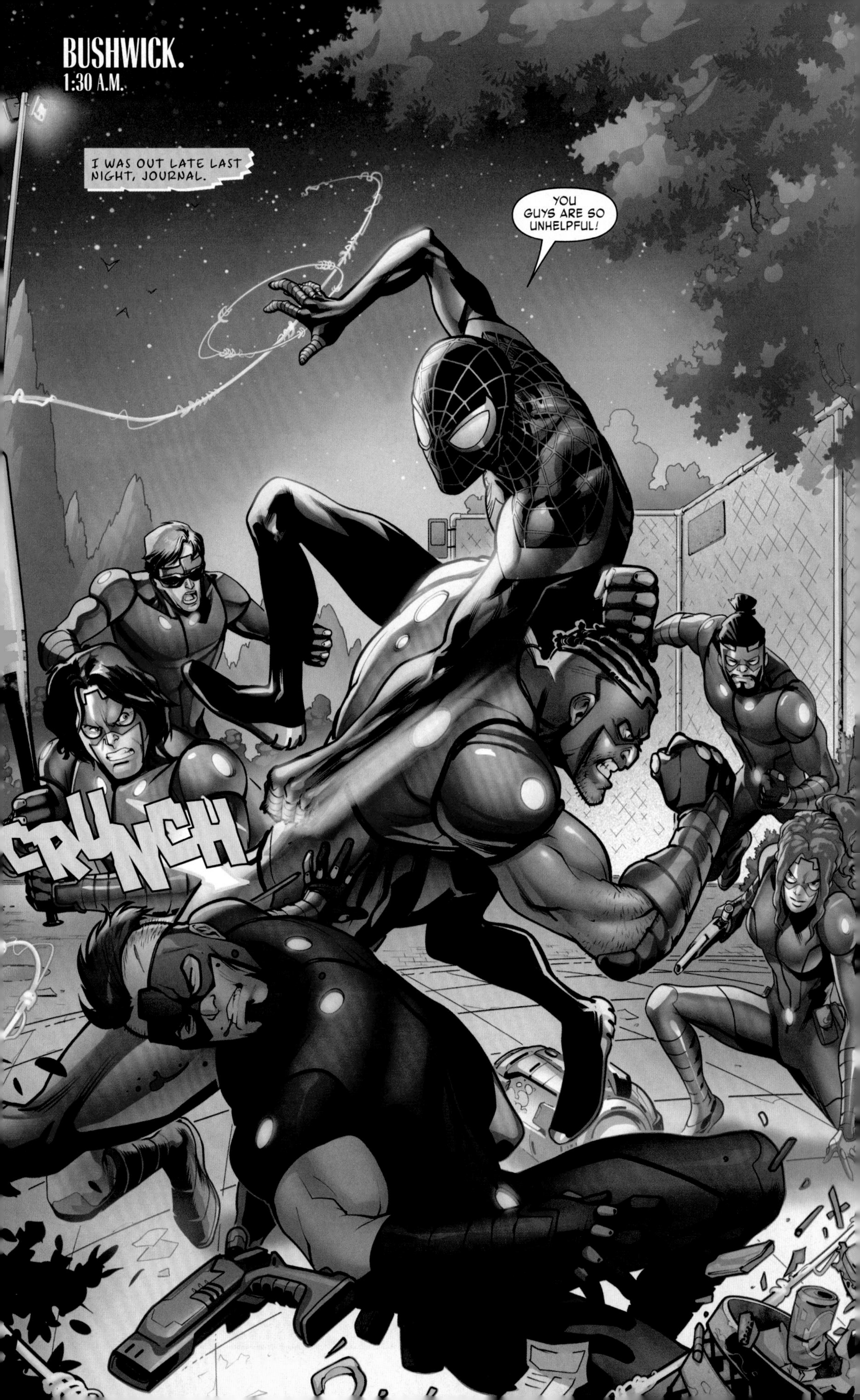
BUSHWICK.
1:30 A.M.
I WAS OUT LATE LAST NIGHT, JOURNAL.
YOU GUYS ARE SO UNHELPFUL!
CRUNCH

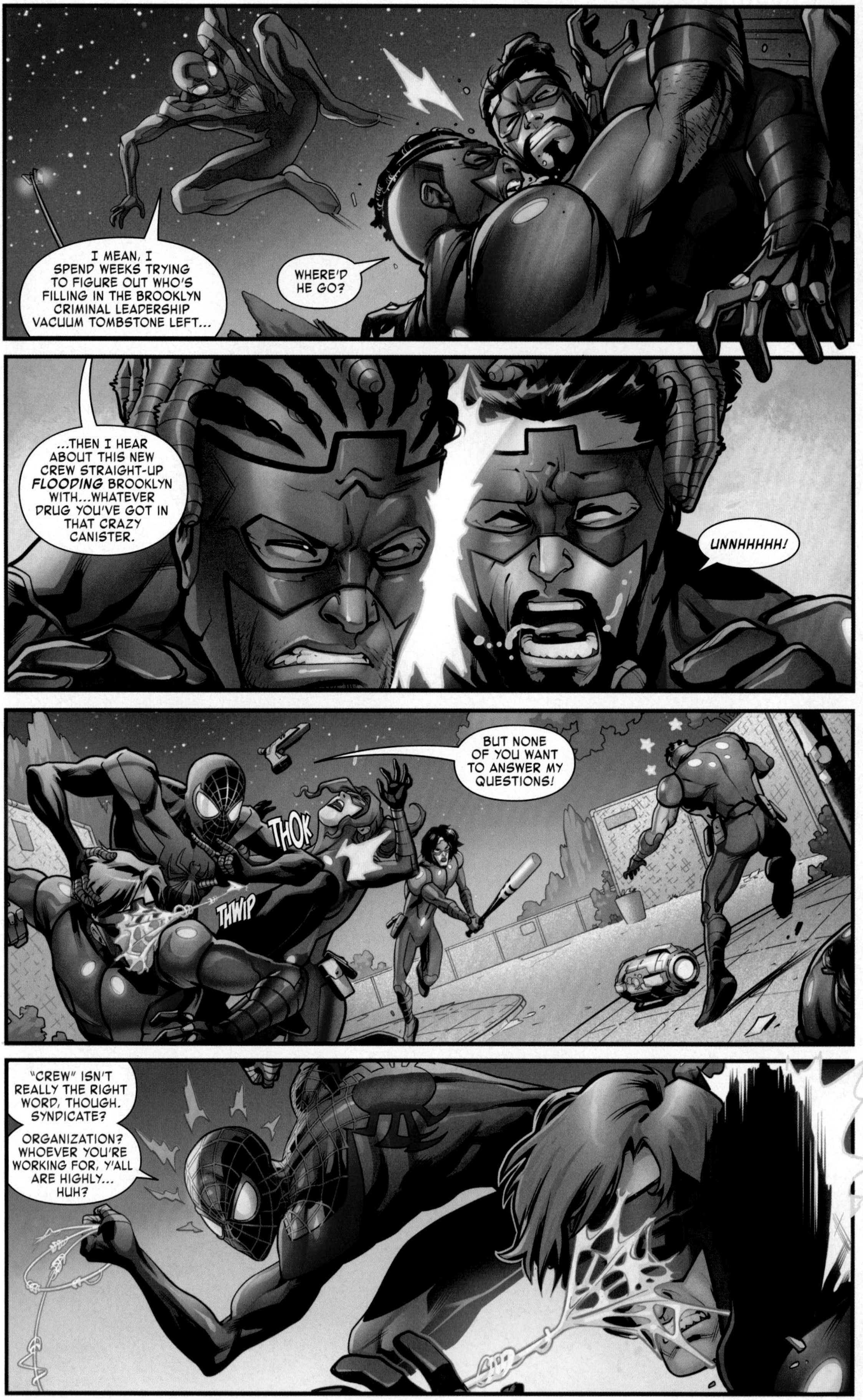
I MEAN, I SPEND WEEKS TRYING TO FIGURE OUT WHO'S FILLING IN THE BROOKLYN CRIMINAL LEADERSHIP VACUUM TOMBSTONE LEFT...
WHERE'D HE GO?
...THEN I HEAR ABOUT THIS NEW CREW STRAIGHT-UP *FLOODING* BROOKLYN WITH...WHATEVER DRUG YOU'VE GOT IN THAT CRAZY CANISTER.
UNNHHHHH!
BUT NONE OF YOU WANT TO ANSWER MY QUESTIONS!
THOK
THWIP
"CREW" ISN'T REALLY THE RIGHT WORD, THOUGH. SYNDICATE?
ORGANIZATION? WHOEVER YOU'RE WORKING FOR, Y'ALL ARE HIGHLY... HUH?

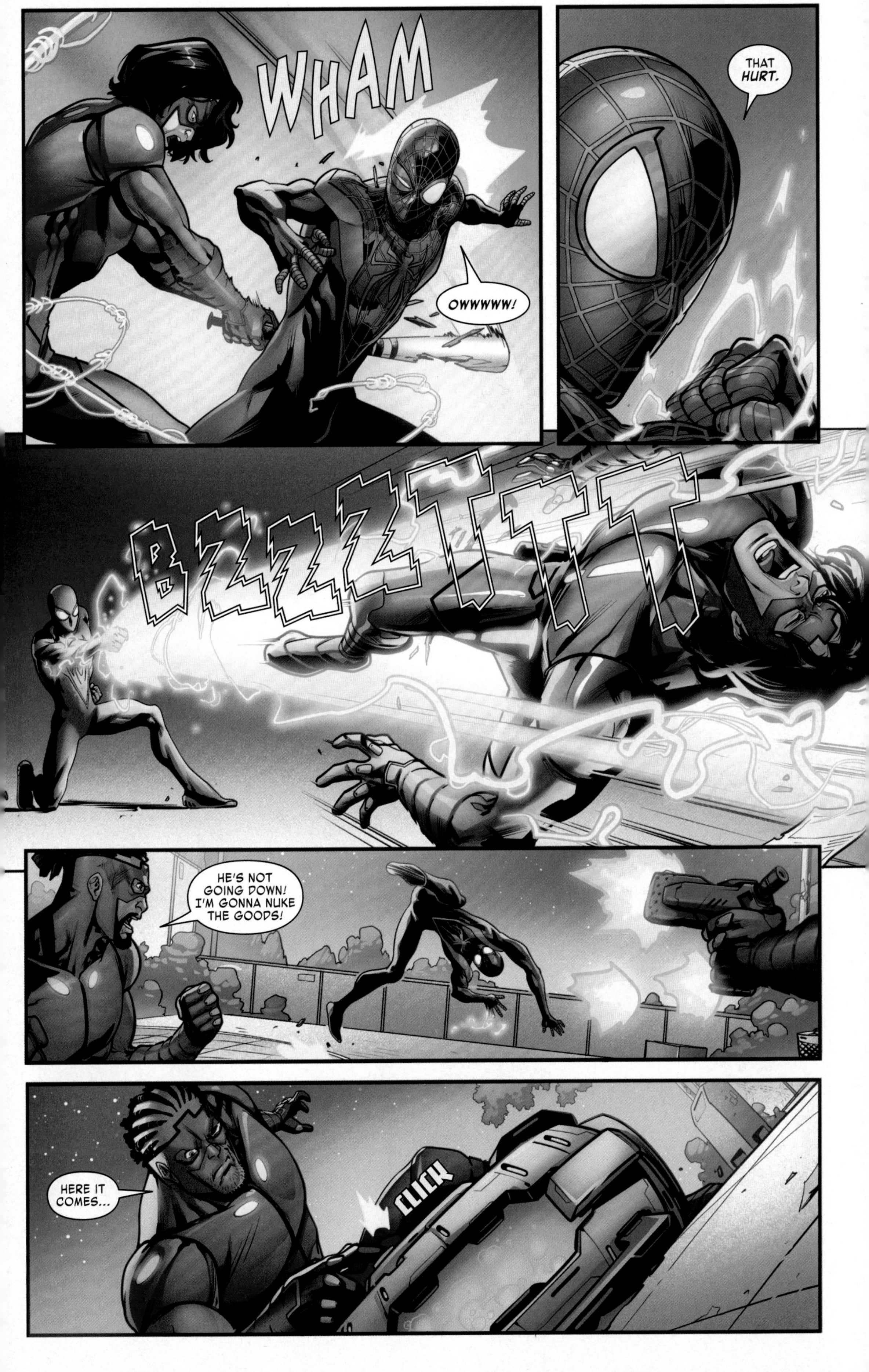
WHAM
OWWWWW!
THAT HURT.
BZZZTTT
HE'S NOT GOING DOWN! I'M GONNA NUKE THE GOODS!
HERE IT COMES...
CLICK

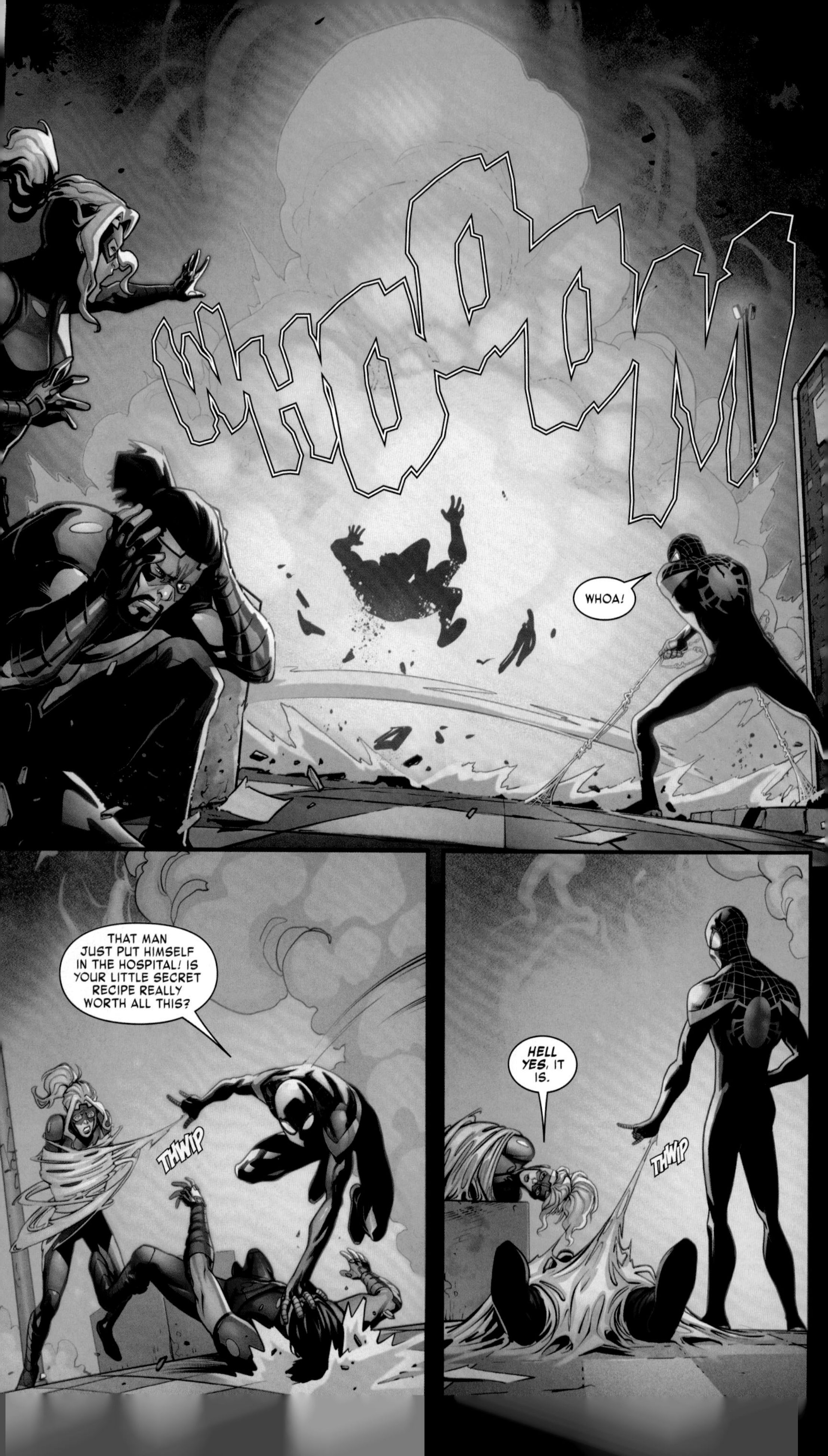
WHOOOM
WHOA!
THAT MAN JUST PUT HIMSELF IN THE HOSPITAL! IS YOUR LITTLE SECRET RECIPE REALLY WORTH ALL THIS?
THWIP
HELL YES, IT IS.
THWIP

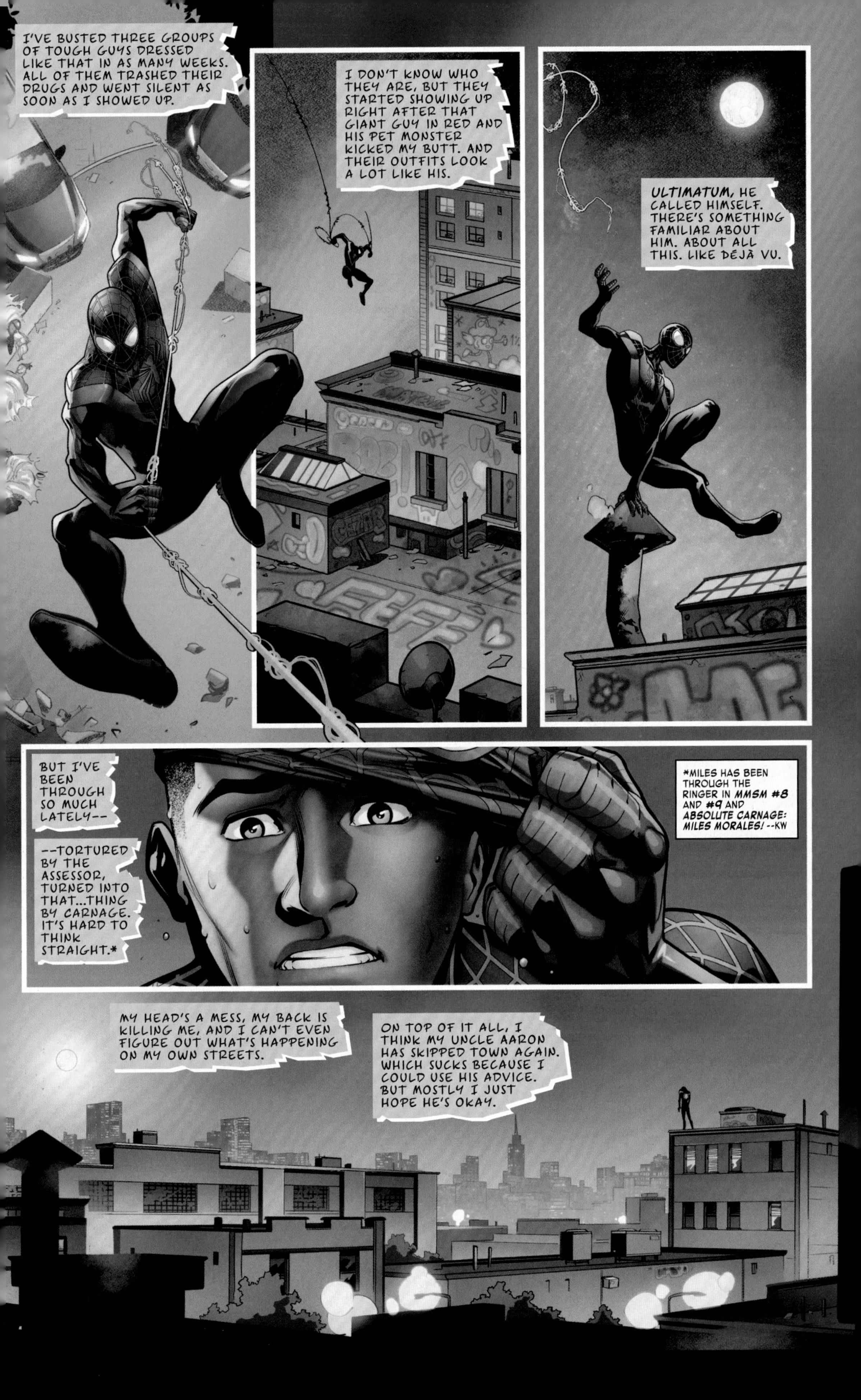
I'VE BUSTED THREE GROUPS OF TOUGH GUYS DRESSED LIKE THAT IN AS MANY WEEKS. ALL OF THEM TRASHED THEIR DRUGS AND WENT SILENT AS SOON AS I SHOWED UP.
I DON'T KNOW WHO THEY ARE, BUT THEY STARTED SHOWING UP RIGHT AFTER THAT GIANT GUY IN RED AND HIS PET MONSTER KICKED MY BUTT. AND THEIR OUTFITS LOOK A LOT LIKE HIS.
ULTIMATUM, HE CALLED HIMSELF. THERE'S SOMETHING FAMILIAR ABOUT HIM. ABOUT ALL THIS. LIKE DÉJÀ VU.
BUT I'VE BEEN THROUGH SO MUCH LATELY--
--TORTURED BY THE ASSESSOR, TURNED INTO THAT...THING BY CARNAGE. IT'S HARD TO THINK STRAIGHT.*
*MILES HAS BEEN THROUGH THE RINGER IN MMSM #8 AND #9 AND ABSOLUTE CARNAGE: MILES MORALES! --KW
MY HEAD'S A MESS, MY BACK IS KILLING ME, AND I CAN'T EVEN FIGURE OUT WHAT'S HAPPENING ON MY OWN STREETS.
ON TOP OF IT ALL, I THINK MY UNCLE AARON HAS SKIPPED TOWN AGAIN. WHICH SUCKS BECAUSE I COULD USE HIS ADVICE. BUT MOSTLY I JUST HOPE HE'S OKAY.

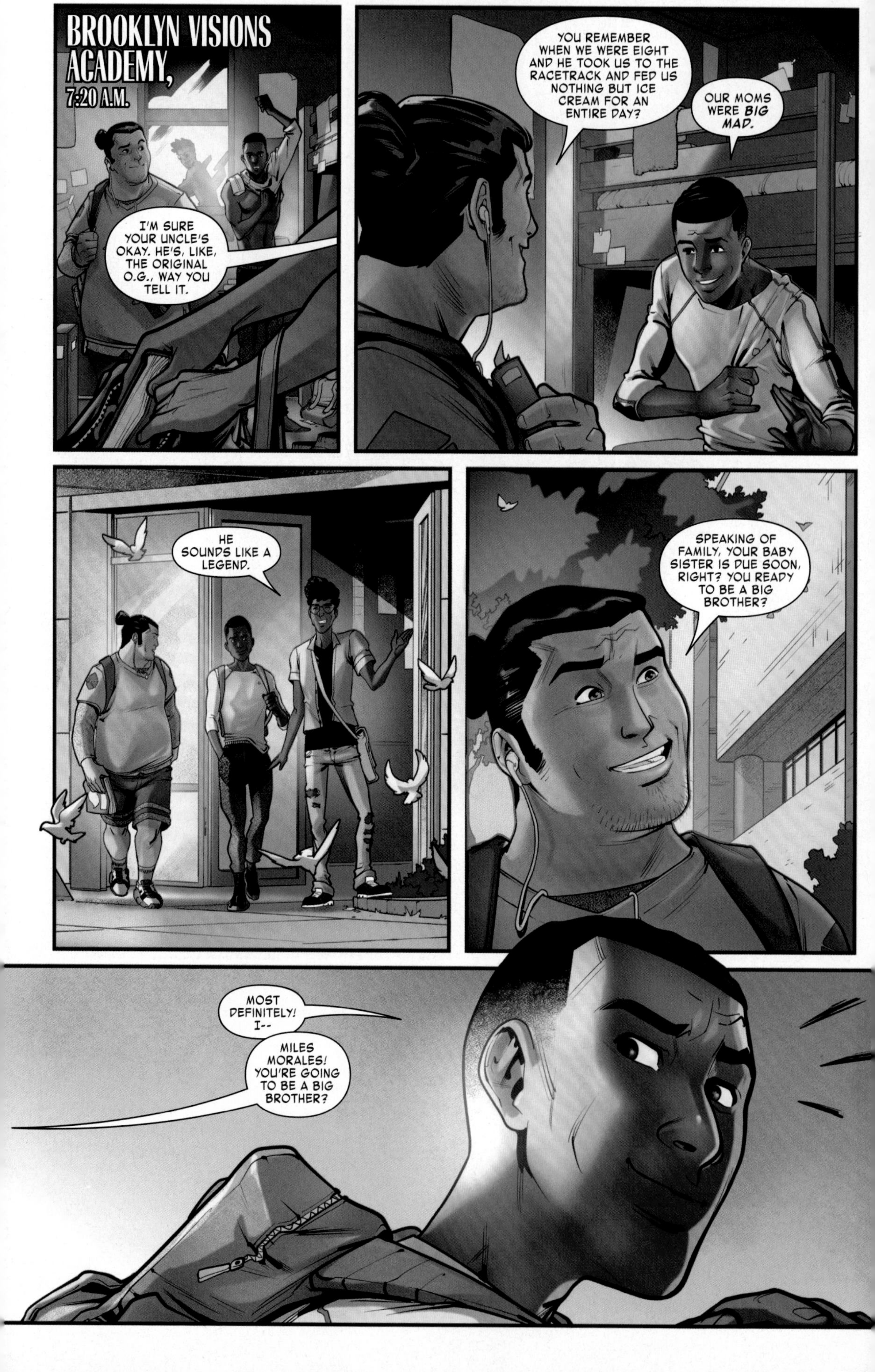
BROOKLYN VISIONS ACADEMY, 7:20 A.M.
I'M SURE YOUR UNCLE'S OKAY. HE'S, LIKE, THE ORIGINAL O.G., WAY YOU TELL IT.
YOU REMEMBER WHEN WE WERE EIGHT AND HE TOOK US TO THE RACETRACK AND FED US NOTHING BUT ICE CREAM FOR AN ENTIRE DAY?
OUR MOMS WERE BIG MAD.
HE SOUNDS LIKE A LEGEND.
SPEAKING OF FAMILY, YOUR BABY SISTER IS DUE SOON, RIGHT? YOU READY TO BE A BIG BROTHER?
MOST DEFINITELY! I--
MILES MORALES! YOU'RE GOING TO BE A BIG BROTHER?

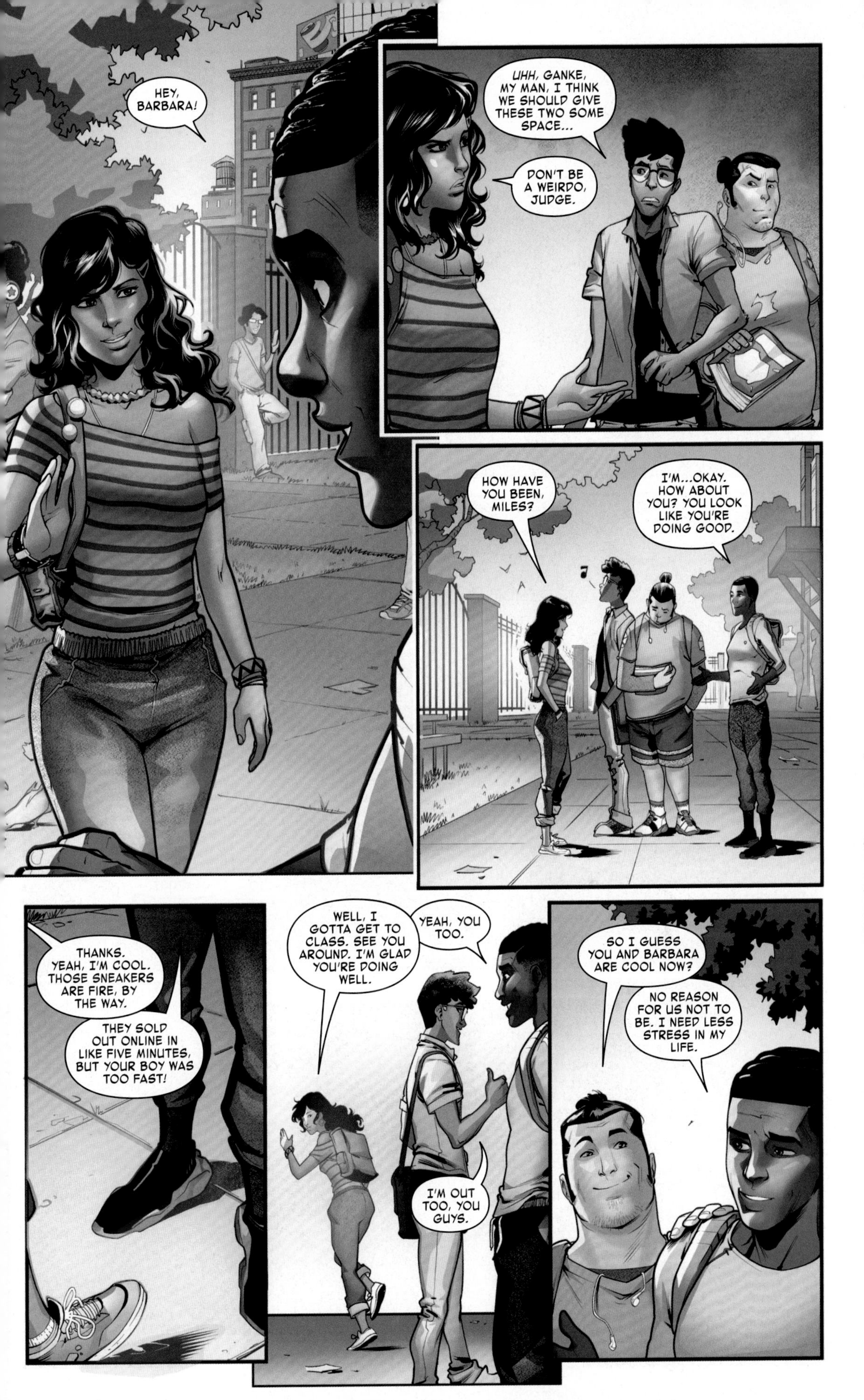
HEY, BARBARA!
UHH, GANKE, MY MAN, I THINK WE SHOULD GIVE THESE TWO SOME SPACE...
DON'T BE A WEIRDO, JUDGE.
HOW HAVE YOU BEEN, MILES?
I'M...OKAY. HOW ABOUT YOU? YOU LOOK LIKE YOU'RE DOING GOOD.
THANKS. YEAH, I'M COOL. THOSE SNEAKERS ARE FIRE, BY THE WAY.
THEY SOLD OUT ONLINE IN LIKE FIVE MINUTES, BUT YOUR BOY WAS TOO FAST!
WELL, I GOTTA GET TO CLASS. SEE YOU AROUND. I'M GLAD YOU'RE DOING WELL.
YEAH, YOU TOO.
I'M OUT TOO, YOU GUYS.
SO I GUESS YOU AND BARBARA ARE COOL NOW?
NO REASON FOR US NOT TO BE. I NEED LESS STRESS IN MY LIFE.

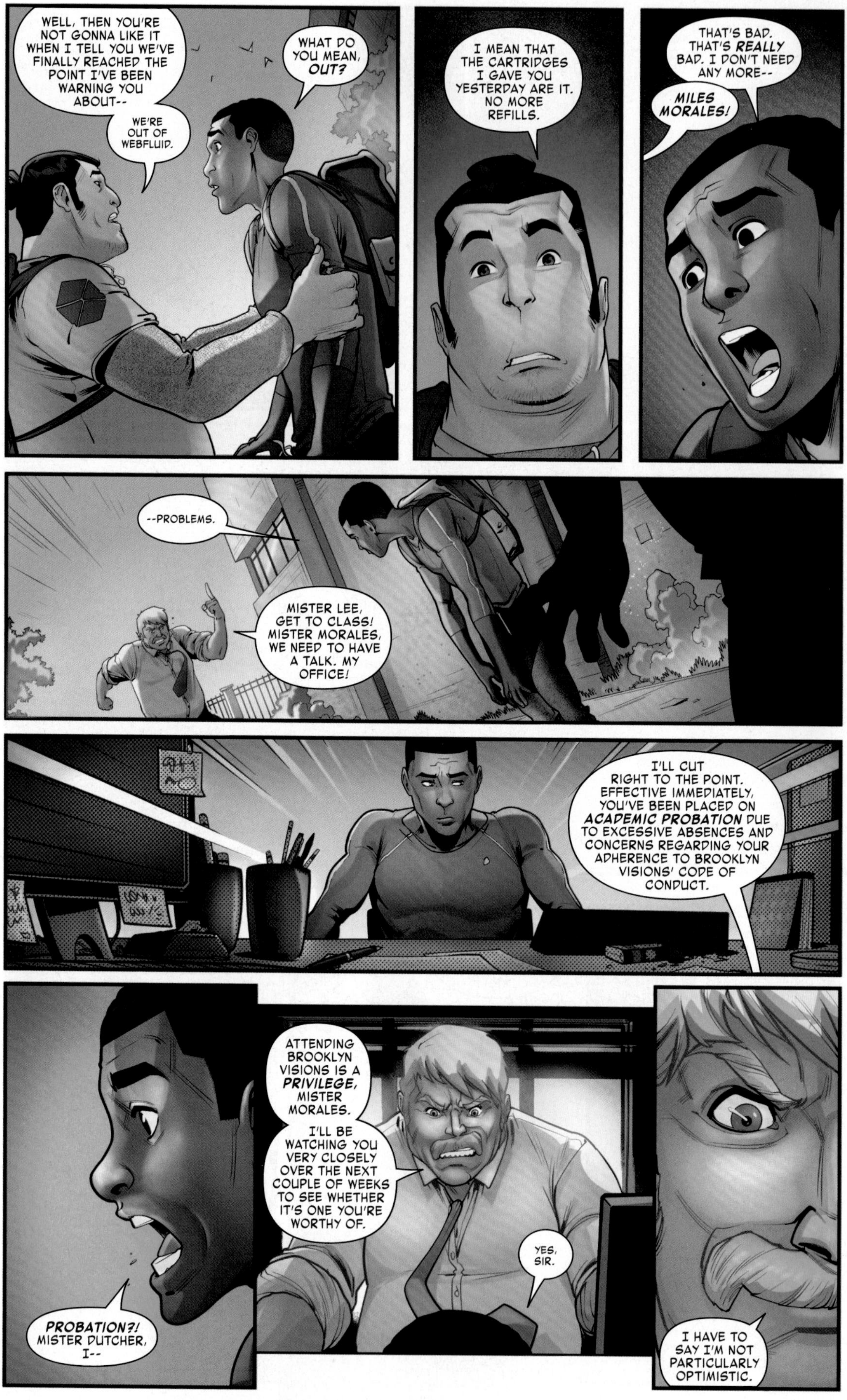
WELL, THEN YOU'RE NOT GONNA LIKE IT WHEN I TELL YOU WE'VE FINALLY REACHED THE POINT I'VE BEEN WARNING YOU ABOUT--
WE'RE OUT OF WEBFLUID.
WHAT DO YOU MEAN, OUT?
I MEAN THAT THE CARTRIDGES I GAVE YOU YESTERDAY ARE IT. NO MORE REFILLS.
THAT'S BAD. THAT'S REALLY BAD. I DON'T NEED ANY MORE--
MILES MORALES!
--PROBLEMS.
MISTER LEE, GET TO CLASS! MISTER MORALES, WE NEED TO HAVE A TALK. MY OFFICE!
I'LL CUT RIGHT TO THE POINT. EFFECTIVE IMMEDIATELY, YOU'VE BEEN PLACED ON ACADEMIC PROBATION DUE TO EXCESSIVE ABSENCES AND CONCERNS REGARDING YOUR ADHERENCE TO BROOKLYN VISIONS' CODE OF CONDUCT.
PROBATION?! MISTER DUTCHER, I--
ATTENDING BROOKLYN VISIONS IS A PRIVILEGE, MISTER MORALES.
I'LL BE WATCHING YOU VERY CLOSELY OVER THE NEXT COUPLE OF WEEKS TO SEE WHETHER IT'S ONE YOU'RE WORTHY OF.
YES, SIR.
I HAVE TO SAY I'M NOT PARTICULARLY OPTIMISTIC.

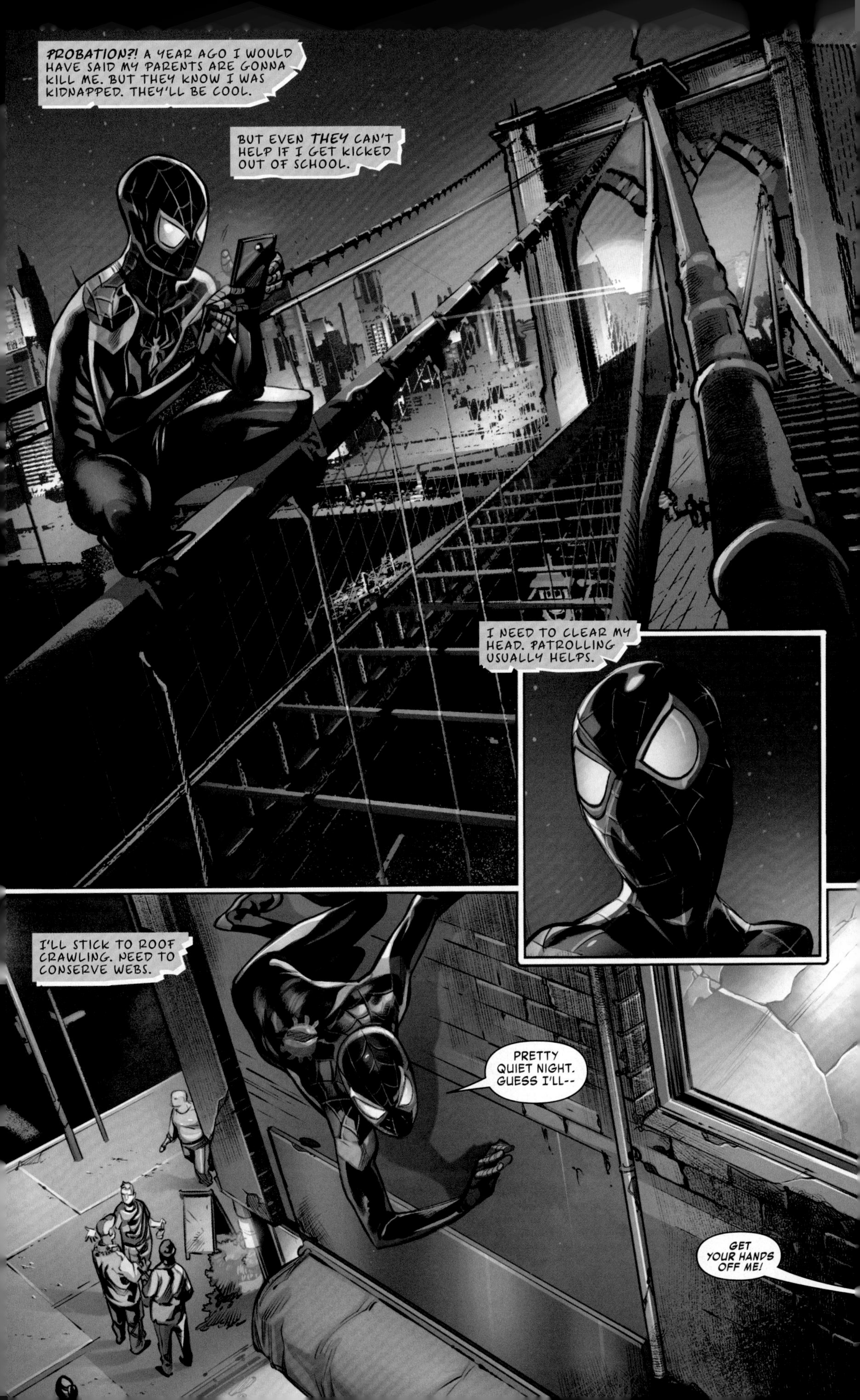
PROBATION?! A YEAR AGO I WOULD HAVE SAID MY PARENTS ARE GONNA KILL ME. BUT THEY KNOW I WAS KIDNAPPED. THEY'LL BE COOL.
BUT EVEN THEY CAN'T HELP IF I GET KICKED OUT OF SCHOOL.
I NEED TO CLEAR MY HEAD. PATROLLING USUALLY HELPS.
I'LL STICK TO ROOF CRAWLING. NEED TO CONSERVE WEBS.
PRETTY QUIET NIGHT. GUESS I'LL--
GET YOUR HANDS OFF ME!

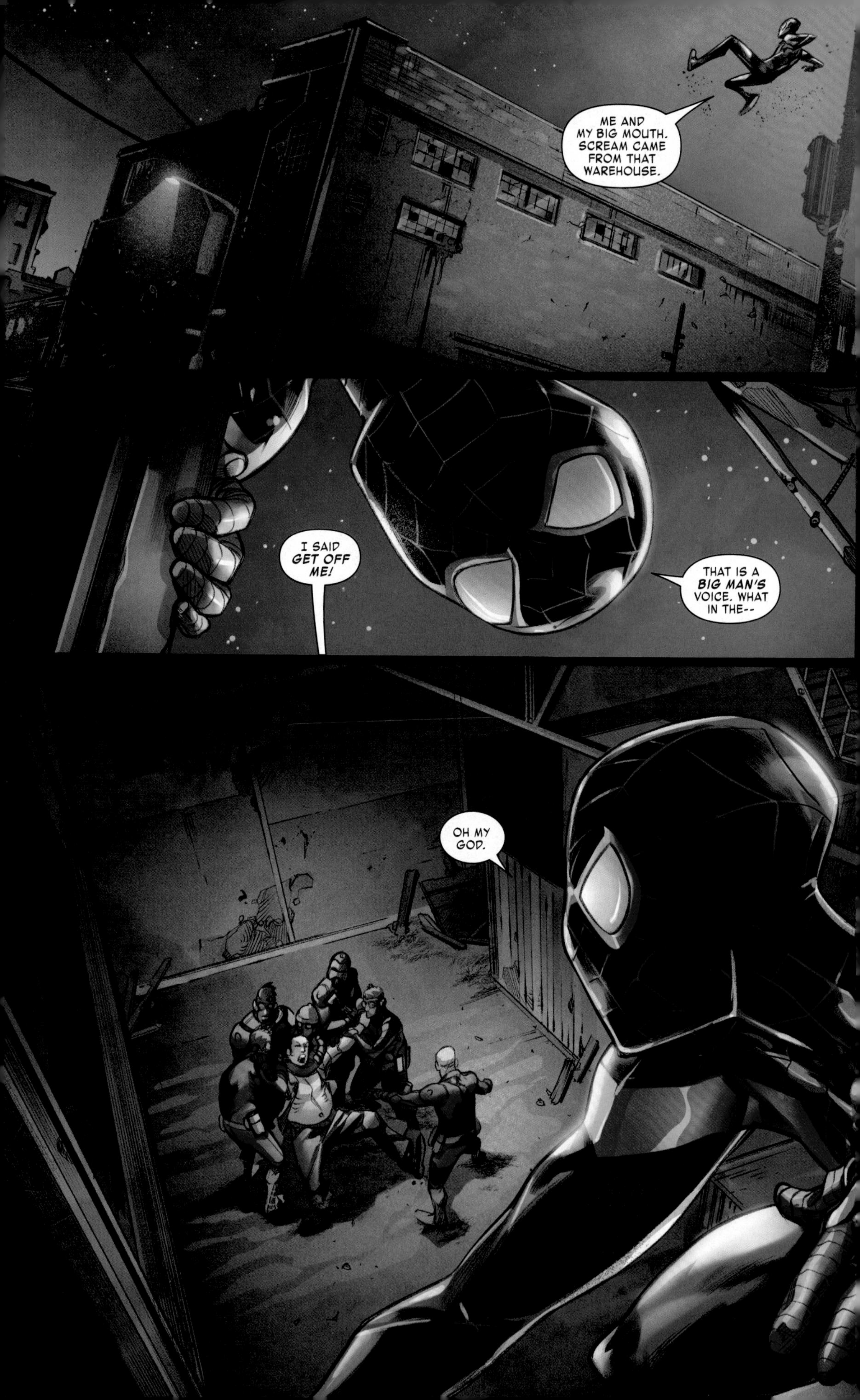
ME AND MY BIG MOUTH. SCREAM CAME FROM THAT WAREHOUSE.
I SAID *GET OFF ME!*
THAT IS A *BIG MAN'S* VOICE. WHAT IN THE--
OH MY GOD.

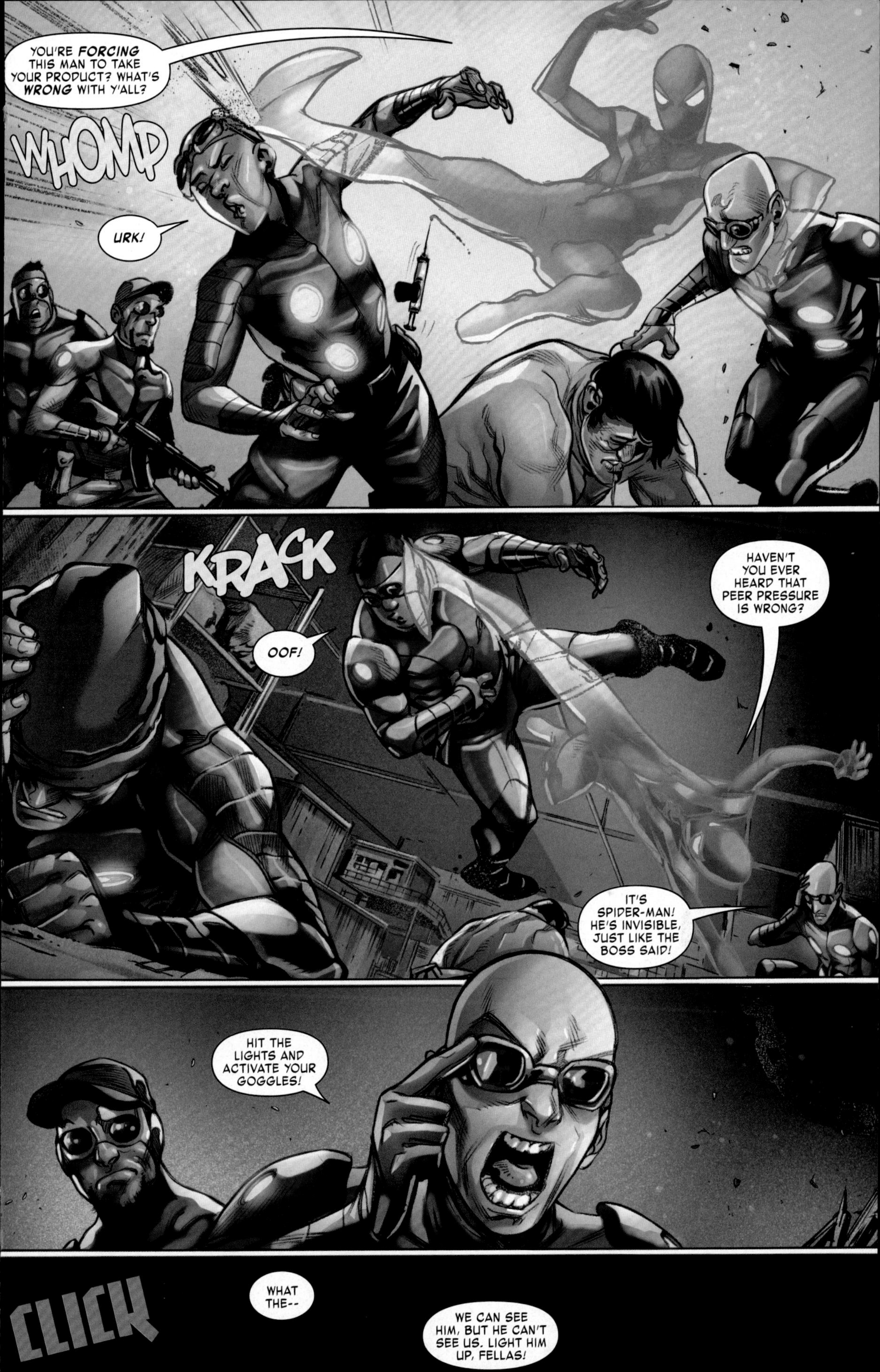
YOU'RE FORCING THIS MAN TO TAKE YOUR PRODUCT? WHAT'S WRONG WITH Y'ALL?
WHOMP
URK!
KRACK
OOF!
HAVEN'T YOU EVER HEARD THAT PEER PRESSURE IS WRONG?
IT'S SPIDER-MAN! HE'S INVISIBLE, JUST LIKE THE BOSS SAID!
HIT THE LIGHTS AND ACTIVATE YOUR GOGGLES!
CLICK
WHAT THE--
WE CAN SEE HIM, BUT HE CAN'T SEE US. LIGHT HIM UP, FELLAS!

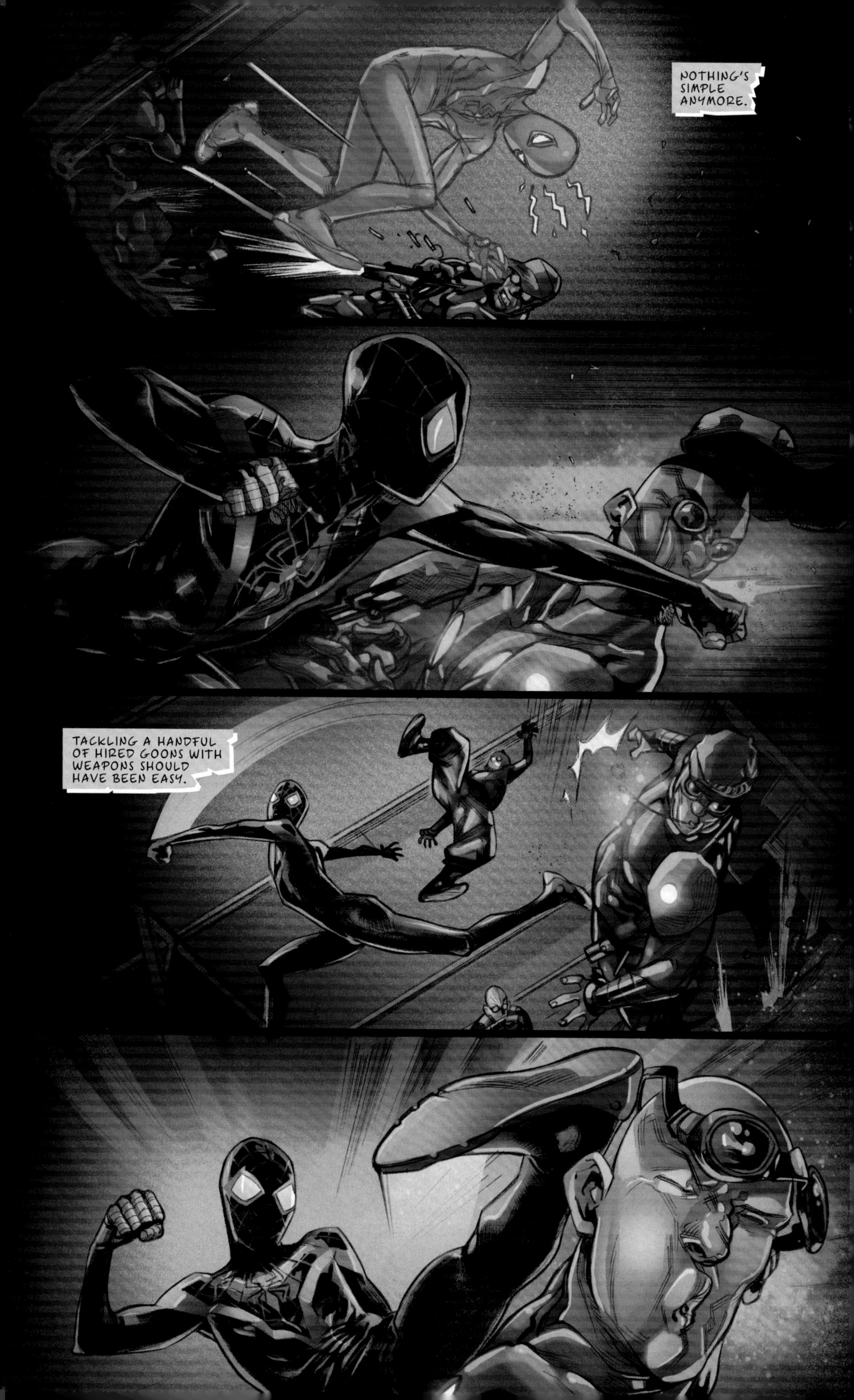
NOTHING'S SIMPLE ANYMORE.
TACKLING A HANDFUL OF HIRED GOONS WITH WEAPONS SHOULD HAVE BEEN EASY.

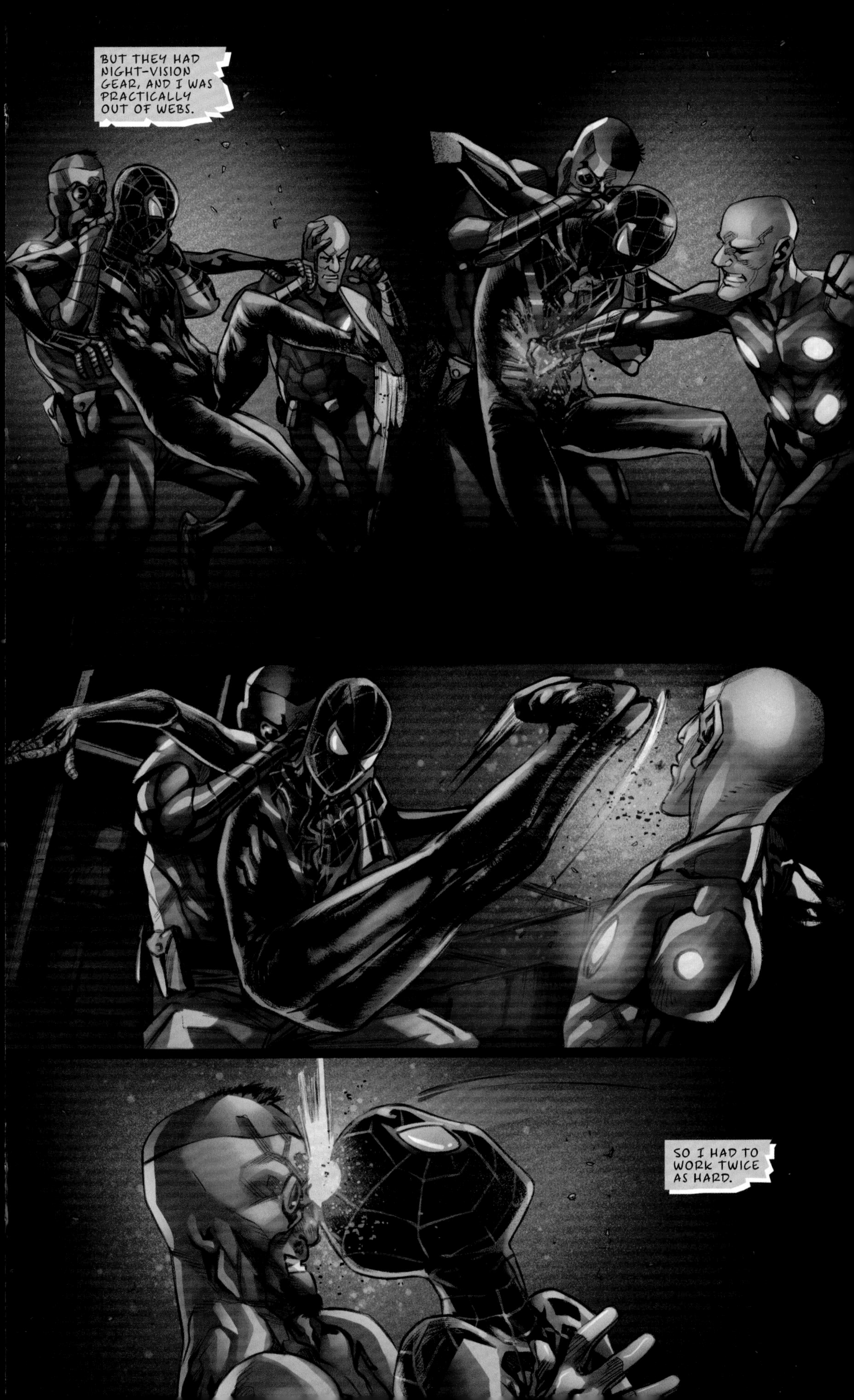
BUT THEY HAD NIGHT-VISION GEAR, AND I WAS PRACTICALLY OUT OF WEBS.
SO I HAD TO WORK TWICE AS HARD.

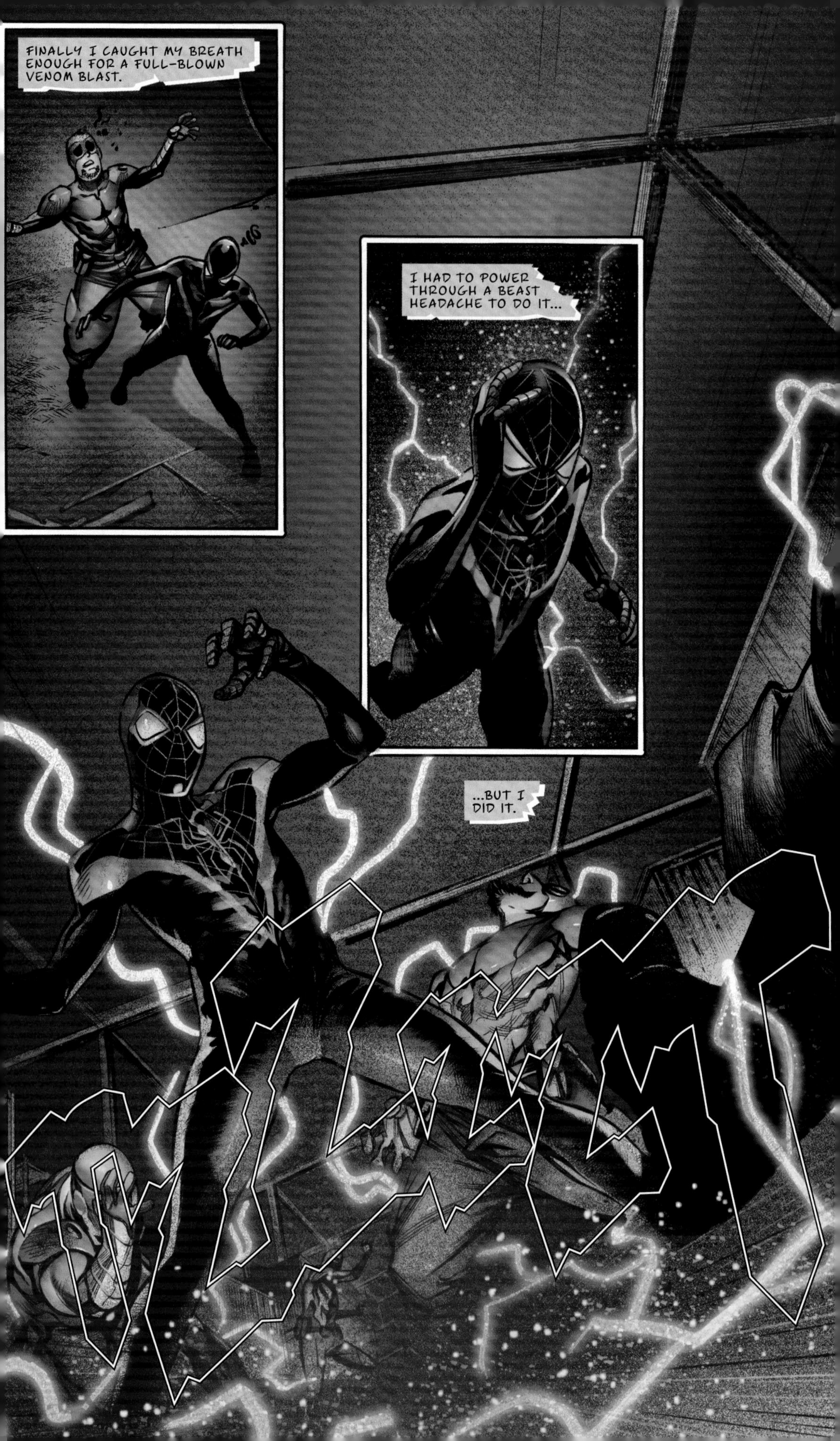
FINALLY I CAUGHT MY BREATH ENOUGH FOR A FULL-BLOWN VENOM BLAST.
I HAD TO POWER THROUGH A BEAST HEADACHE TO DO IT...
...BUT I DID IT.

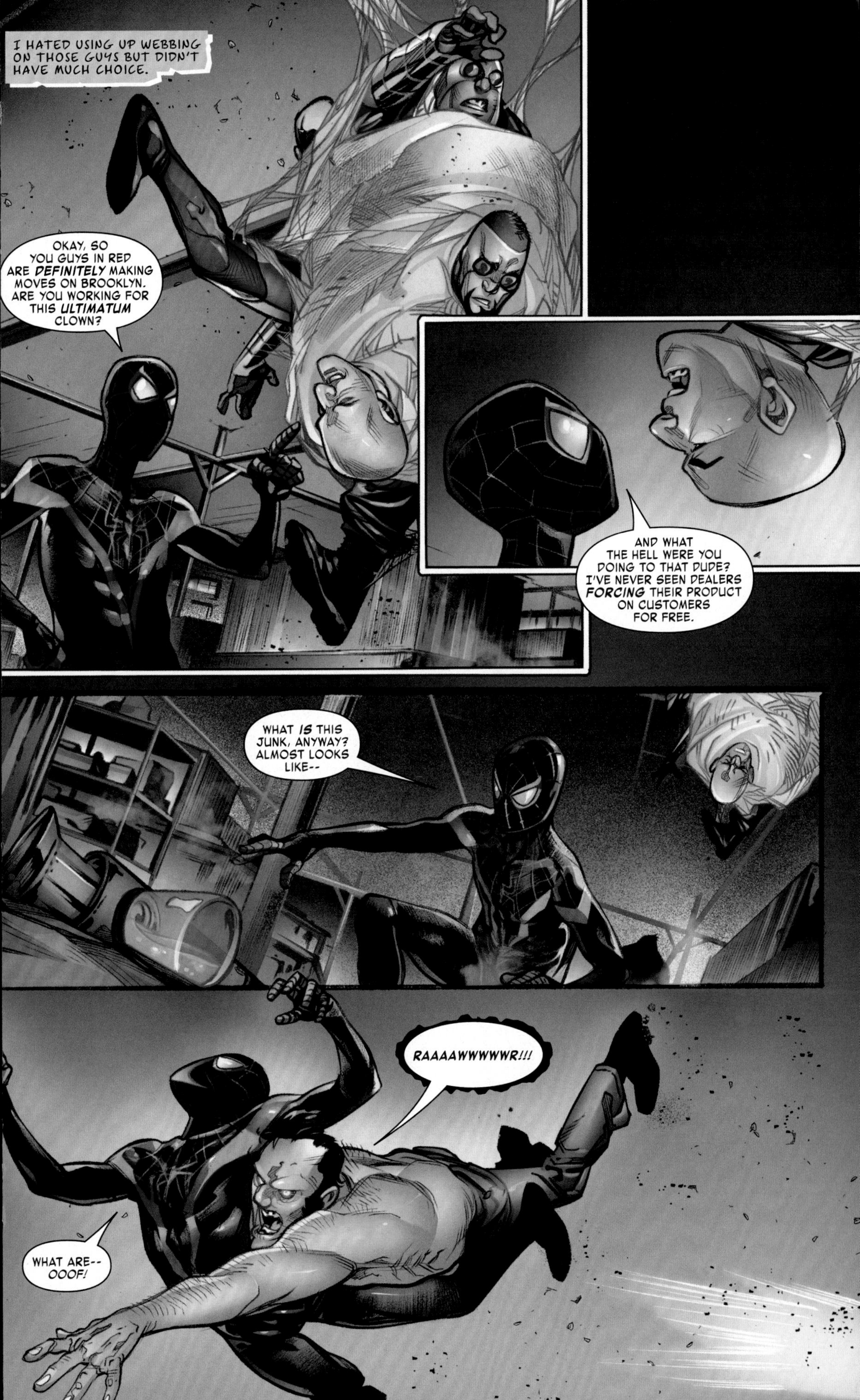
I HATED USING UP WEBBING ON THOSE GUYS BUT DIDN'T HAVE MUCH CHOICE.
OKAY, SO YOU GUYS IN RED ARE *DEFINITELY* MAKING MOVES ON BROOKLYN. ARE YOU WORKING FOR THIS *ULTIMATUM* CLOWN?
AND WHAT THE HELL WERE YOU DOING TO THAT DUDE? I'VE NEVER SEEN DEALERS *FORCING* THEIR PRODUCT ON CUSTOMERS FOR FREE.
WHAT *IS* THIS JUNK, ANYWAY? ALMOST LOOKS LIKE--
RAAAAWWWWWR!!!
WHAT ARE-- *OOOF!*

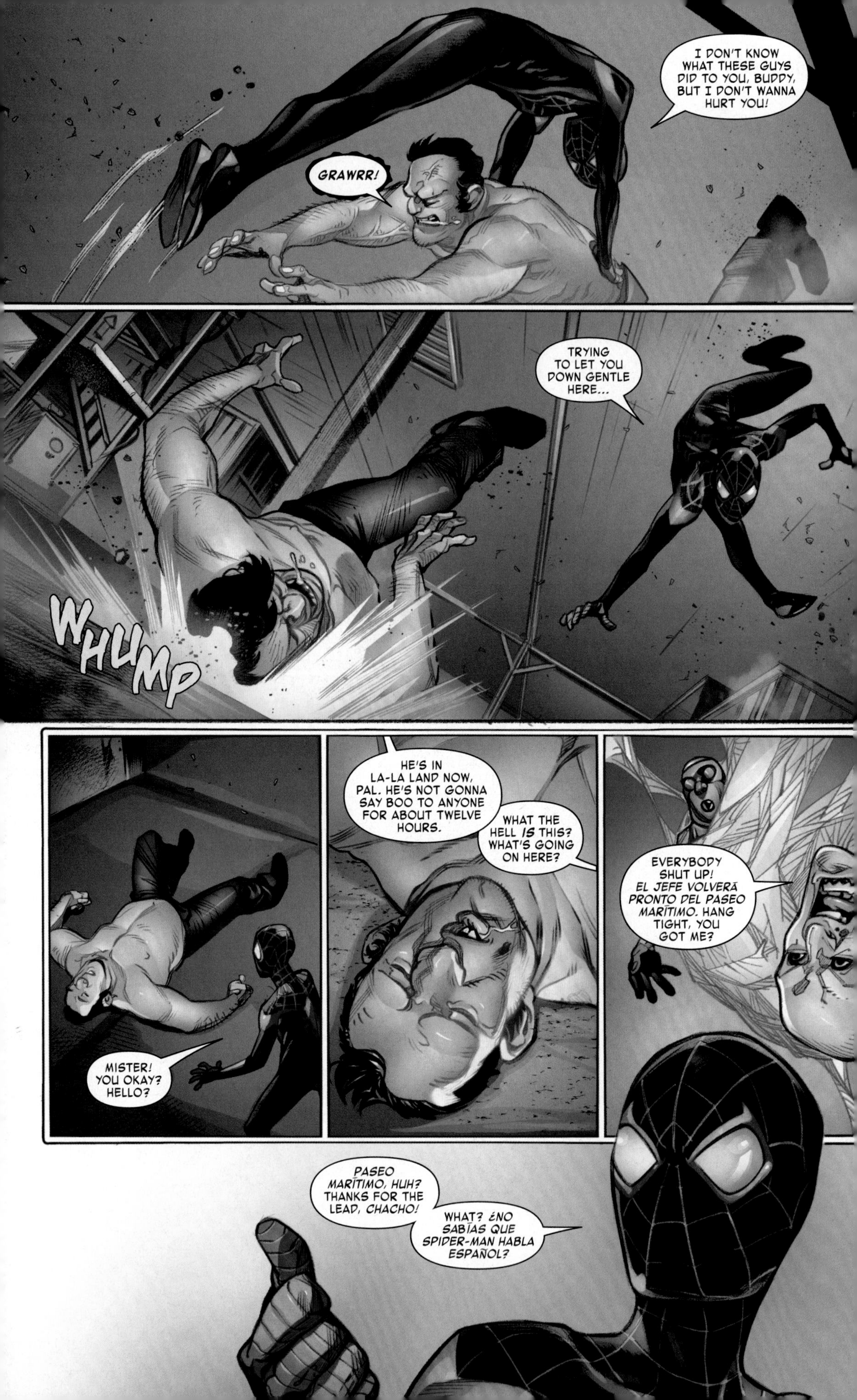
I DON'T KNOW WHAT THESE GUYS DID TO YOU, BUDDY, BUT I DON'T WANNA HURT YOU!
GRAWRR!
TRYING TO LET YOU DOWN GENTLE HERE...
WHUMP
MISTER! YOU OKAY? HELLO?
HE'S IN LA-LA LAND NOW, PAL. HE'S NOT GONNA SAY BOO TO ANYONE FOR ABOUT TWELVE HOURS.
WHAT THE HELL *IS* THIS? WHAT'S GOING ON HERE?
EVERYBODY SHUT UP! EL JEFE VOLVERÁ PRONTO DEL PASEO MARÍTIMO. HANG TIGHT, YOU GOT ME?
PASEO MARÍTIMO, HUH? THANKS FOR THE LEAD, CHACHO!
WHAT? ¿NO SABÍAS QUE SPIDER-MAN HABLA ESPAÑOL?

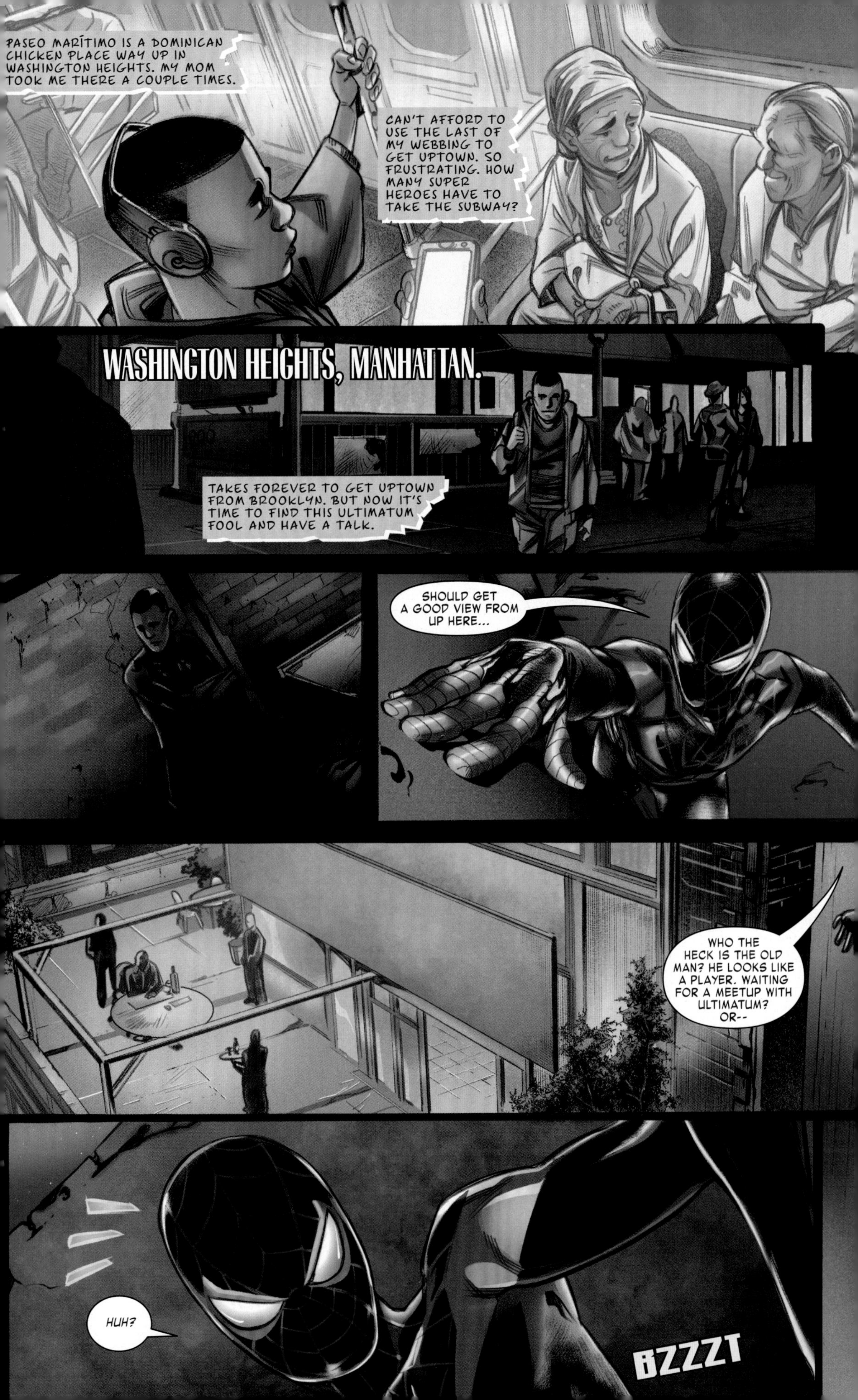
PASEO MARÍTIMO IS A DOMINICAN CHICKEN PLACE WAY UP IN WASHINGTON HEIGHTS. MY MOM TOOK ME THERE A COUPLE TIMES.
CAN'T AFFORD TO USE THE LAST OF MY WEBBING TO GET UPTOWN. SO FRUSTRATING. HOW MANY SUPER HEROES HAVE TO TAKE THE SUBWAY?
WASHINGTON HEIGHTS, MANHATTAN.
TAKES FOREVER TO GET UPTOWN FROM BROOKLYN. BUT NOW IT'S TIME TO FIND THIS ULTIMATUM FOOL AND HAVE A TALK.
SHOULD GET A GOOD VIEW FROM UP HERE...
WHO THE HECK IS THE OLD MAN? HE LOOKS LIKE A PLAYER. WAITING FOR A MEETUP WITH ULTIMATUM? OR--
HUH?
BZZZT

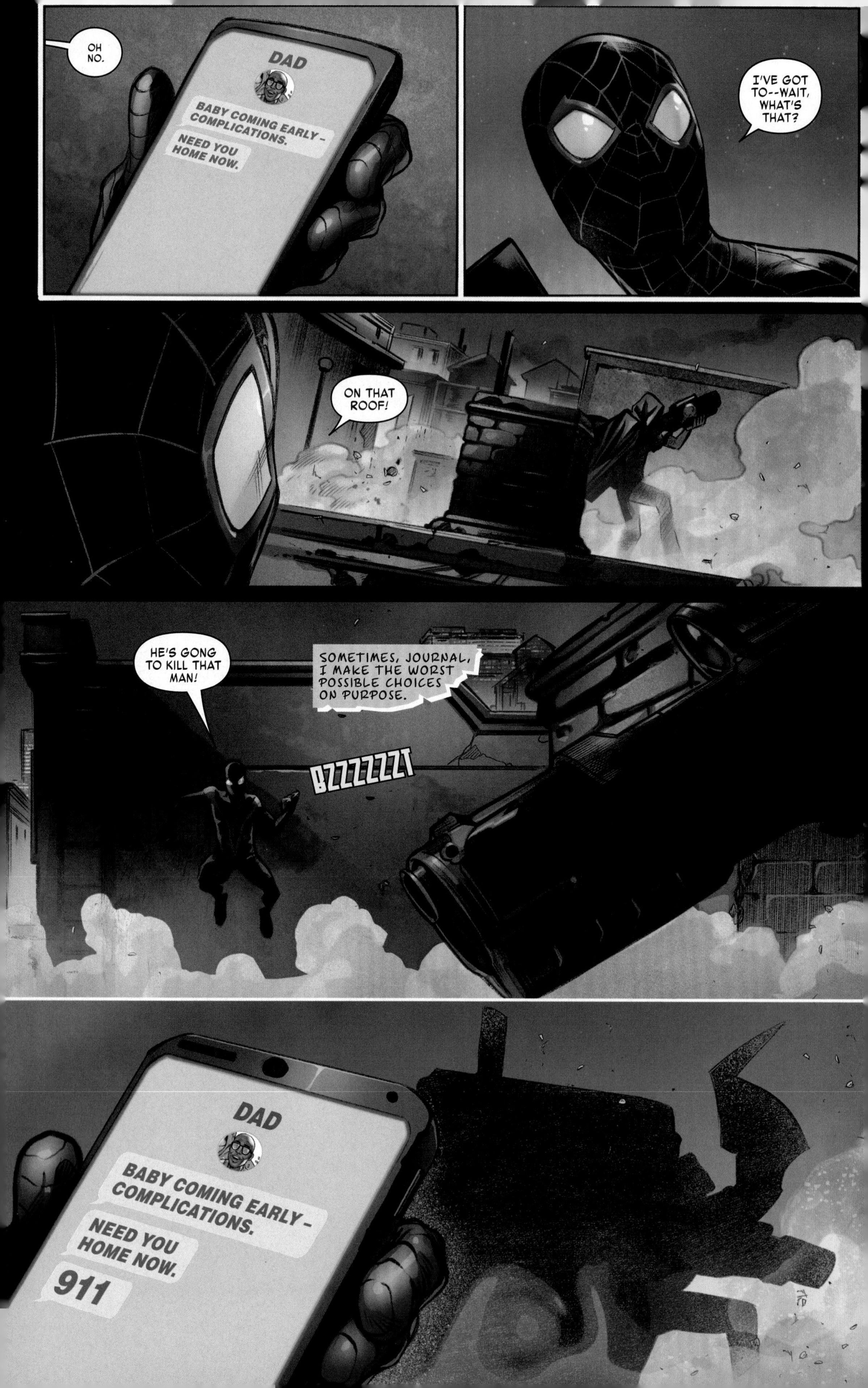
OH NO.
DAD
BABY COMING EARLY – COMPLICATIONS.
NEED YOU HOME NOW.
I'VE GOT TO--WAIT, WHAT'S THAT?
ON THAT ROOF!
HE'S GONG TO KILL THAT MAN!
SOMETIMES, JOURNAL, I MAKE THE WORST POSSIBLE CHOICES ON PURPOSE.
BZZZZZZT
DAD
BABY COMING EARLY – COMPLICATIONS.
NEED YOU HOME NOW.
911

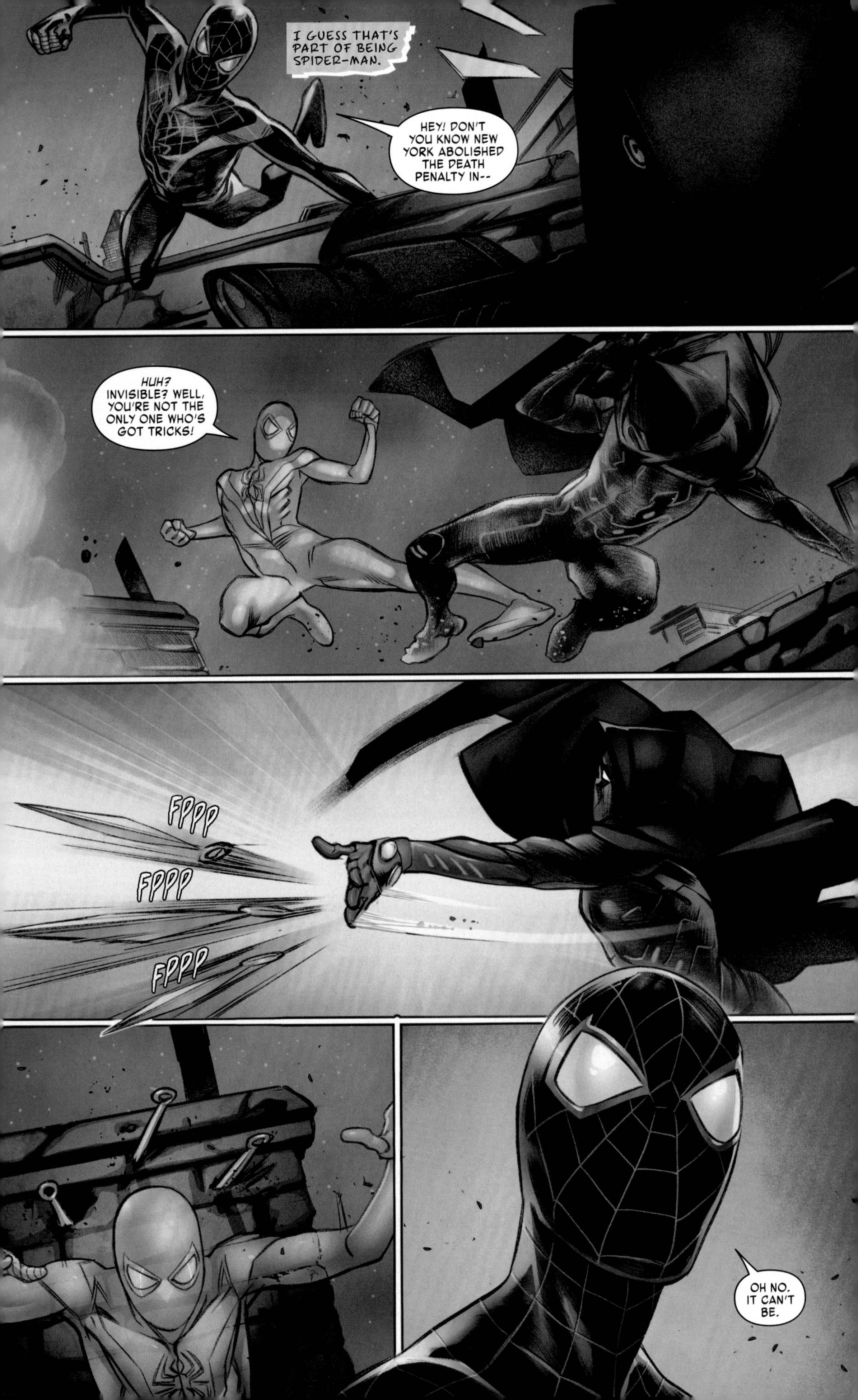
I GUESS THAT'S PART OF BEING SPIDER-MAN.
HEY! DON'T YOU KNOW NEW YORK ABOLISHED THE DEATH PENALTY IN--
HUH? INVISIBLE? WELL, YOU'RE NOT THE ONLY ONE WHO'S GOT TRICKS!
FPPP
FPPP
FPPP
OH NO. IT CAN'T BE.

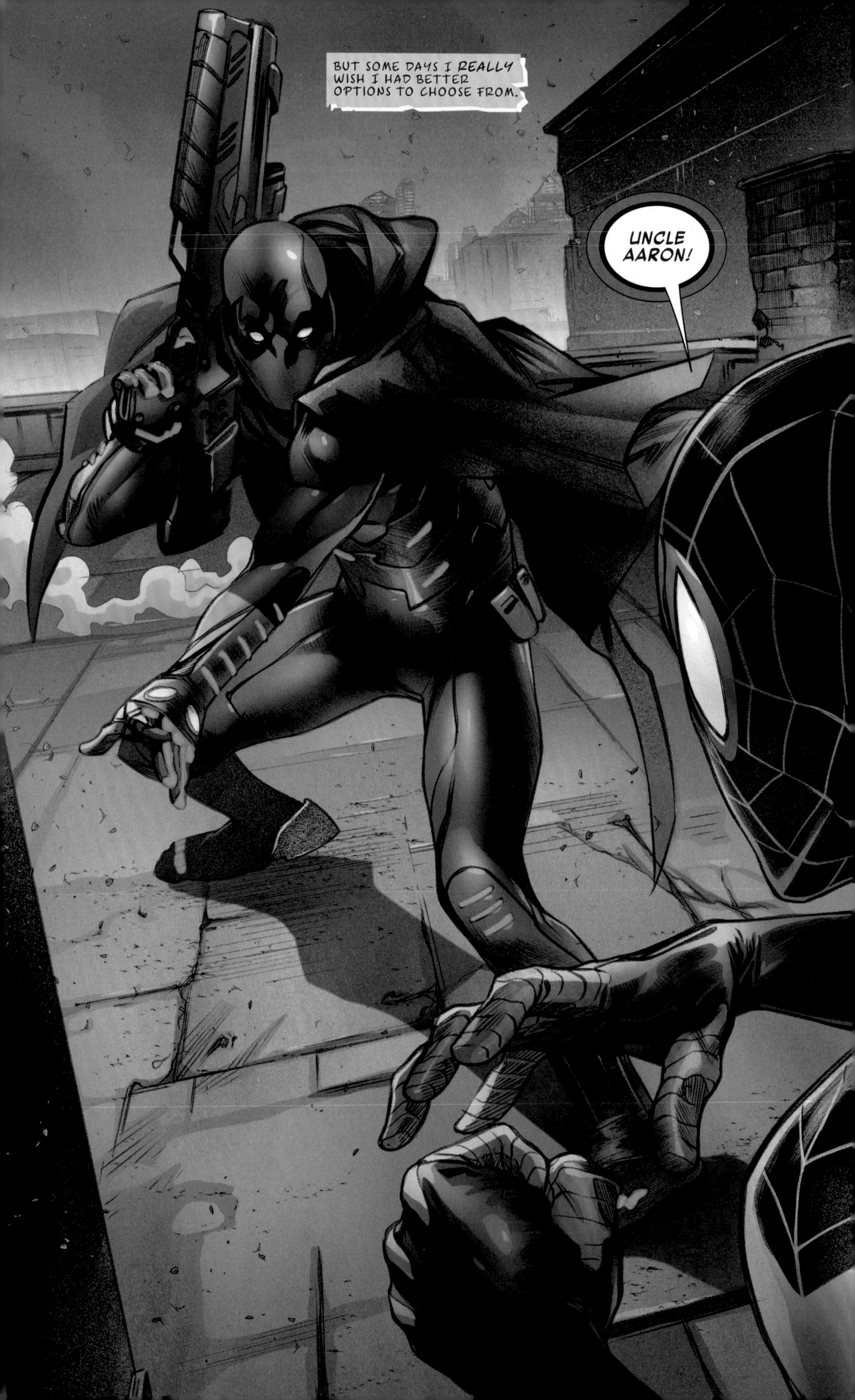
BUT SOME DAYS I REALLY WISH I HAD BETTER OPTIONS TO CHOOSE FROM.
UNCLE AARON!

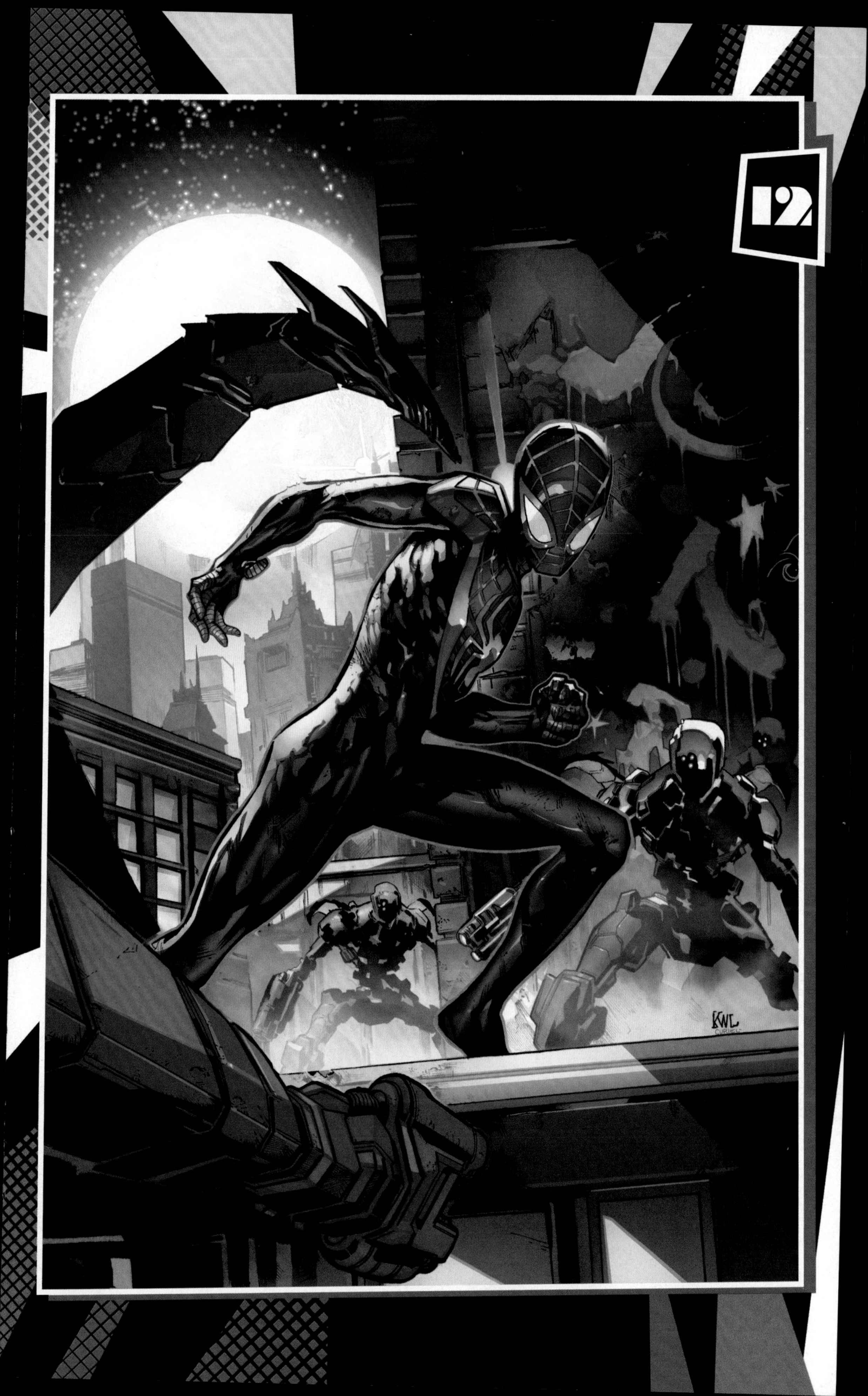
12

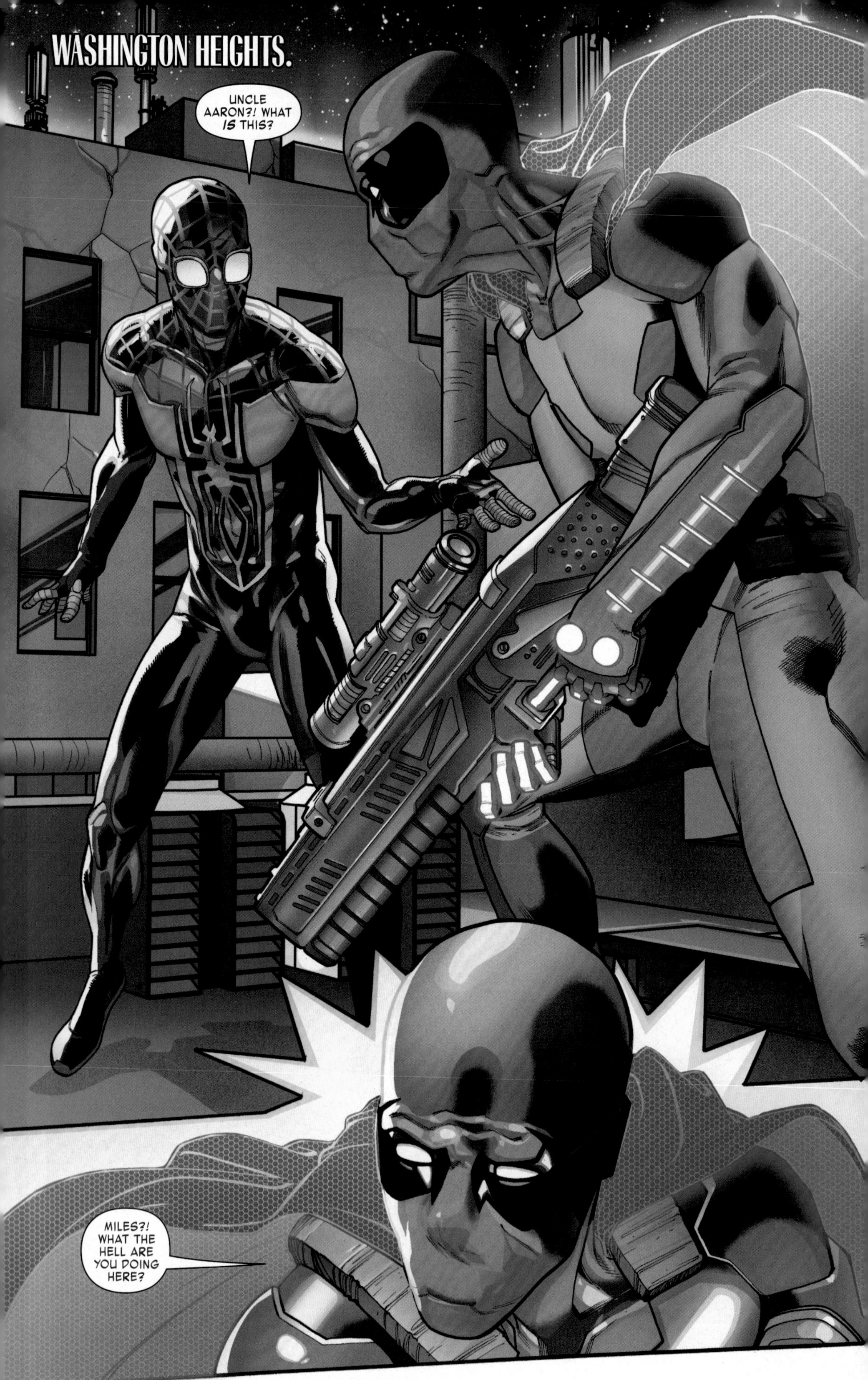
WASHINGTON HEIGHTS.
UNCLE AARON?! WHAT IS THIS?
MILES?! WHAT THE HELL ARE YOU DOING HERE?

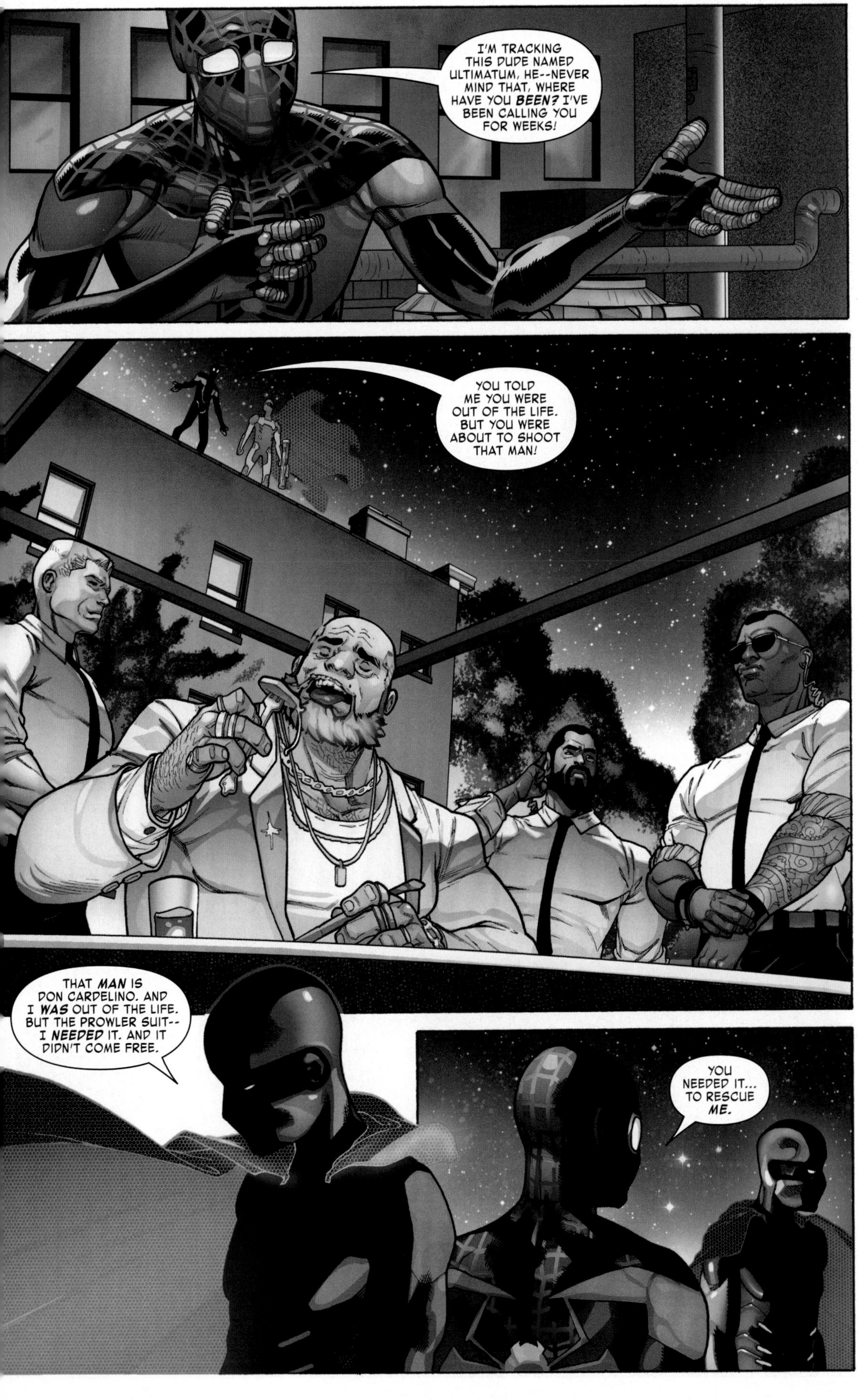
I'M TRACKING THIS DUDE NAMED ULTIMATUM, HE--NEVER MIND THAT, WHERE HAVE YOU BEEN? I'VE BEEN CALLING YOU FOR WEEKS!
YOU TOLD ME YOU WERE OUT OF THE LIFE. BUT YOU WERE ABOUT TO SHOOT THAT MAN!
THAT MAN IS DON CARDELINO. AND I WAS OUT OF THE LIFE. BUT THE PROWLER SUIT-- I NEEDED IT. AND IT DIDN'T COME FREE.
YOU NEEDED IT... TO RESCUE ME.

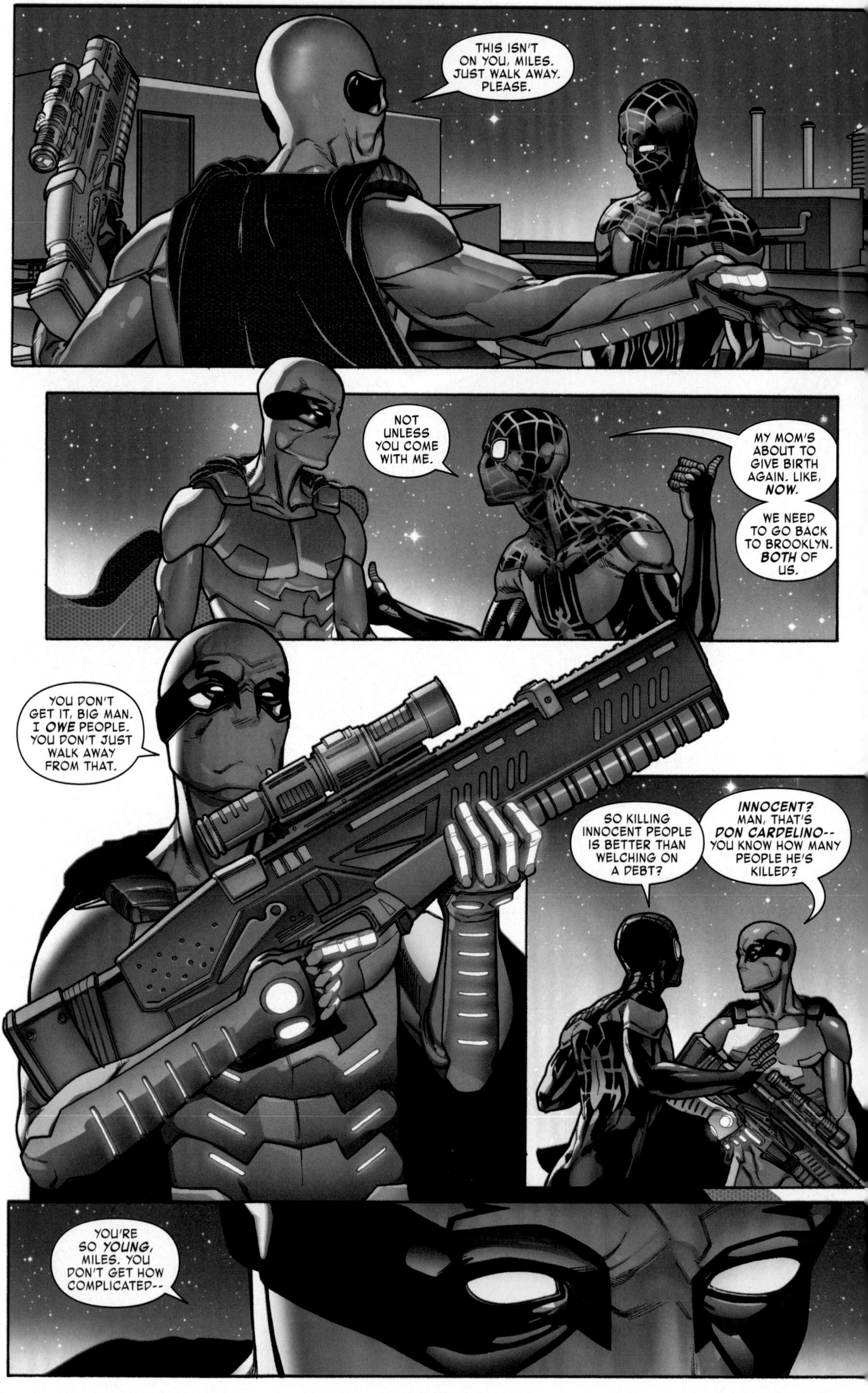
THIS ISN'T ON YOU, MILES. JUST WALK AWAY. PLEASE.
NOT UNLESS YOU COME WITH ME.
MY MOM'S ABOUT TO GIVE BIRTH AGAIN. LIKE, NOW.
WE NEED TO GO BACK TO BROOKLYN. BOTH OF US.
YOU DON'T GET IT, BIG MAN. I OWE PEOPLE. YOU DON'T JUST WALK AWAY FROM THAT.
SO KILLING INNOCENT PEOPLE IS BETTER THAN WELCHING ON A DEBT?
INNOCENT? MAN, THAT'S DON CARDELINO-- YOU KNOW HOW MANY PEOPLE HE'S KILLED?
YOU'RE SO YOUNG, MILES. YOU DON'T GET HOW COMPLICATED--

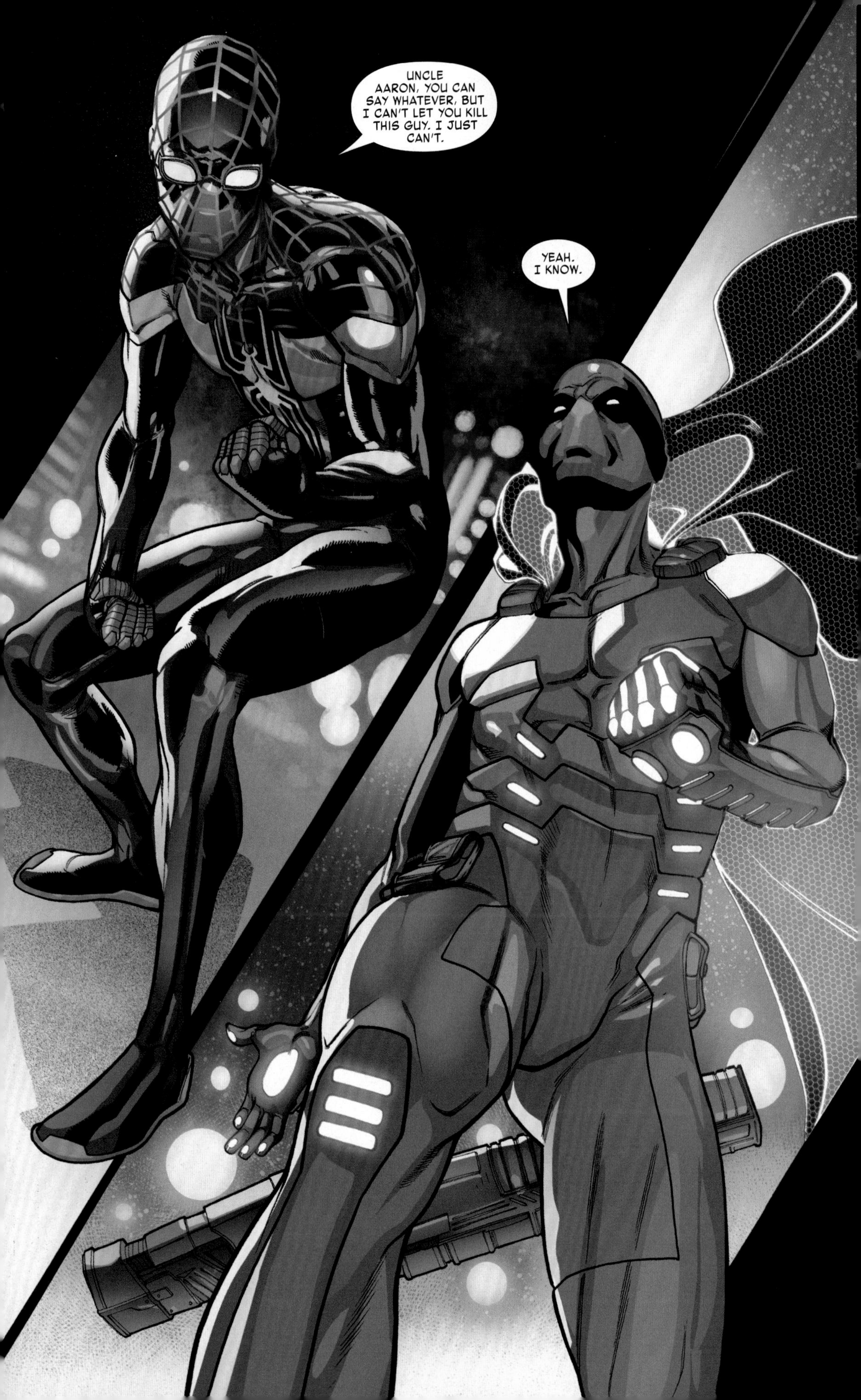
UNCLE AARON, YOU CAN SAY WHATEVER, BUT I CAN'T LET YOU KILL THIS GUY. I JUST CAN'T.
YEAH. I KNOW.

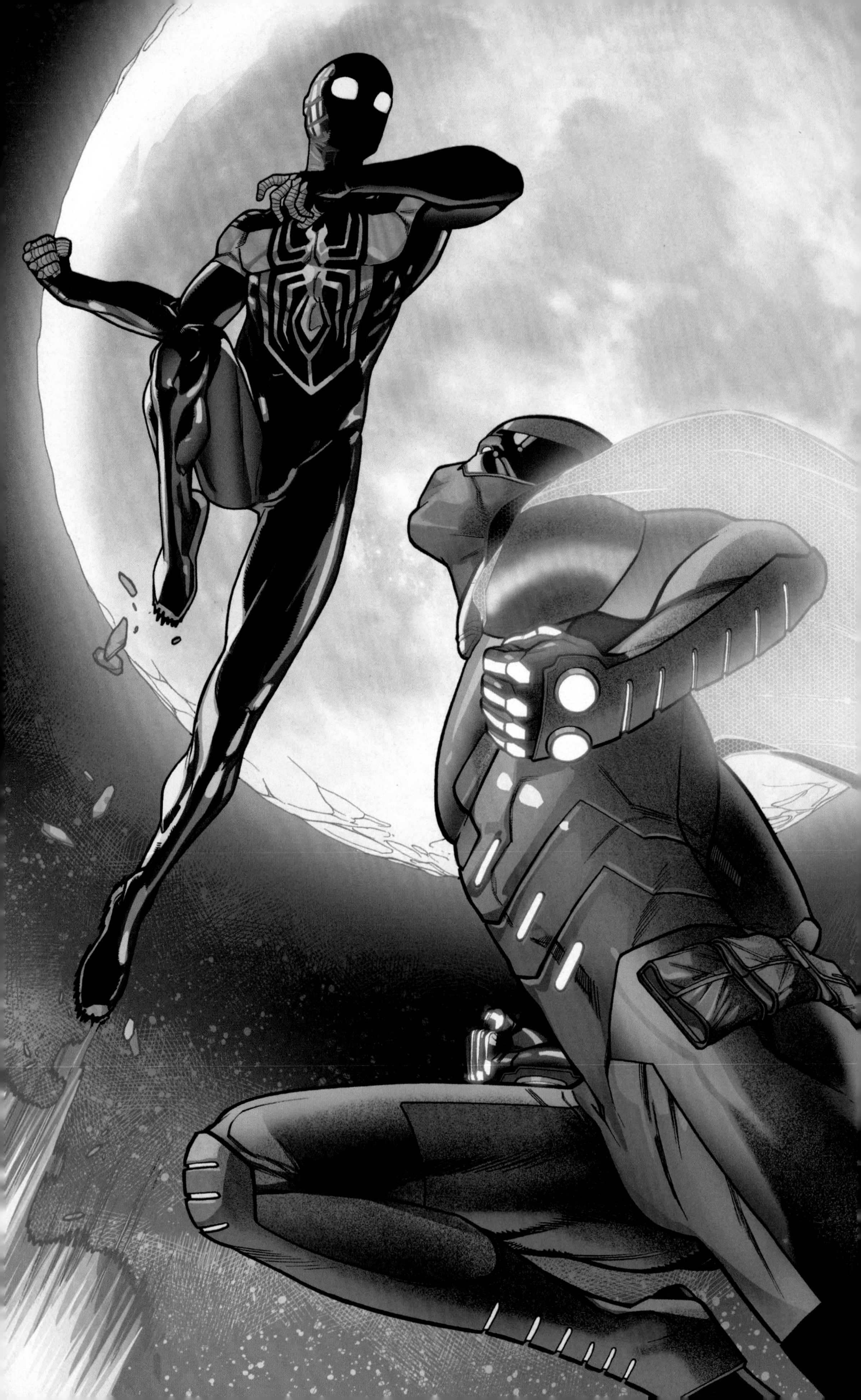

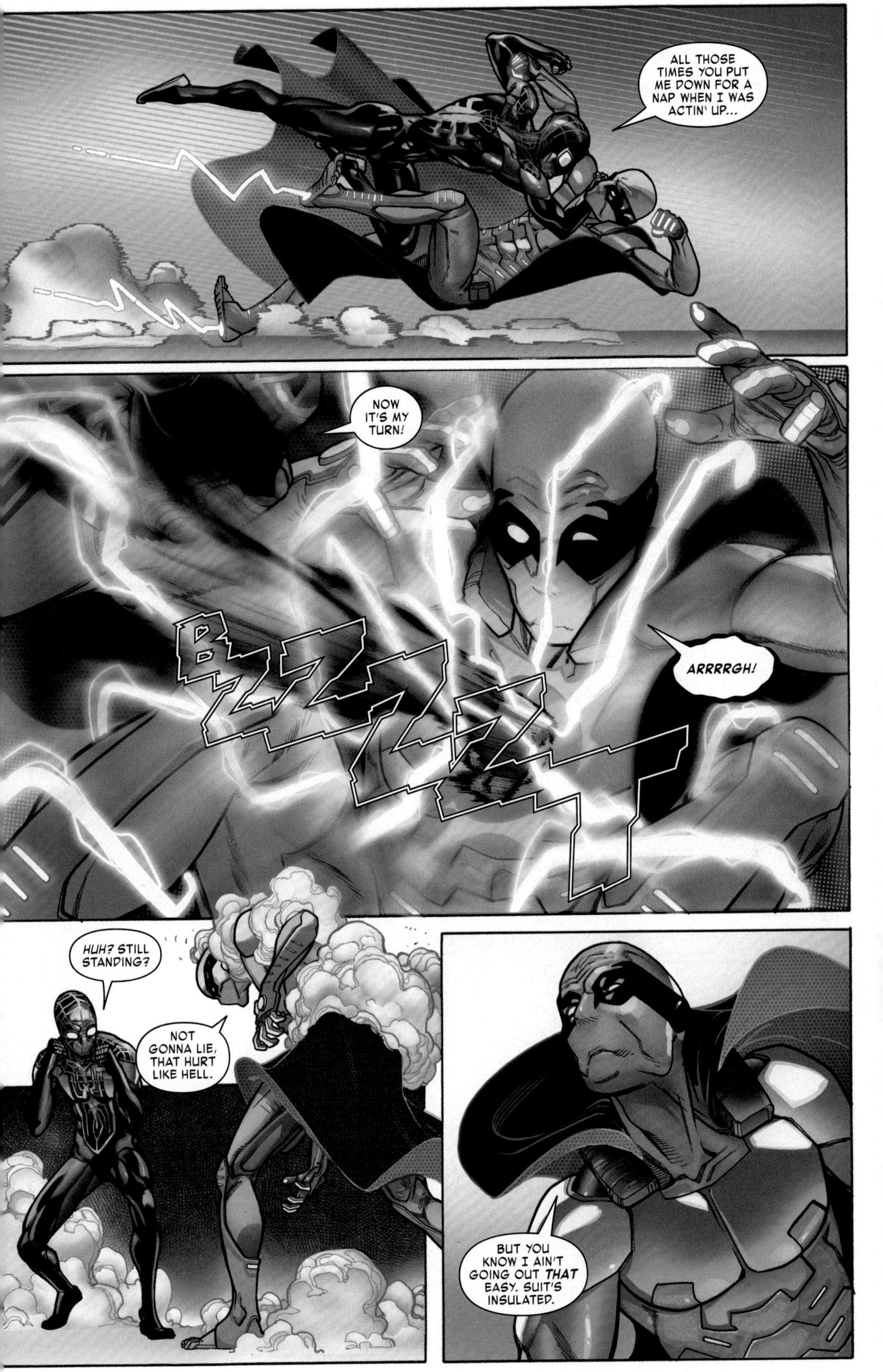
ALL THOSE TIMES YOU PUT ME DOWN FOR A NAP WHEN I WAS ACTIN' UP...
NOW IT'S MY TURN!
BZZZZT
ARRRRGH!
HUH? STILL STANDING?
NOT GONNA LIE, THAT HURT LIKE HELL.
BUT YOU KNOW I AIN'T GOING OUT *THAT* EASY. SUIT'S INSULATED.

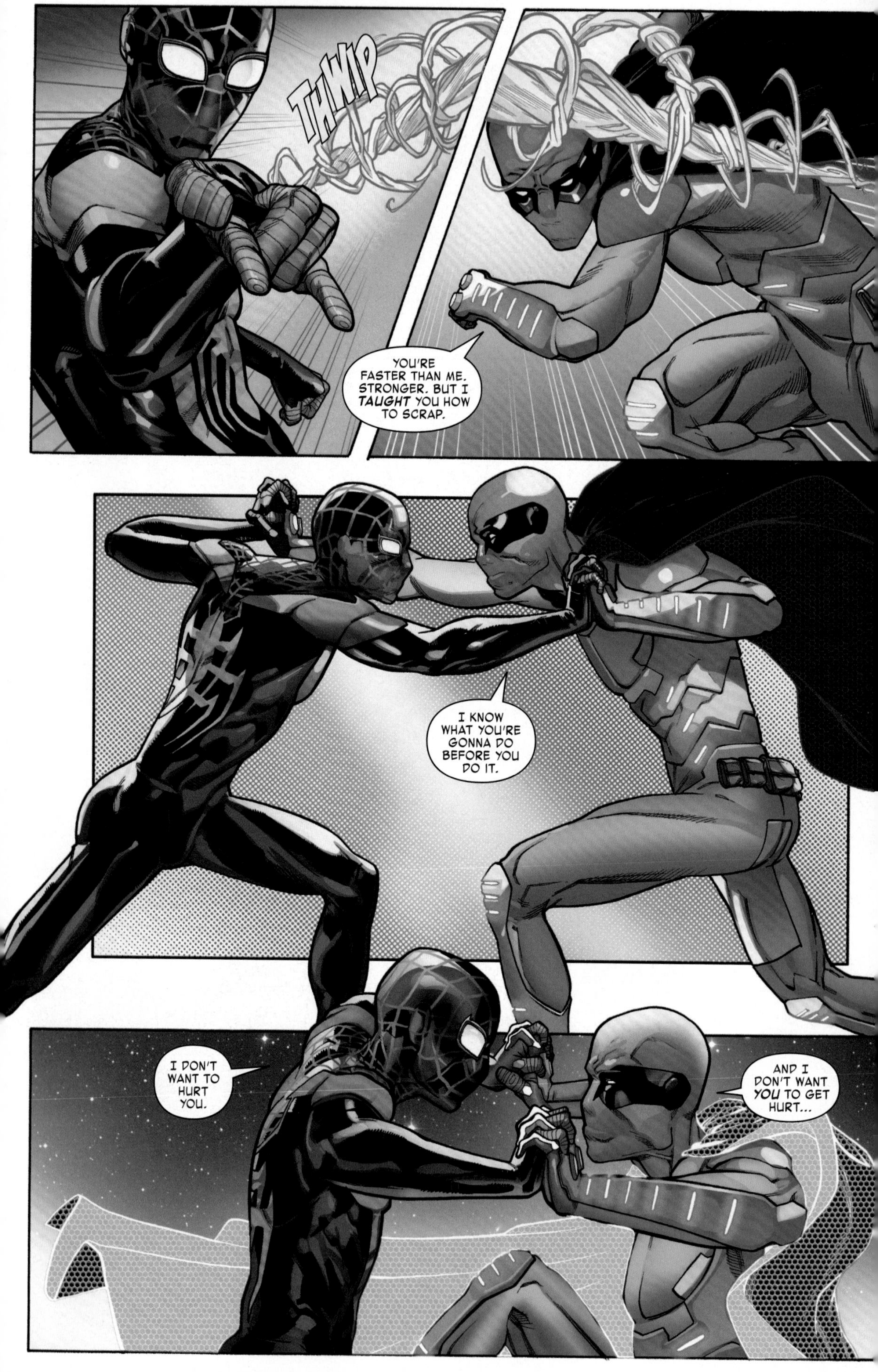
THWIP
YOU'RE FASTER THAN ME. STRONGER. BUT I TAUGHT YOU HOW TO SCRAP.
I KNOW WHAT YOU'RE GONNA DO BEFORE YOU DO IT.
I DON'T WANT TO HURT YOU.
AND I DON'T WANT YOU TO GET HURT...

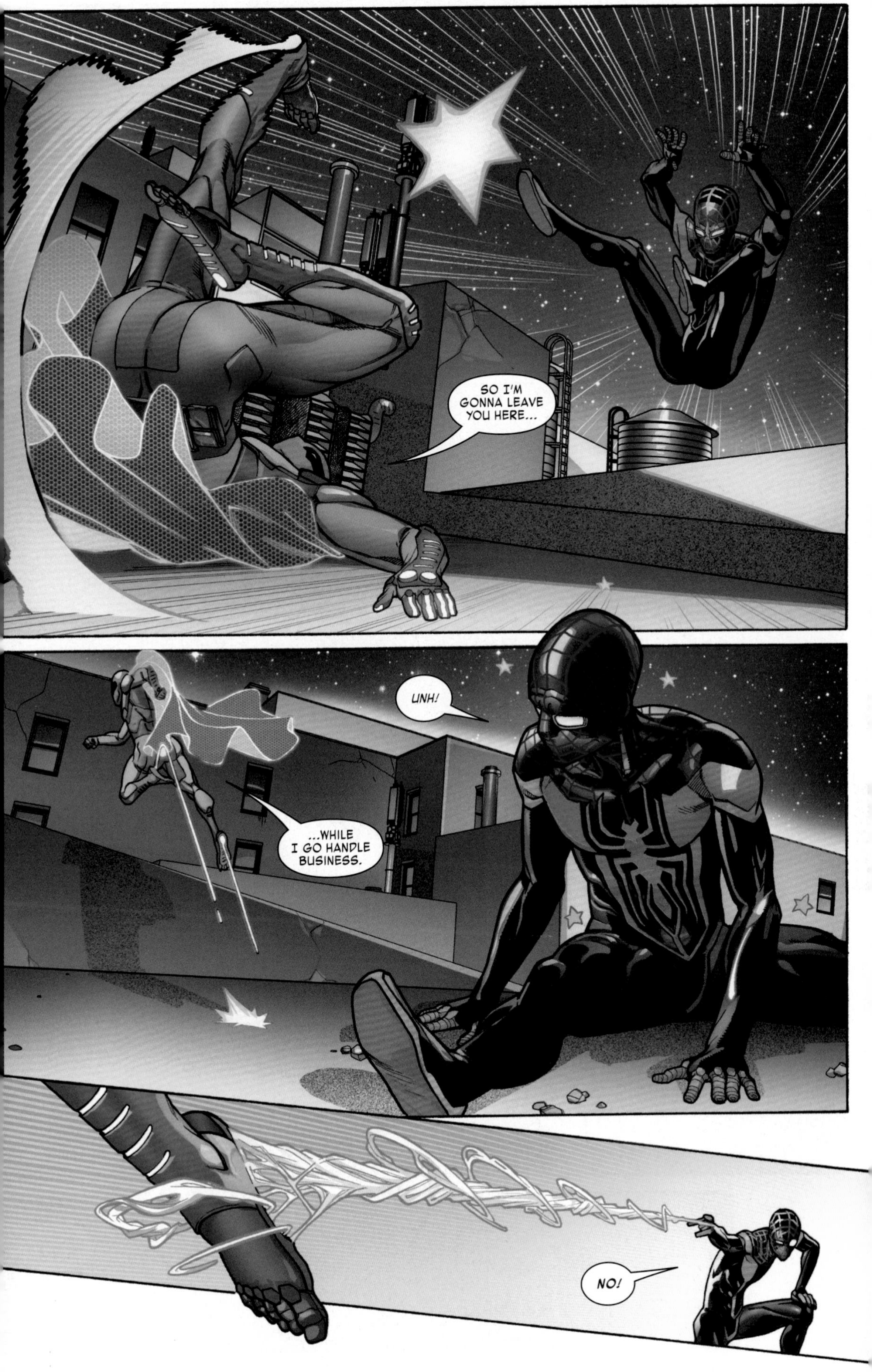
SO I'M GONNA LEAVE YOU HERE...
UNH!
...WHILE I GO HANDLE BUSINESS.
NO!

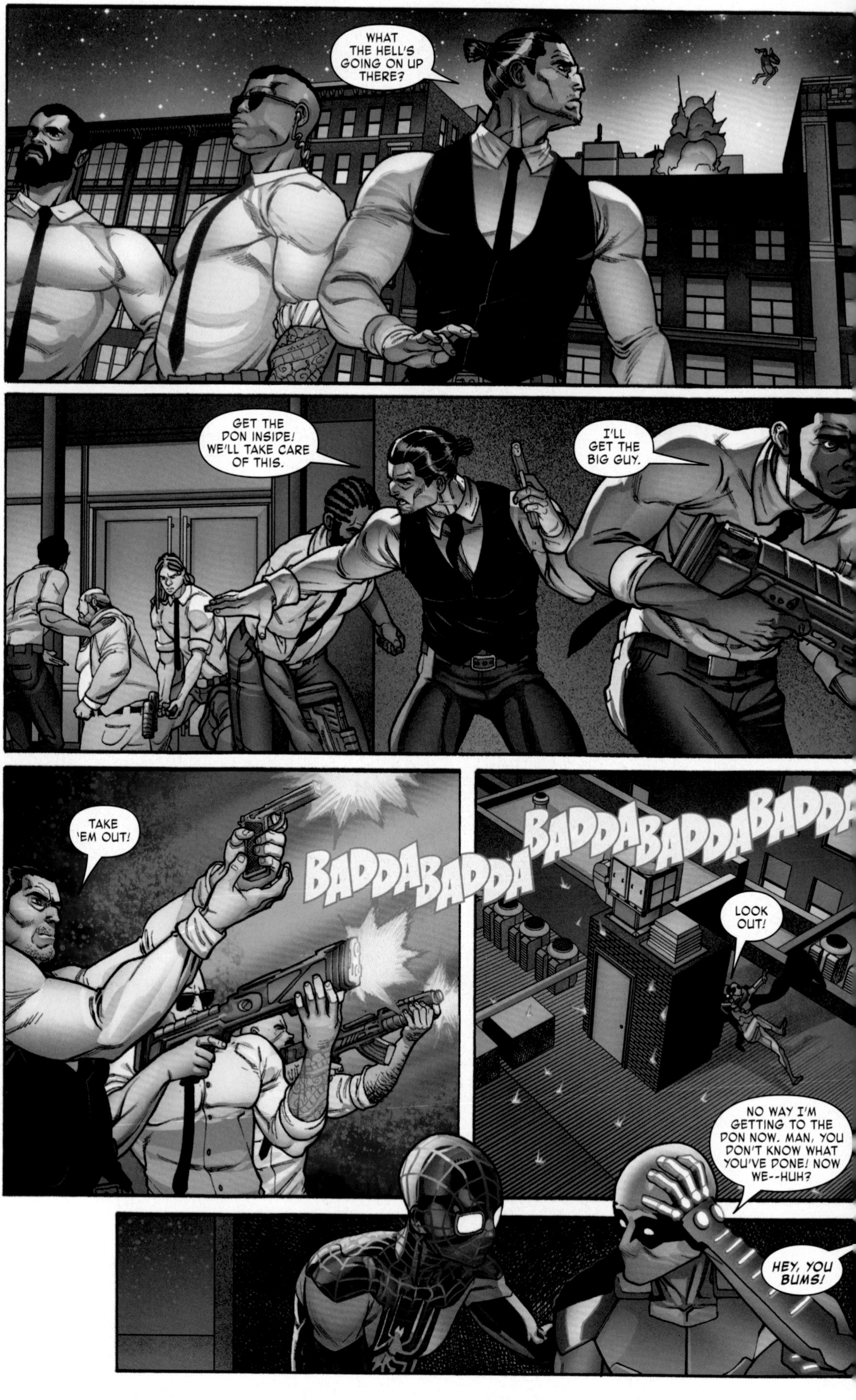
WHAT THE HELL'S GOING ON UP THERE?
GET THE DON INSIDE! WE'LL TAKE CARE OF THIS.
I'LL GET THE BIG GUY.
TAKE 'EM OUT!
BADDABADDABADDABADDABADDABADDA
LOOK OUT!
NO WAY I'M GETTING TO THE DON NOW. MAN, YOU DON'T KNOW WHAT YOU'VE DONE! NOW WE--HUH?
HEY, YOU BUMS!

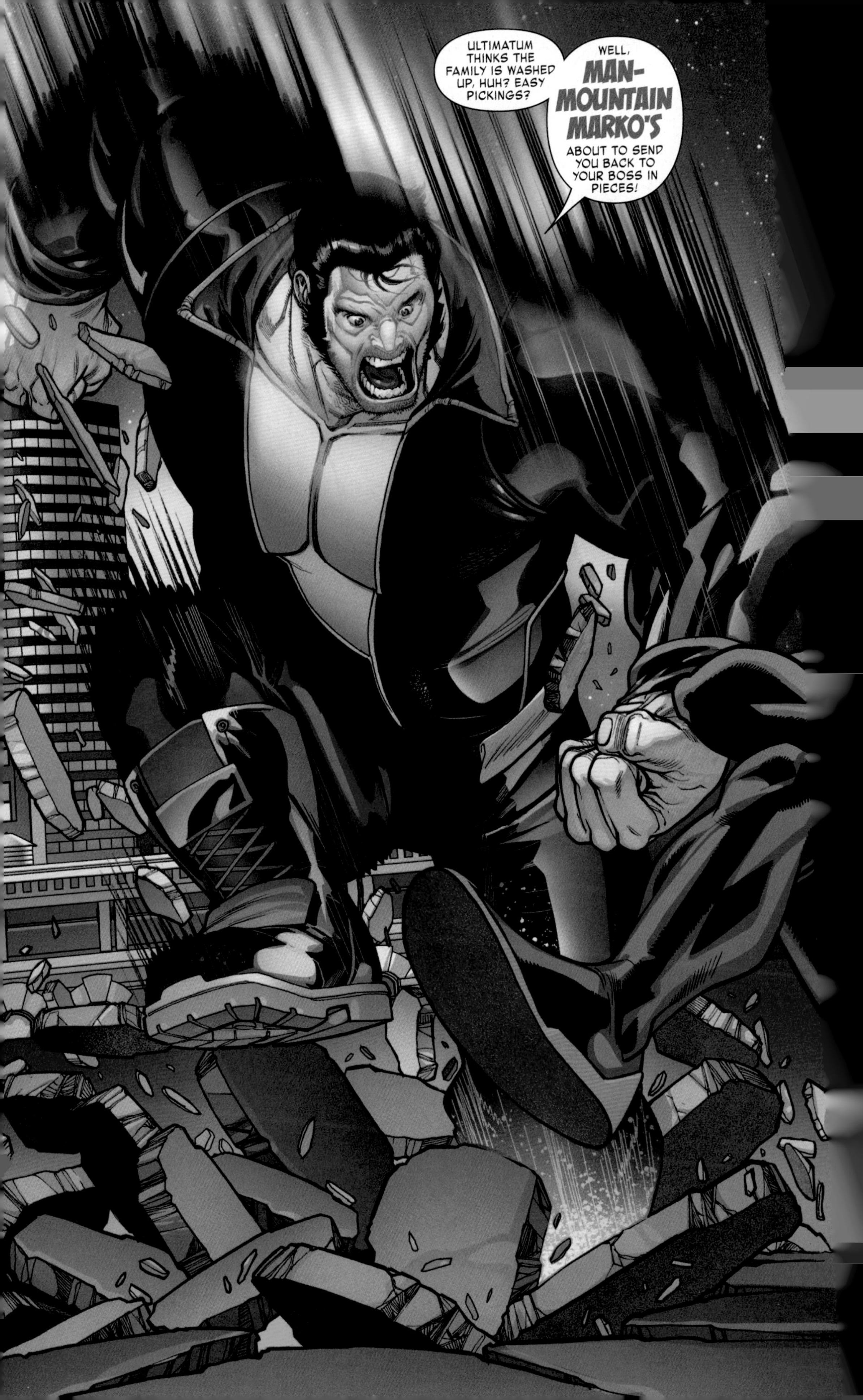
ULTIMATUM THINKS THE FAMILY IS WASHED UP, HUH? EASY PICKINGS?
WELL, MAN-MOUNTAIN MARKO'S ABOUT TO SEND YOU BACK TO YOUR BOSS IN PIECES!

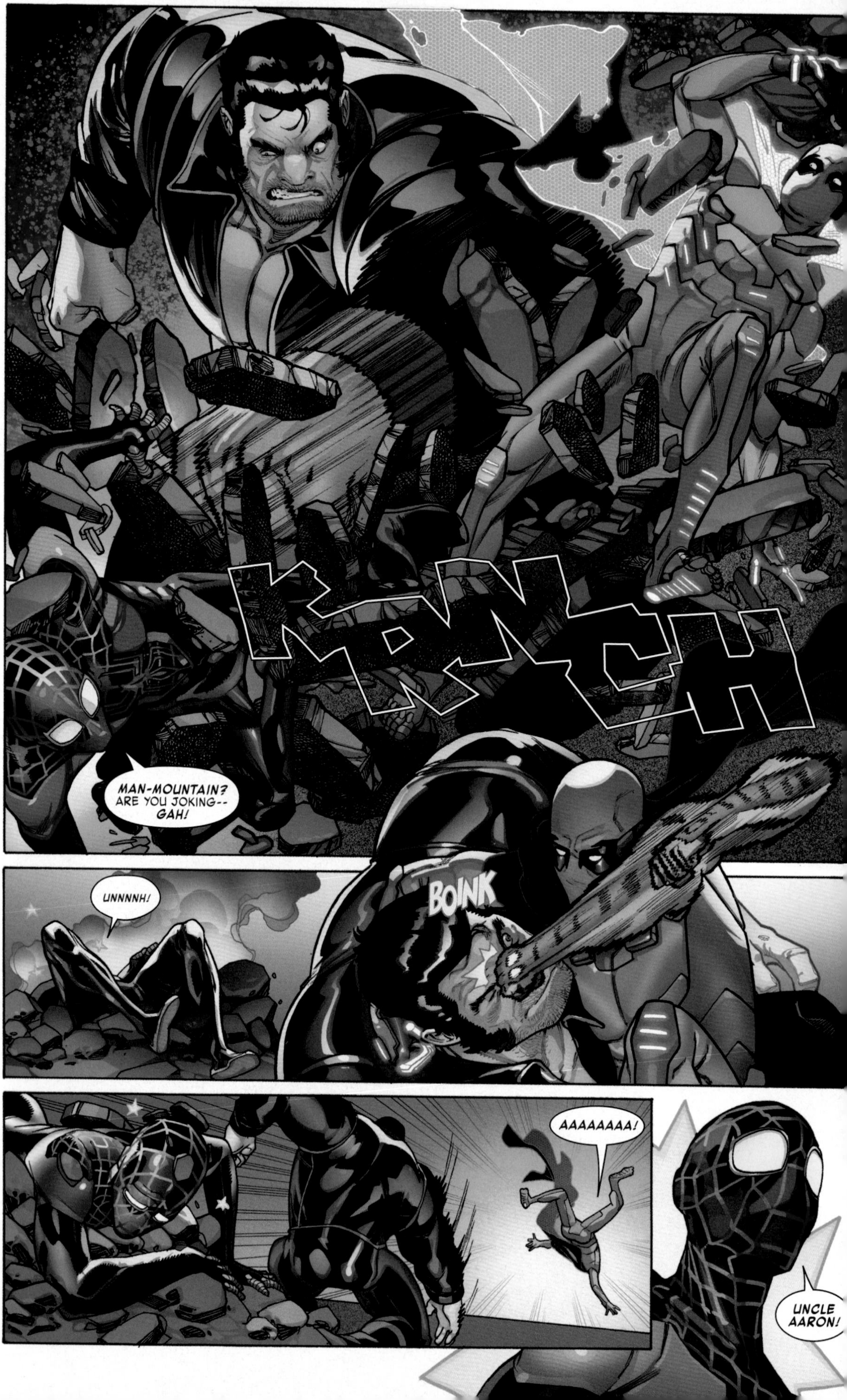
KRUNCH
MAN-MOUNTAIN? ARE YOU JOKING-- GAH!
UNNNNH!
BOINK
AAAAAAAA!
UNCLE AARON!

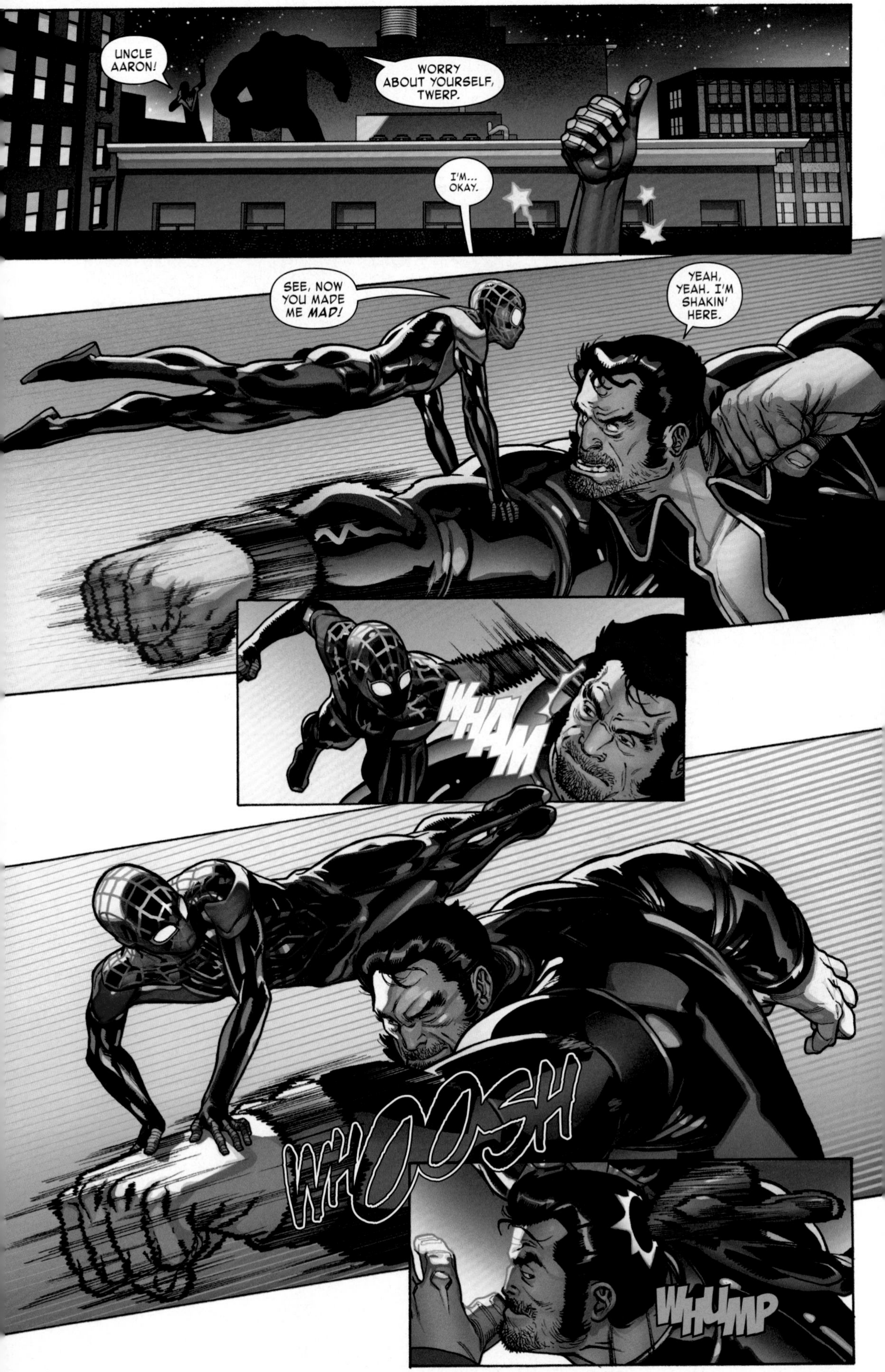
UNCLE AARON!
WORRY ABOUT YOURSELF, TWERP.
I'M... OKAY.
SEE, NOW YOU MADE ME MAD!
YEAH, YEAH. I'M SHAKIN' HERE.
WHAM
WHOOSH
WHUMP

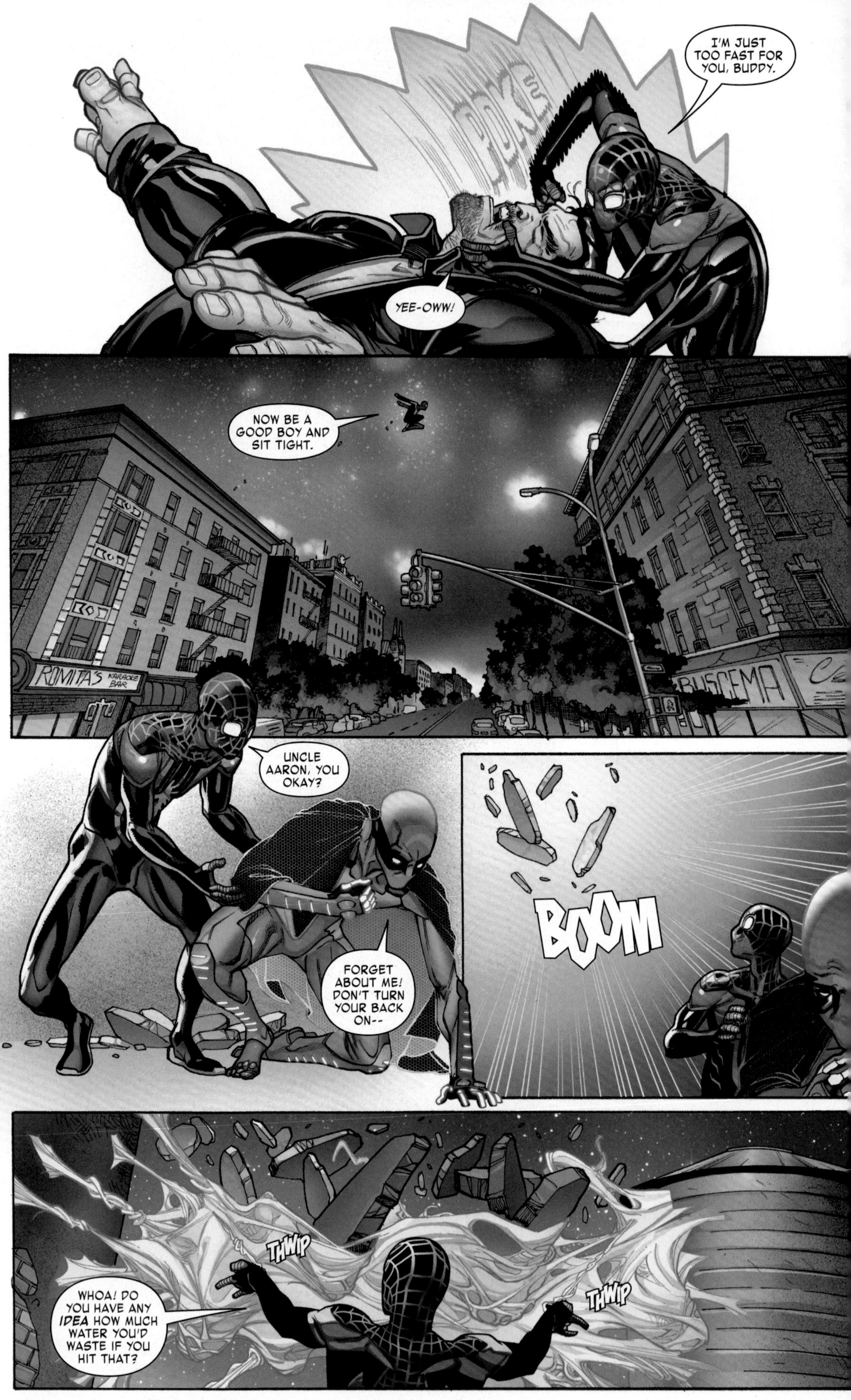
I'M JUST TOO FAST FOR YOU, BUDDY.
YEE-OWW!
NOW BE A GOOD BOY AND SIT TIGHT.
ROMITA'S KARAOKE BAR
BUSCEMA
UNCLE AARON, YOU OKAY?
FORGET ABOUT ME! DON'T TURN YOUR BACK ON--
BOOM
THWIP
THWIP
WHOA! DO YOU HAVE ANY *IDEA* HOW MUCH WATER YOU'D WASTE IF YOU HIT THAT?

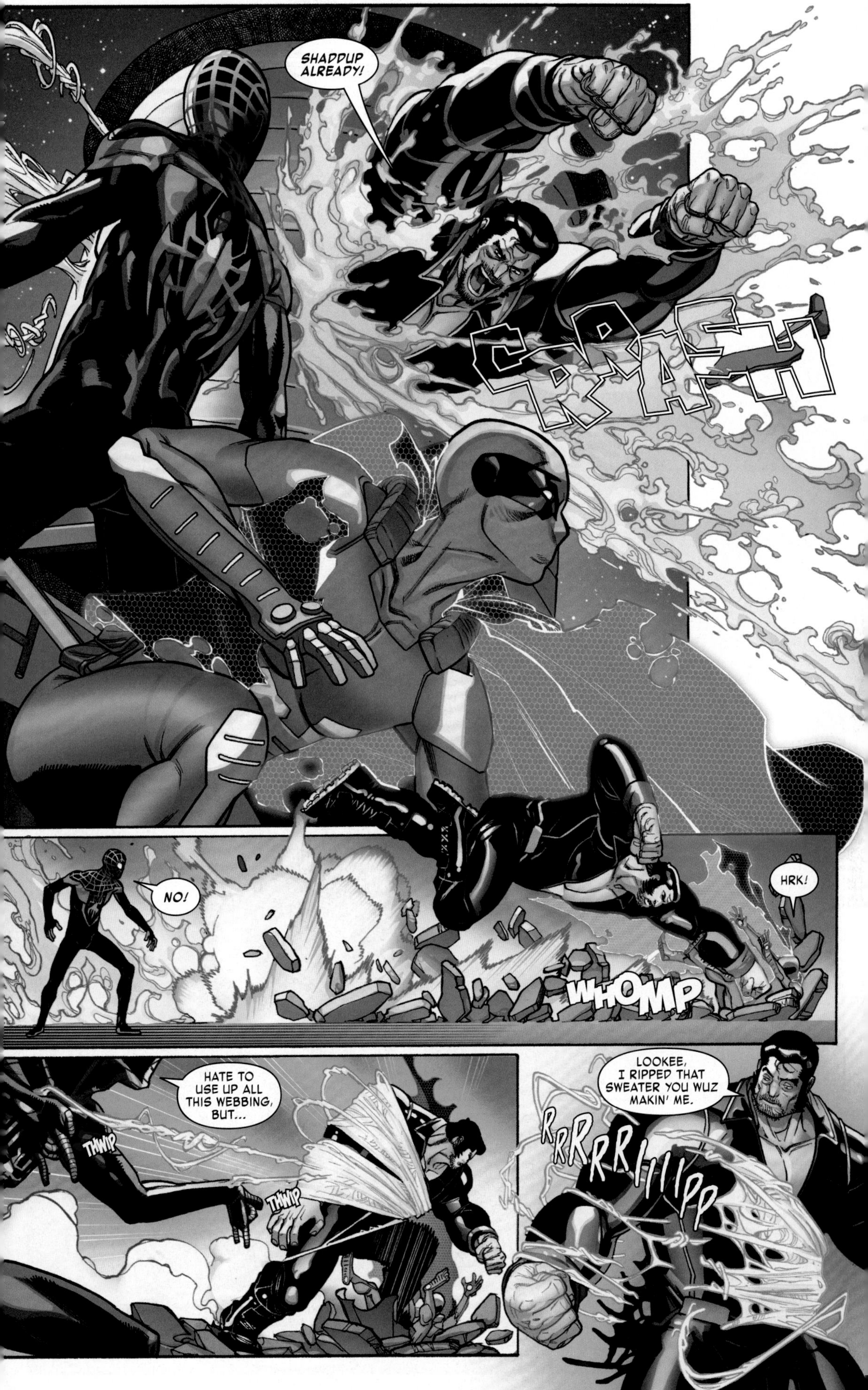
SHADDUP ALREADY!
CRASH
NO!
HRK!
WHOMP
HATE TO USE UP ALL THIS WEBBING, BUT...
THWIP
THWIP
LOOKEE, I RIPPED THAT SWEATER YOU WUZ MAKIN' ME.
RRRRIIIIPP

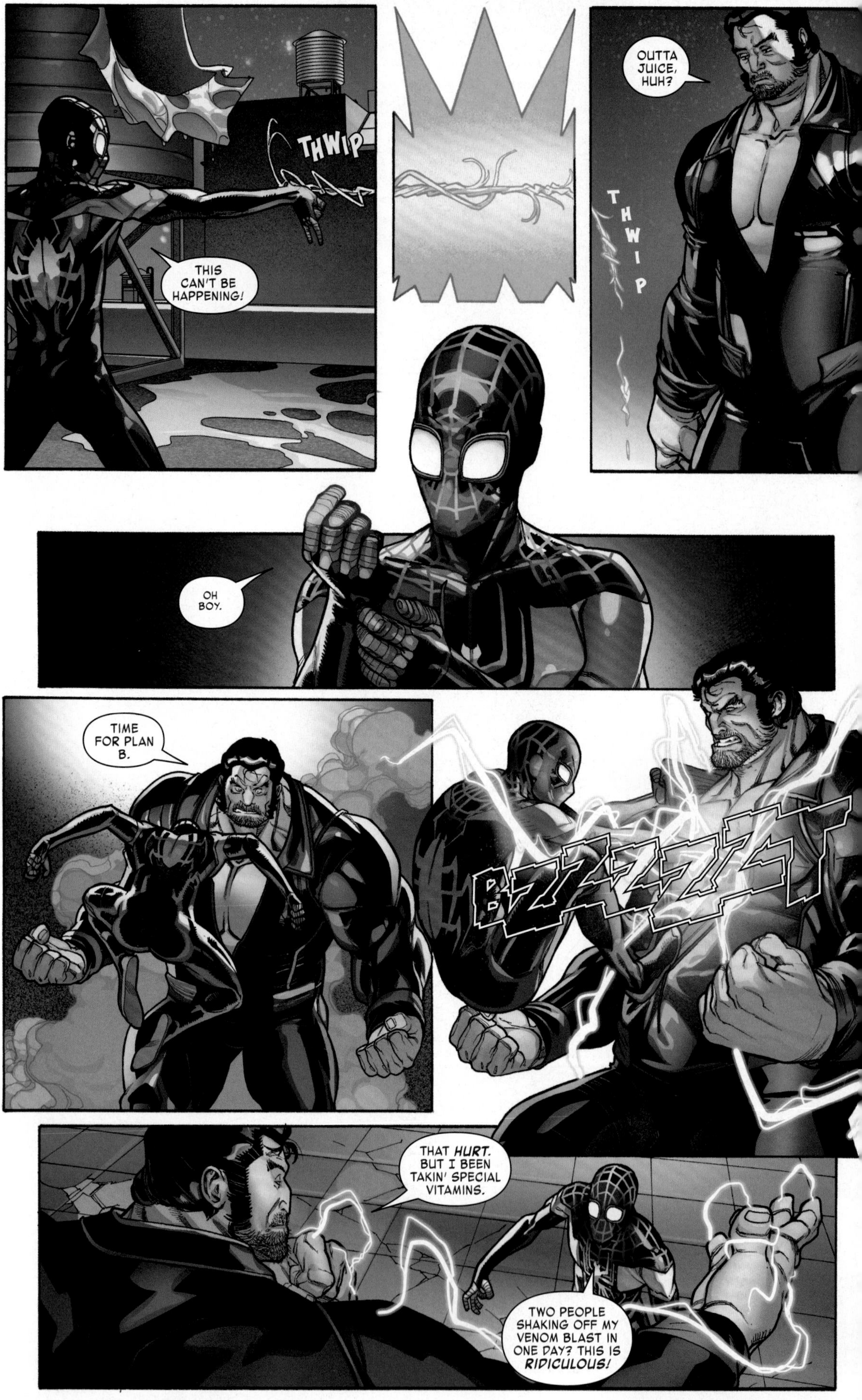
THWIP
THIS CAN'T BE HAPPENING!
OUTTA JUICE, HUH?
THWIP
OH BOY.
TIME FOR PLAN B.
BZZZZZT
THAT *HURT.* BUT I BEEN TAKIN' SPECIAL VITAMINS.
TWO PEOPLE SHAKING OFF MY VENOM BLAST IN ONE DAY? THIS IS *RIDICULOUS!*

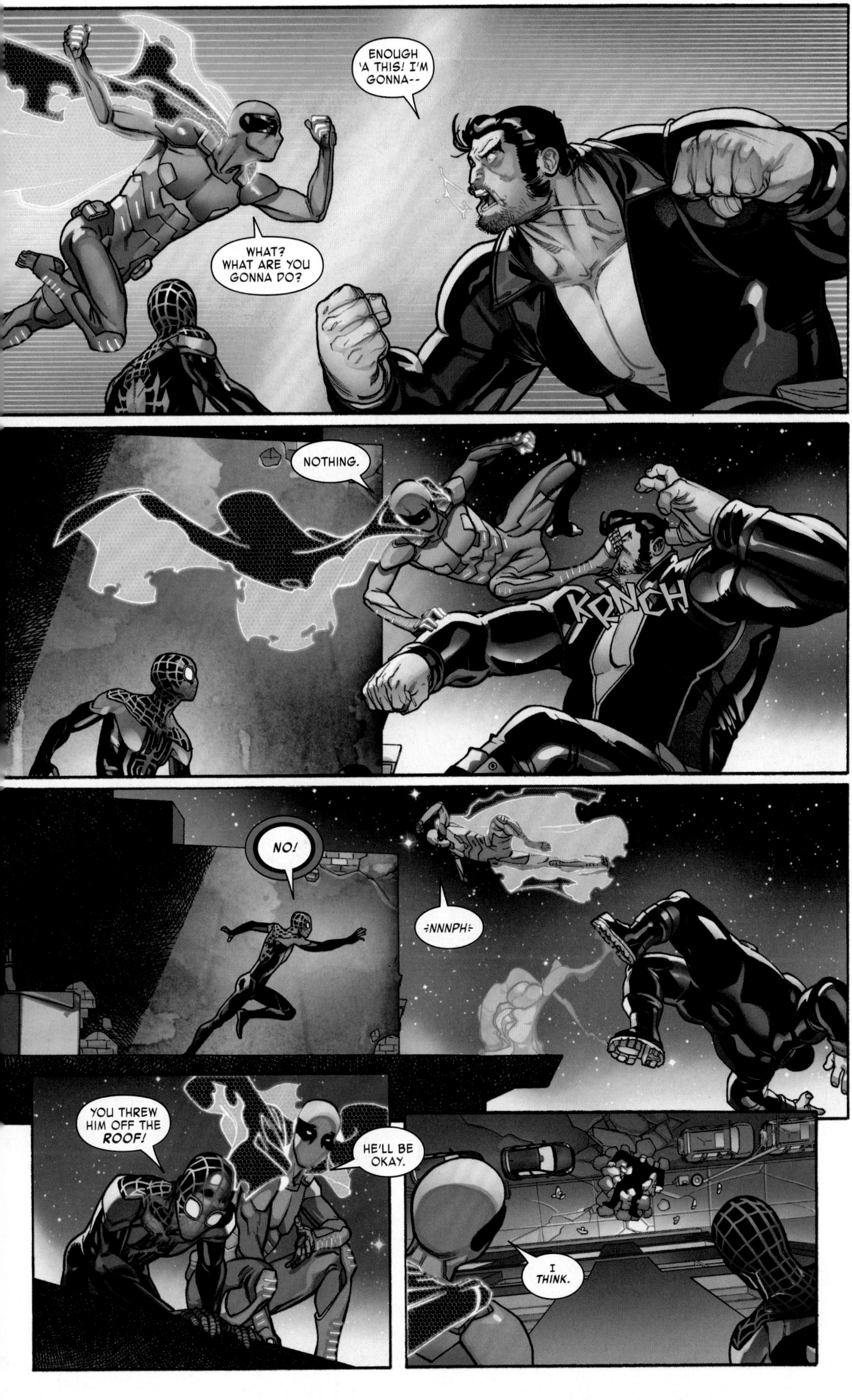
ENOUGH 'A THIS! I'M GONNA--
WHAT? WHAT ARE YOU GONNA DO?
NOTHING.
KRNCH
NO!
NNNPH
YOU THREW HIM OFF THE ROOF!
HE'LL BE OKAY.
I THINK.

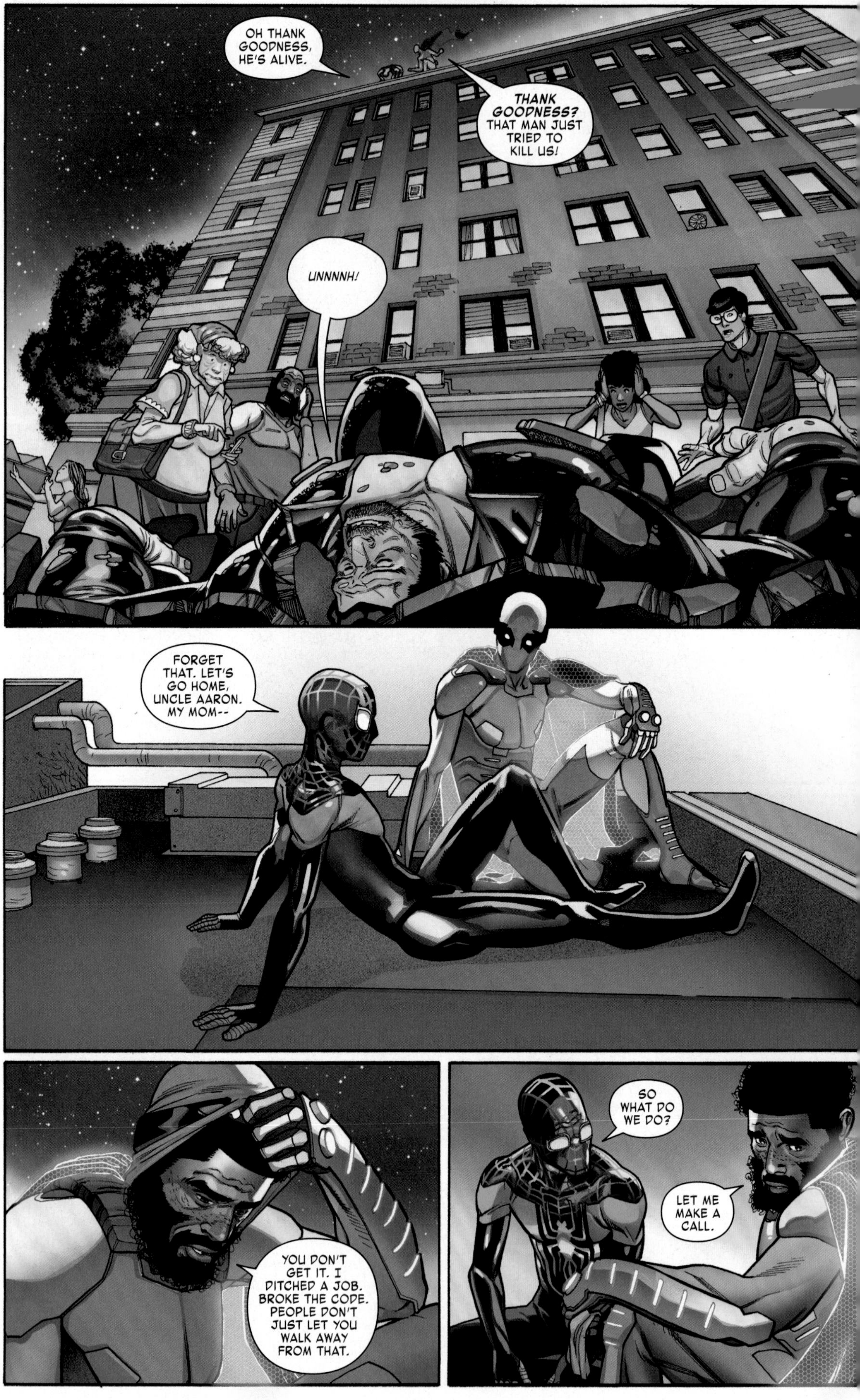
OH THANK GOODNESS, HE'S ALIVE.
THANK GOODNESS? THAT MAN JUST TRIED TO *KILL* US!
UNNNNH!
FORGET THAT. LET'S GO HOME, UNCLE AARON. MY MOM--
YOU DON'T GET IT. I DITCHED A JOB. BROKE THE CODE. PEOPLE DON'T JUST LET YOU WALK AWAY FROM THAT.
SO WHAT DO WE DO?
LET ME MAKE A CALL.

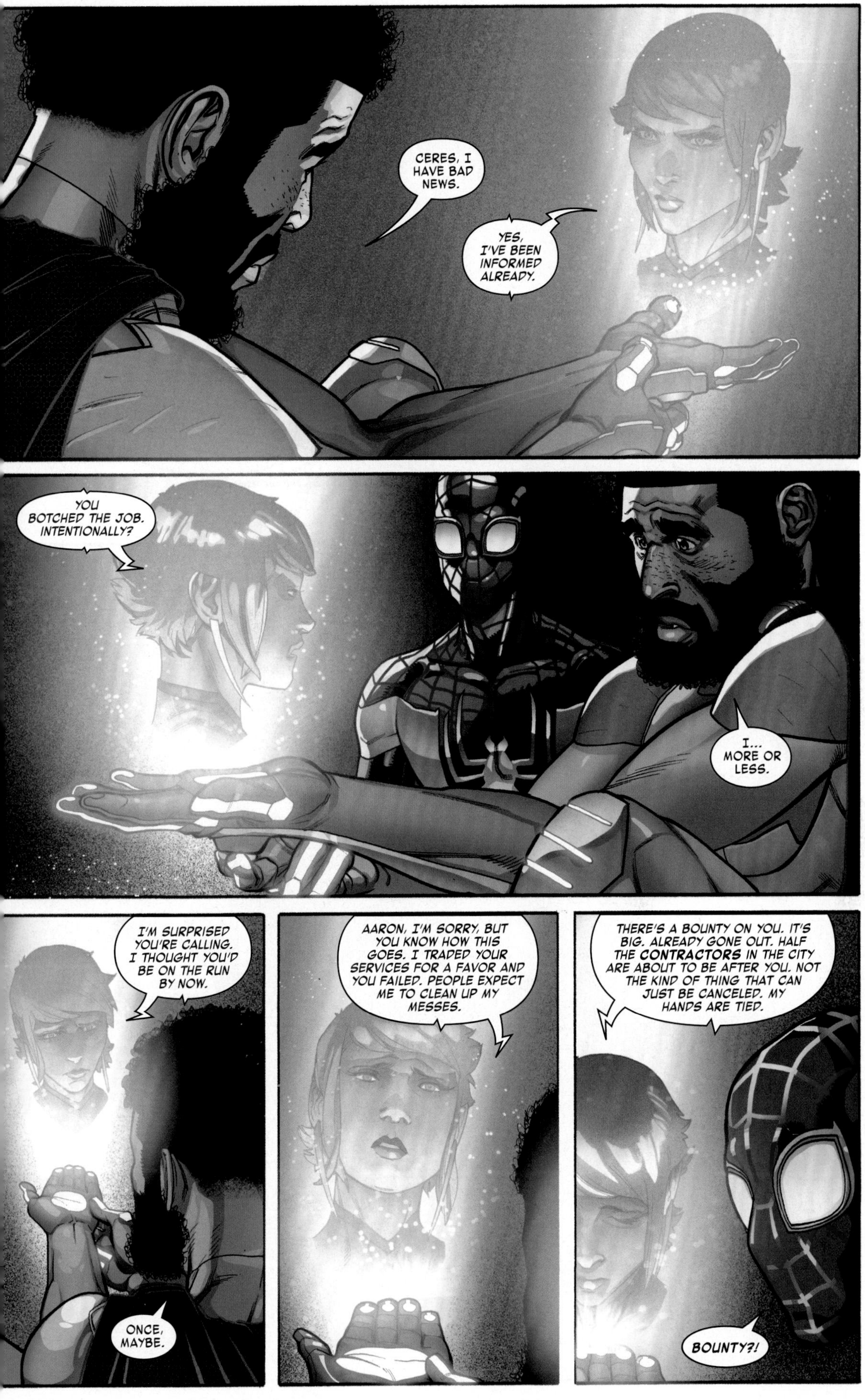
CERES, I HAVE BAD NEWS.
YES, I'VE BEEN INFORMED ALREADY.
YOU BOTCHED THE JOB. INTENTIONALLY?
I... MORE OR LESS.
I'M SURPRISED YOU'RE CALLING. I THOUGHT YOU'D BE ON THE RUN BY NOW.
ONCE, MAYBE.
AARON, I'M SORRY, BUT YOU KNOW HOW THIS GOES. I TRADED YOUR SERVICES FOR A FAVOR AND YOU FAILED. PEOPLE EXPECT ME TO CLEAN UP MY MESSES.
THERE'S A BOUNTY ON YOU. IT'S BIG. ALREADY GONE OUT. HALF THE CONTRACTORS IN THE CITY ARE ABOUT TO BE AFTER YOU. NOT THE KIND OF THING THAT CAN JUST BE CANCELED. MY HANDS ARE TIED.
BOUNTY?!

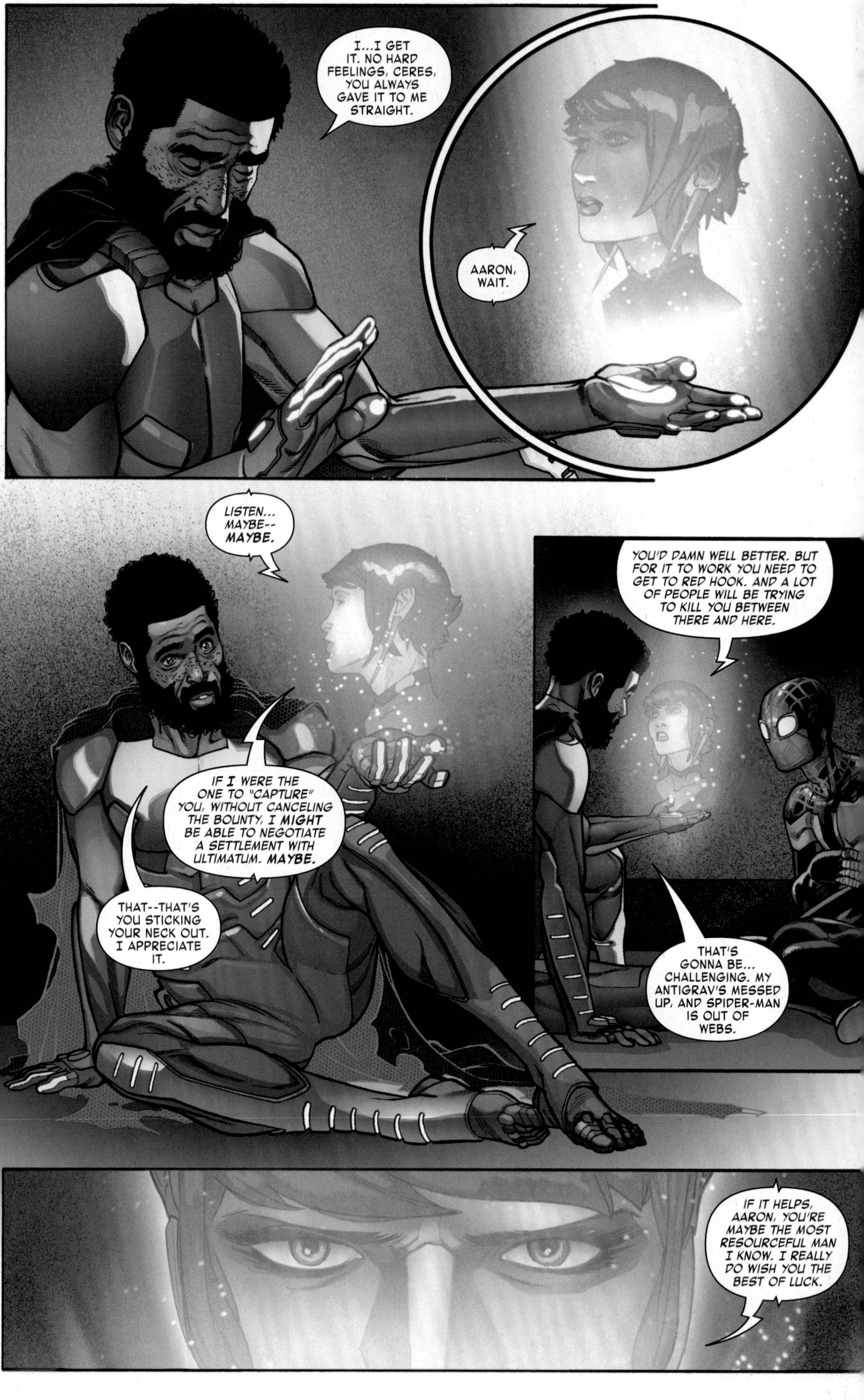
I...I GET IT. NO HARD FEELINGS, CERES, YOU ALWAYS GAVE IT TO ME STRAIGHT.
AARON, WAIT.
LISTEN... MAYBE-- MAYBE.
IF I WERE THE ONE TO "CAPTURE" YOU, WITHOUT CANCELING THE BOUNTY, I MIGHT BE ABLE TO NEGOTIATE A SETTLEMENT WITH ULTIMATUM. MAYBE.
THAT--THAT'S YOU STICKING YOUR NECK OUT. I APPRECIATE IT.
YOU'D DAMN WELL BETTER. BUT FOR IT TO WORK YOU NEED TO GET TO RED HOOK. AND A LOT OF PEOPLE WILL BE TRYING TO KILL YOU BETWEEN THERE AND HERE.
THAT'S GONNA BE... CHALLENGING. MY ANTIGRAV'S MESSED UP, AND SPIDER-MAN IS OUT OF WEBS.
IF IT HELPS, AARON, YOU'RE MAYBE THE MOST RESOURCEFUL MAN I KNOW. I REALLY DO WISH YOU THE BEST OF LUCK.

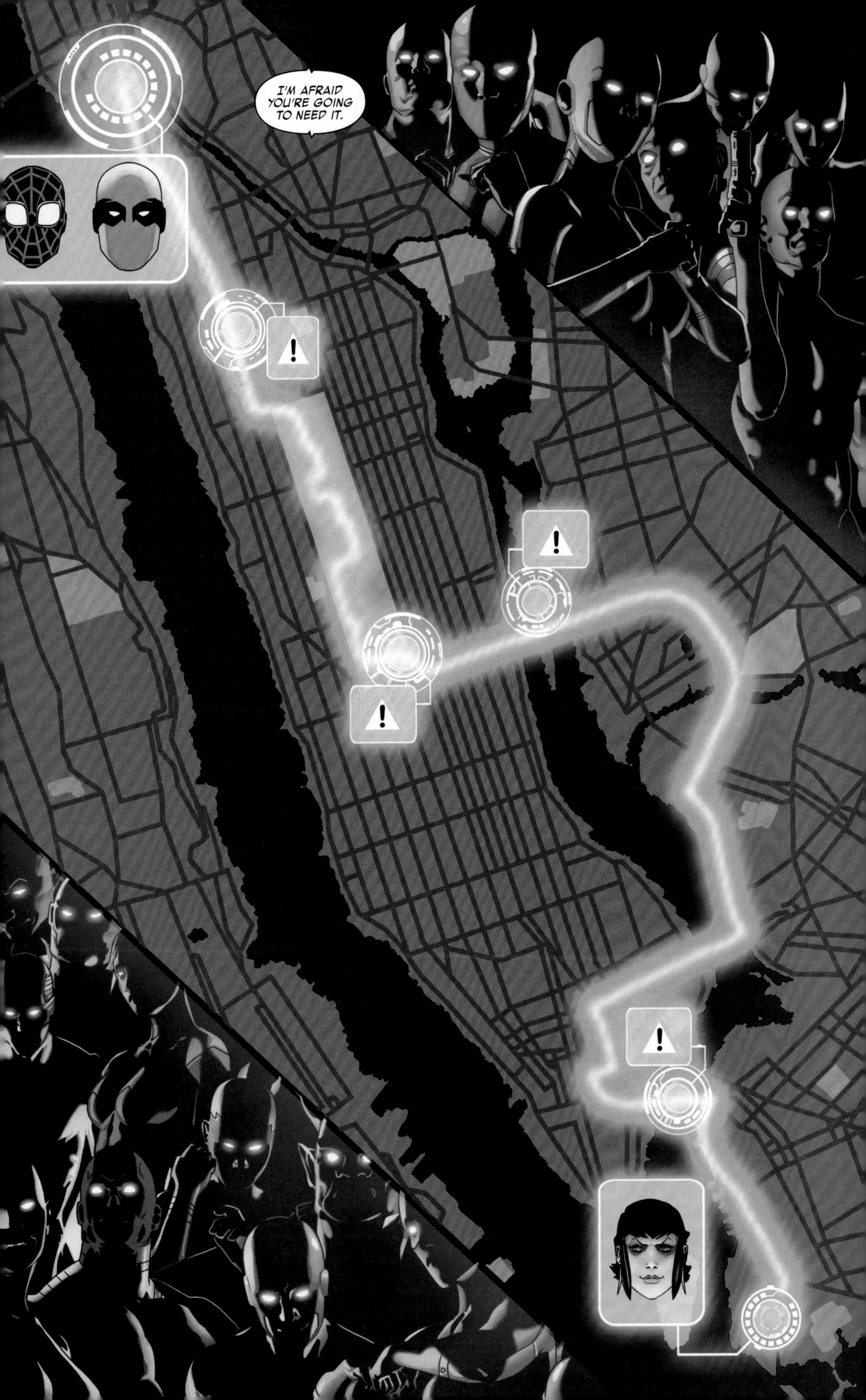
I'M AFRAID YOU'RE GOING TO NEED IT.

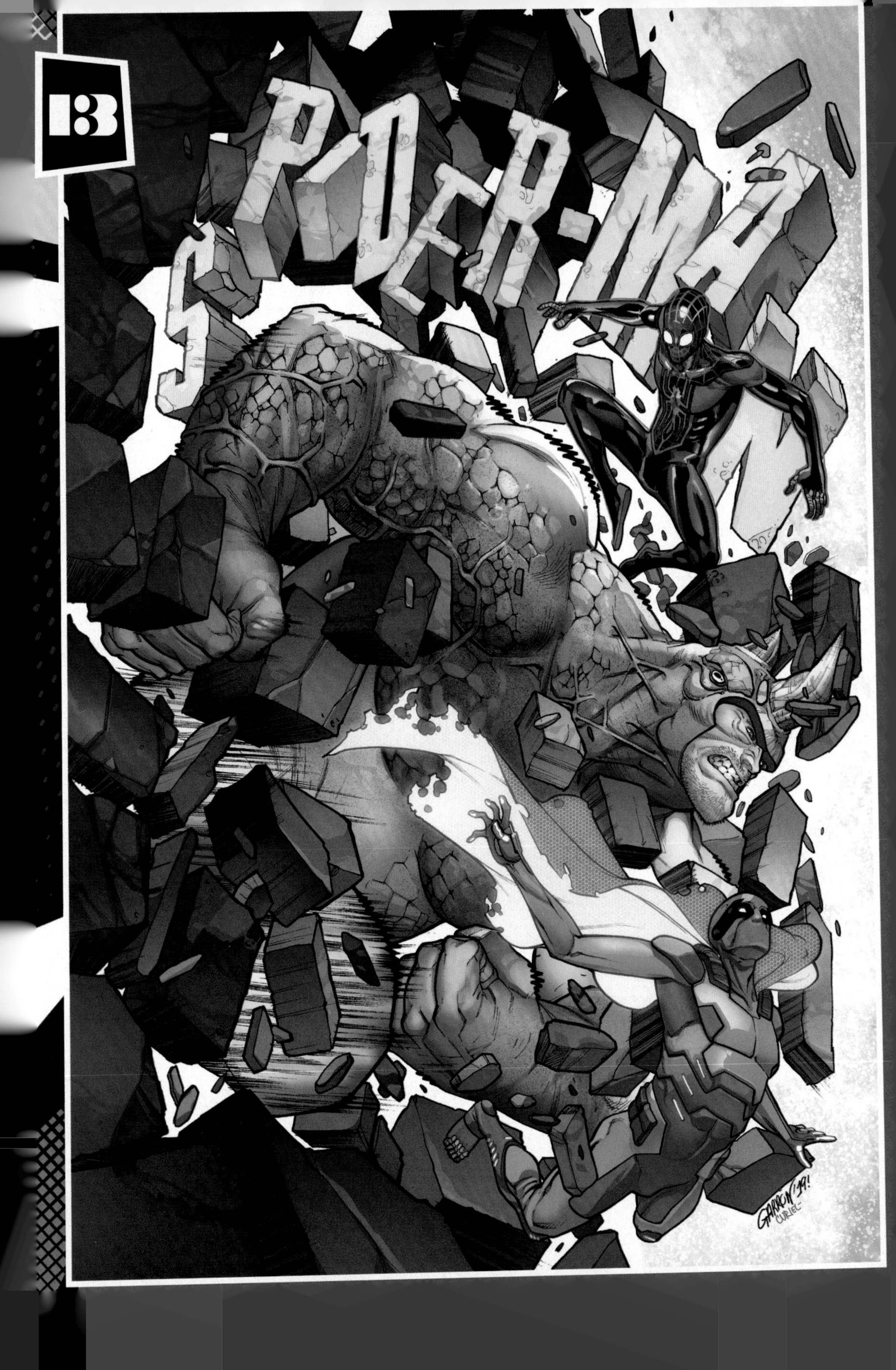

13
GARRON '19!
CURIEL

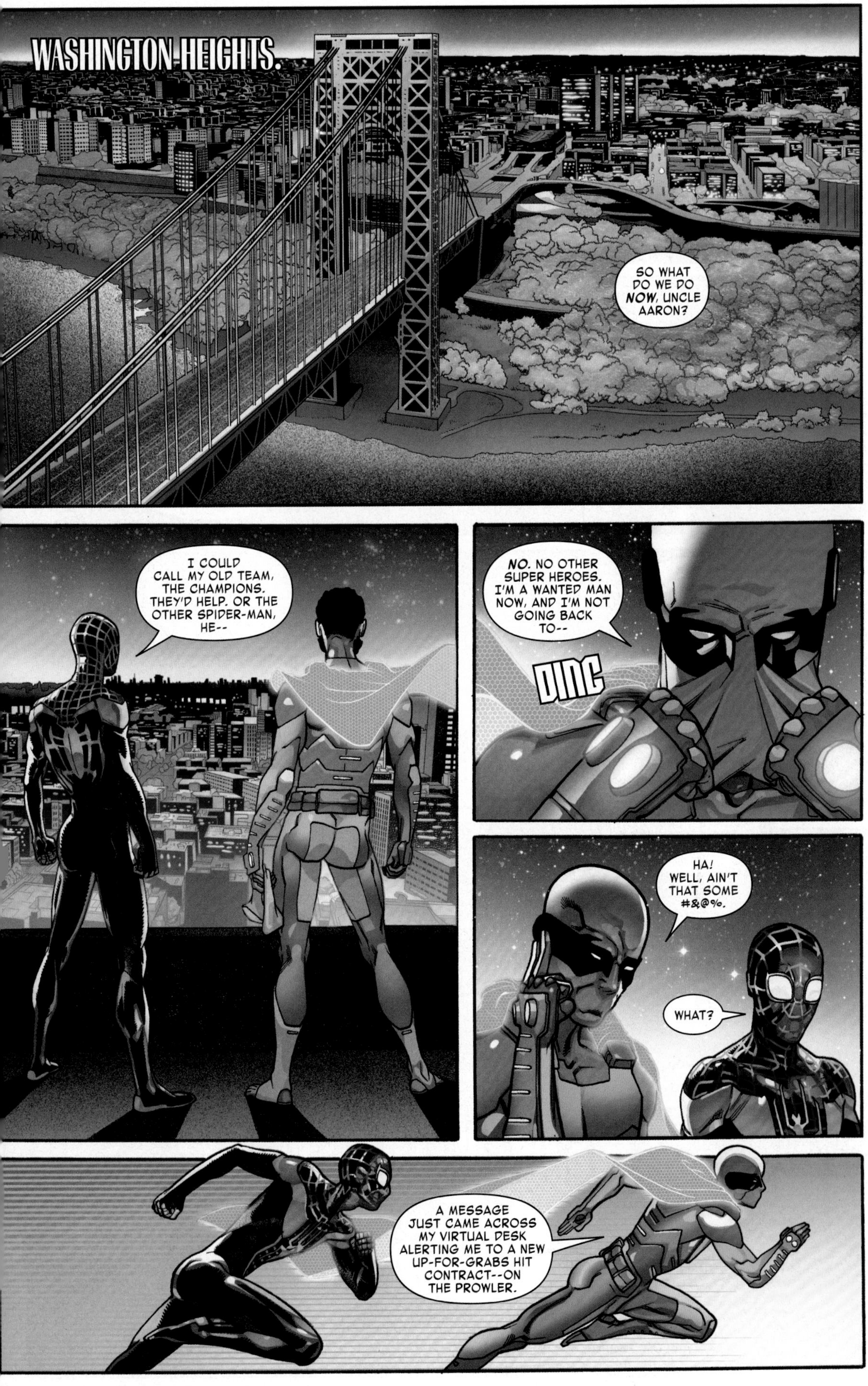
WASHINGTON HEIGHTS.
SO WHAT DO WE DO NOW, UNCLE AARON?
I COULD CALL MY OLD TEAM, THE CHAMPIONS. THEY'D HELP. OR THE OTHER SPIDER-MAN, HE--
NO. NO OTHER SUPER HEROES. I'M A WANTED MAN NOW, AND I'M NOT GOING BACK TO--
DINC
HA! WELL, AIN'T THAT SOME #&@%.
WHAT?
A MESSAGE JUST CAME ACROSS MY VIRTUAL DESK ALERTING ME TO A NEW UP-FOR-GRABS HIT CONTRACT--ON THE PROWLER.

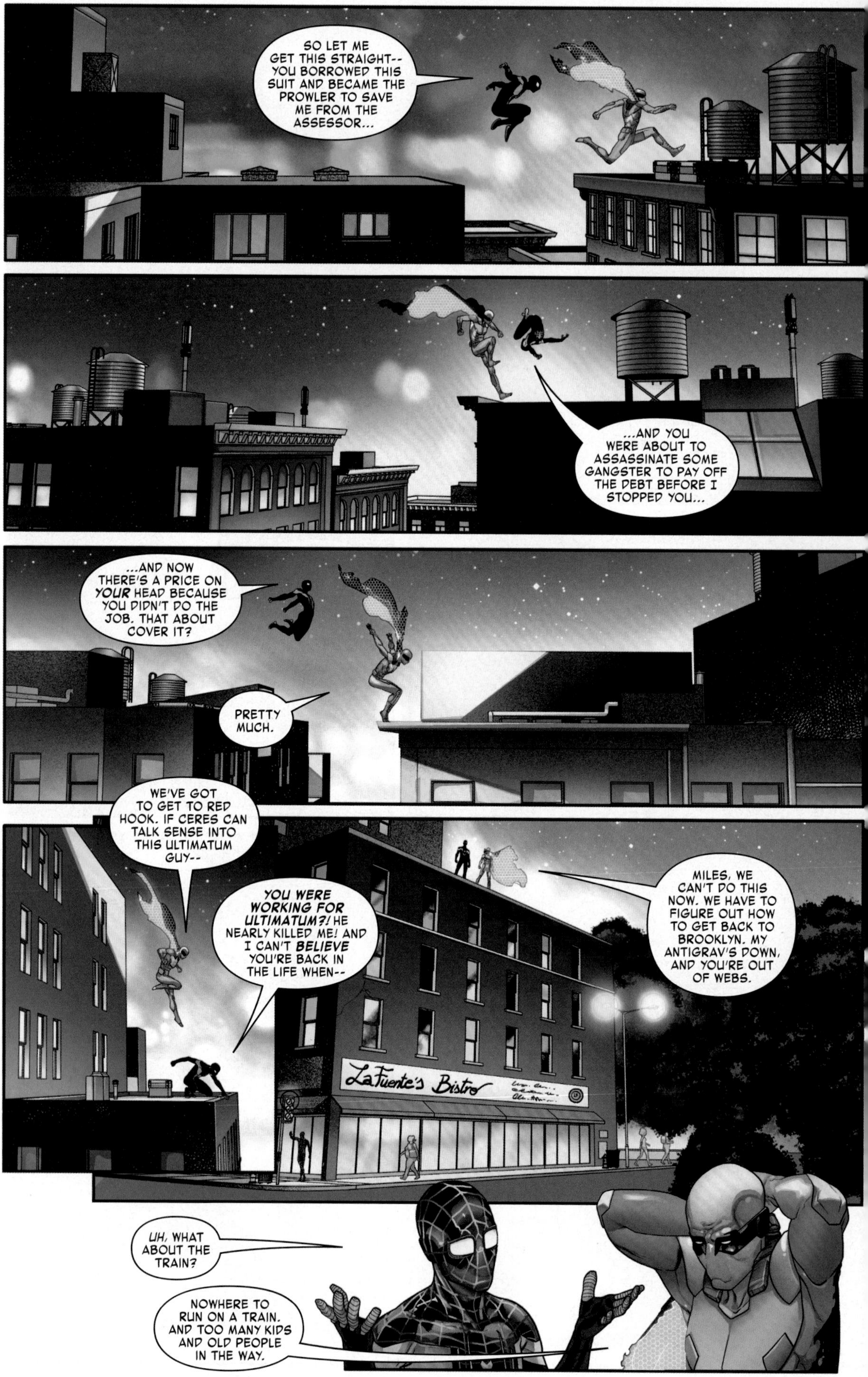
SO LET ME GET THIS STRAIGHT-- YOU BORROWED THIS SUIT AND BECAME THE PROWLER TO SAVE ME FROM THE ASSESSOR...
...AND YOU WERE ABOUT TO ASSASSINATE SOME GANGSTER TO PAY OFF THE DEBT BEFORE I STOPPED YOU...
...AND NOW THERE'S A PRICE ON YOUR HEAD BECAUSE YOU DIDN'T DO THE JOB. THAT ABOUT COVER IT?
PRETTY MUCH.
WE'VE GOT TO GET TO RED HOOK. IF CERES CAN TALK SENSE INTO THIS ULTIMATUM GUY--
YOU WERE WORKING FOR ULTIMATUM?! HE NEARLY KILLED ME! AND I CAN'T BELIEVE YOU'RE BACK IN THE LIFE WHEN--
MILES, WE CAN'T DO THIS NOW. WE HAVE TO FIGURE OUT HOW TO GET BACK TO BROOKLYN. MY ANTIGRAV'S DOWN, AND YOU'RE OUT OF WEBS.
LaFuente's Bistro
UH, WHAT ABOUT THE TRAIN?
NOWHERE TO RUN ON A TRAIN. AND TOO MANY KIDS AND OLD PEOPLE IN THE WAY.

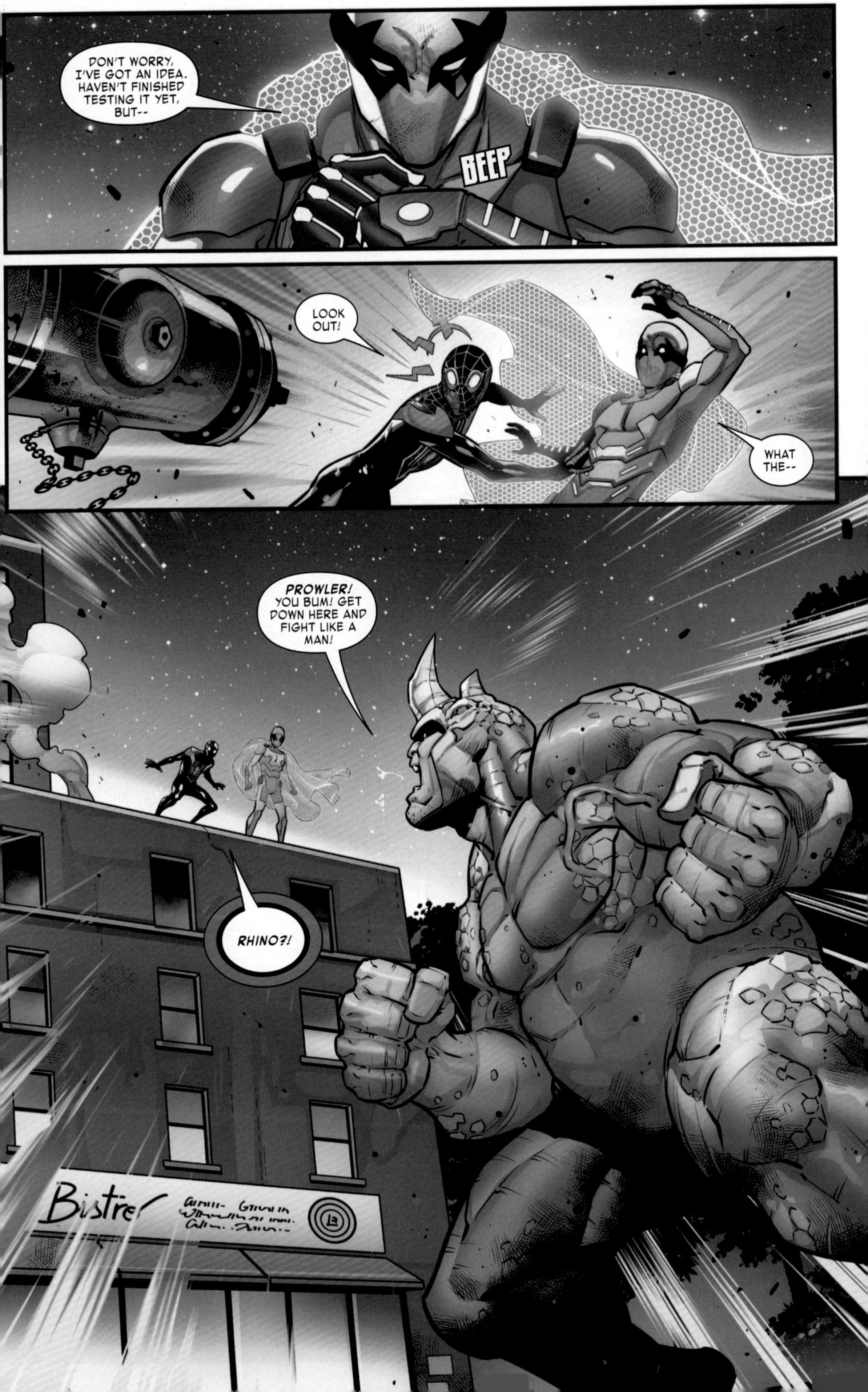
DON'T WORRY, I'VE GOT AN IDEA. HAVEN'T FINISHED TESTING IT YET, BUT--
BEEP
LOOK OUT!
WHAT THE--
PROWLER! YOU BUM! GET DOWN HERE AND FIGHT LIKE A MAN!
RHINO?!
Bistro

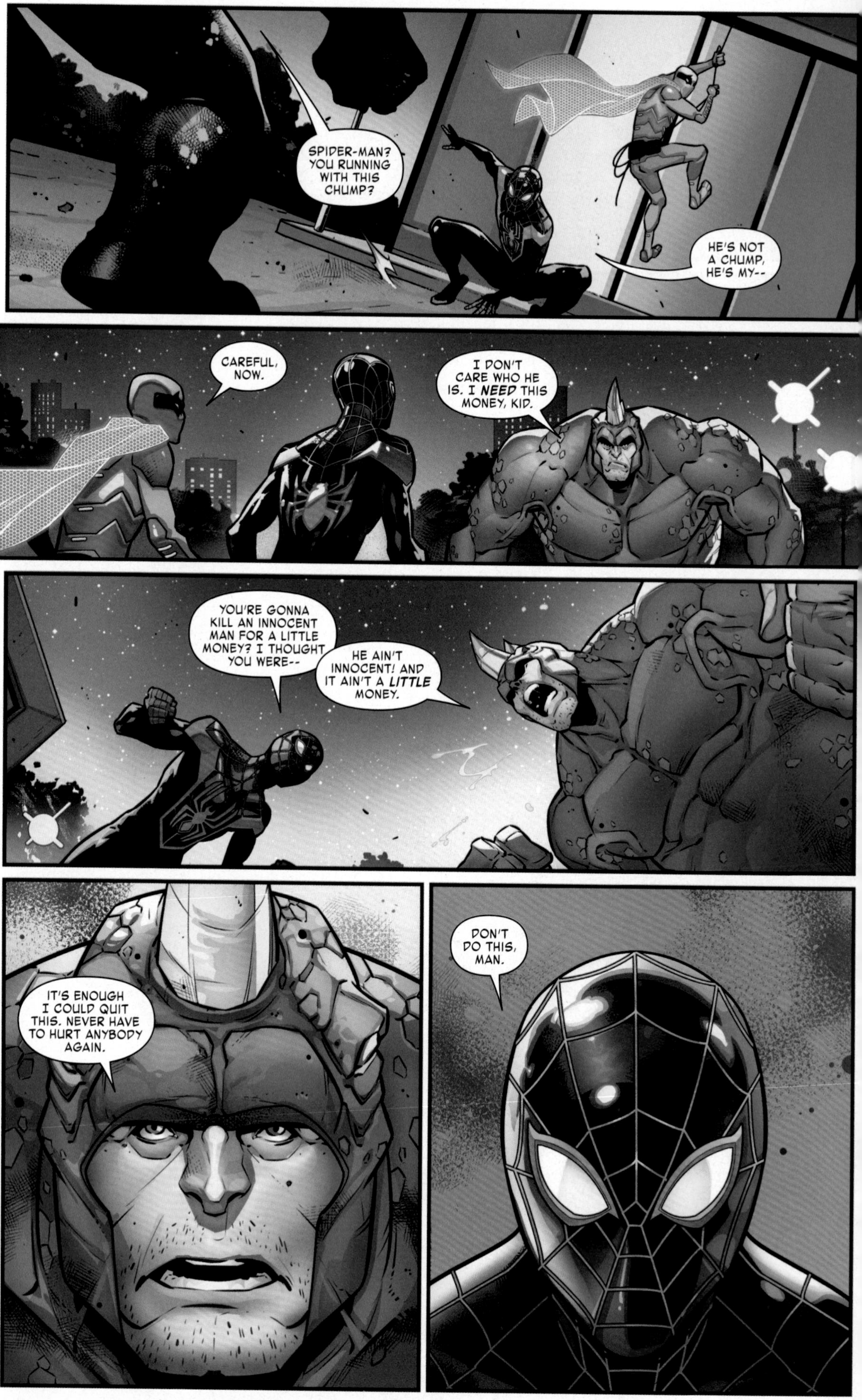
SPIDER-MAN? YOU RUNNING WITH THIS CHUMP?
HE'S NOT A CHUMP, HE'S MY--
CAREFUL, NOW.
I DON'T CARE WHO HE IS. I NEED THIS MONEY, KID.
YOU'RE GONNA KILL AN INNOCENT MAN FOR A LITTLE MONEY? I THOUGHT YOU WERE--
HE AIN'T INNOCENT! AND IT AIN'T A LITTLE MONEY.
IT'S ENOUGH I COULD QUIT THIS. NEVER HAVE TO HURT ANYBODY AGAIN.
DON'T DO THIS, MAN.

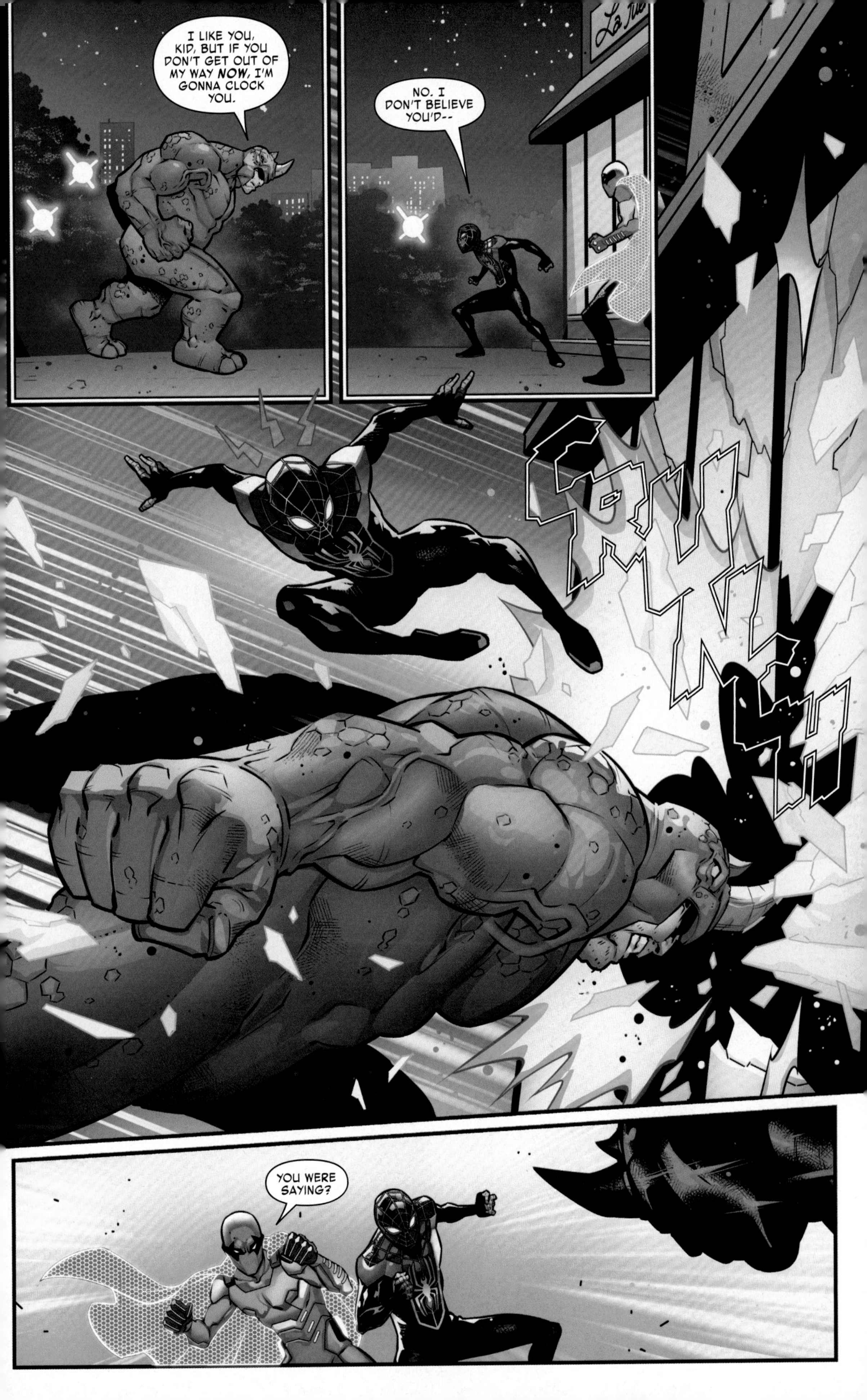
I LIKE YOU, KID, BUT IF YOU DON'T GET OUT OF MY WAY NOW, I'M GONNA CLOCK YOU.
NO. I DON'T BELIEVE YOU'D--
CRUNCH
YOU WERE SAYING?

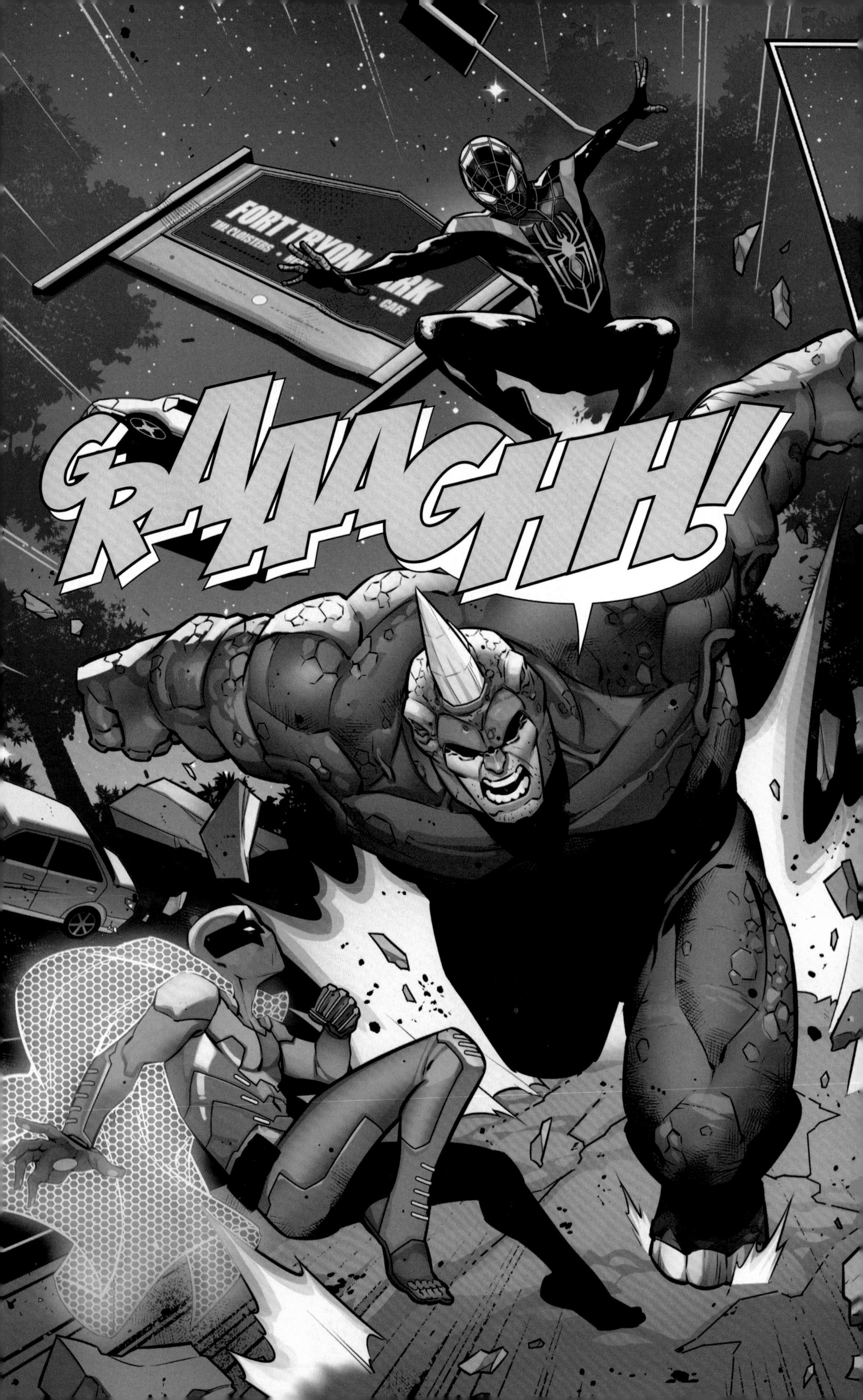
FORT TRYON
ARK
THE CLOISTERS
CAFE
GRAAAGHH!

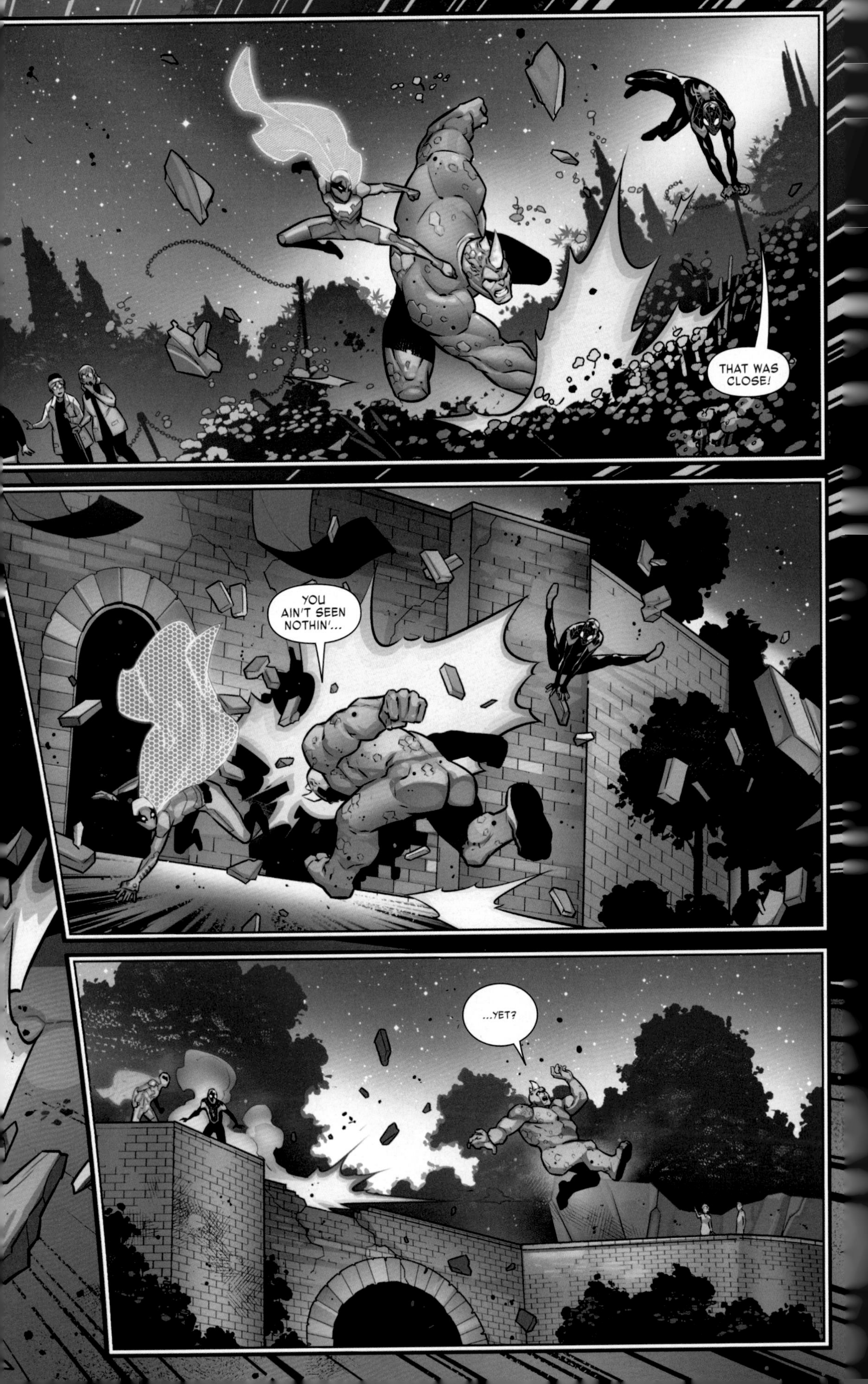
THAT WAS CLOSE!
YOU AIN'T SEEN NOTHIN'...
...YET?

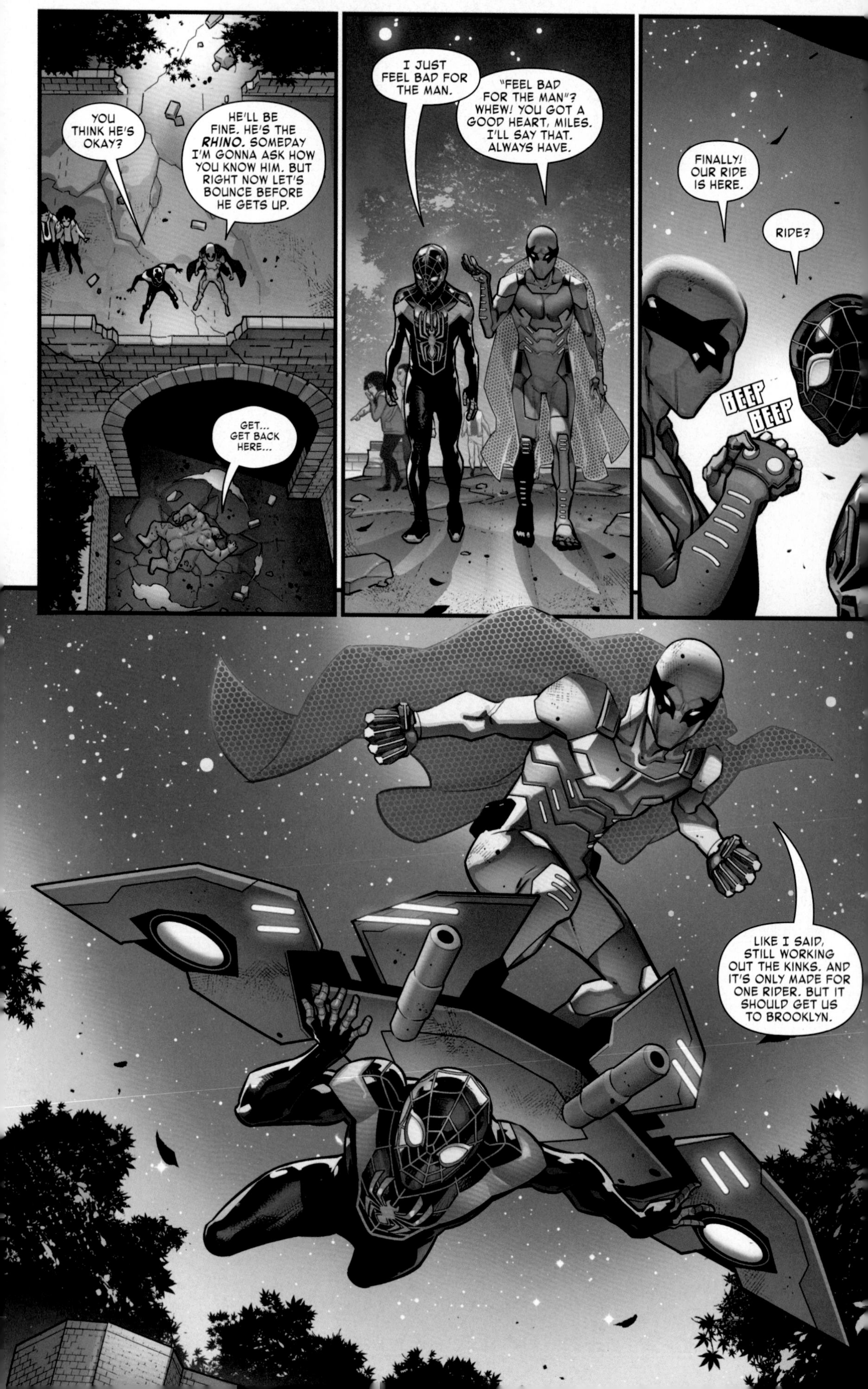

YOU THINK HE'S OKAY?
HE'LL BE FINE. HE'S THE RHINO. SOMEDAY I'M GONNA ASK HOW YOU KNOW HIM. BUT RIGHT NOW LET'S BOUNCE BEFORE HE GETS UP.
GET... GET BACK HERE...
I JUST FEEL BAD FOR THE MAN.
"FEEL BAD FOR THE MAN"? WHEW! YOU GOT A GOOD HEART, MILES. I'LL SAY THAT. ALWAYS HAVE.
FINALLY! OUR RIDE IS HERE.
RIDE?
BEEP BEEP
LIKE I SAID, STILL WORKING OUT THE KINKS. AND IT'S ONLY MADE FOR ONE RIDER. BUT IT SHOULD GET US TO BROOKLYN.

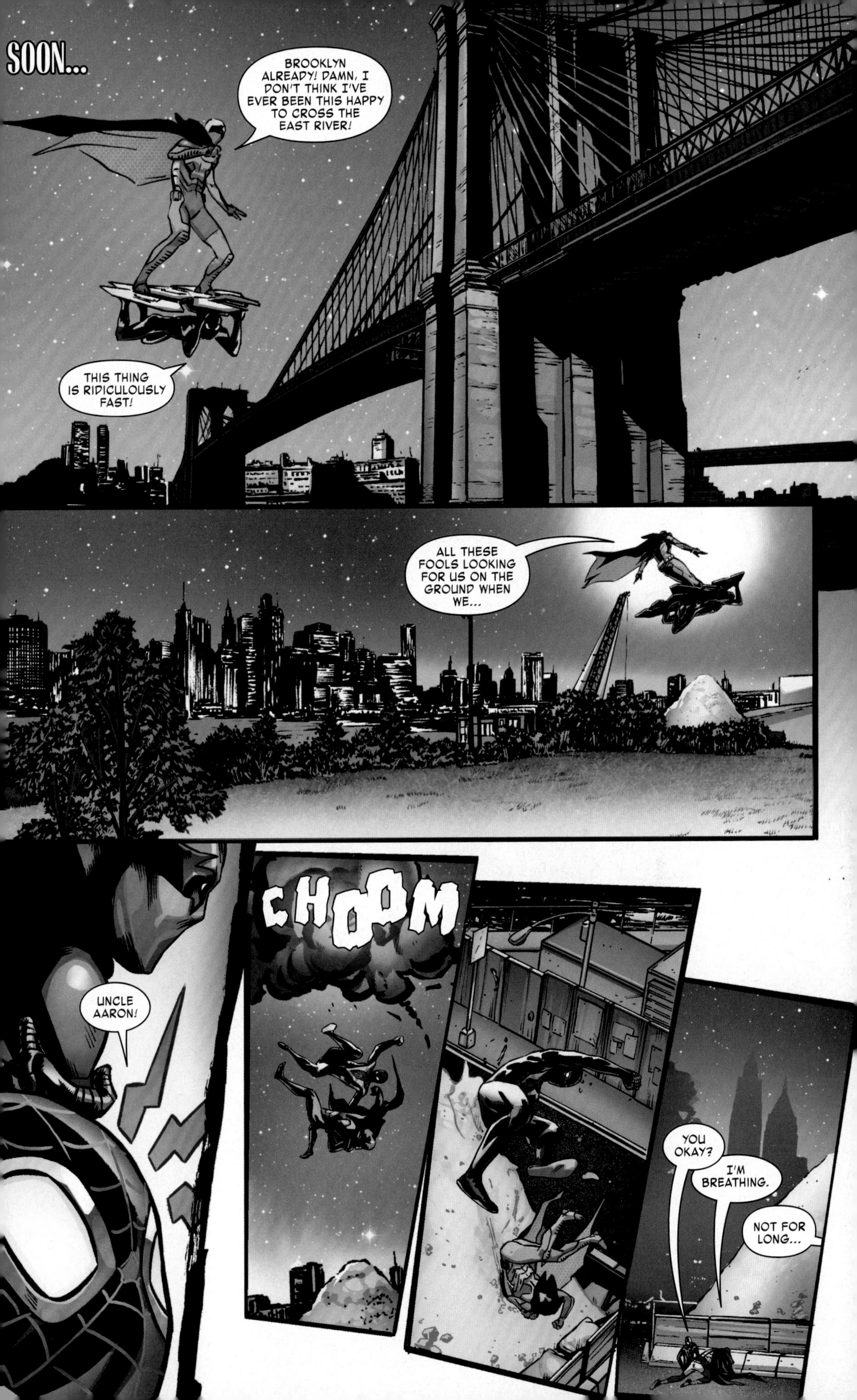
SOON...
BROOKLYN ALREADY! DAMN, I DON'T THINK I'VE EVER BEEN THIS HAPPY TO CROSS THE EAST RIVER!
THIS THING IS RIDICULOUSLY FAST!
ALL THESE FOOLS LOOKING FOR US ON THE GROUND WHEN WE...
UNCLE AARON!
CHOOM
YOU OKAY?
I'M BREATHING.
NOT FOR LONG...

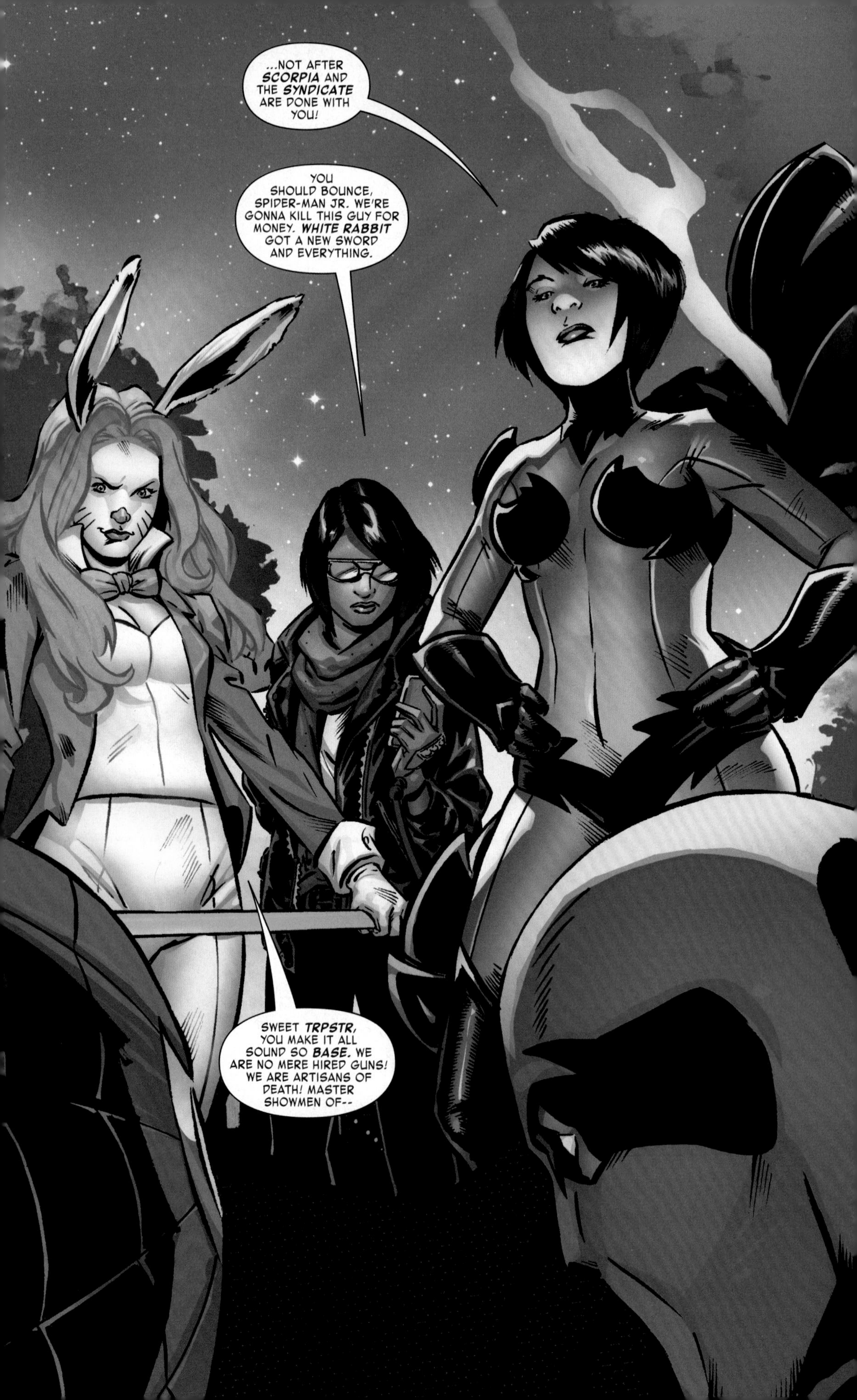
...NOT AFTER SCORPIA AND THE SYNDICATE ARE DONE WITH YOU!
YOU SHOULD BOUNCE, SPIDER-MAN JR. WE'RE GONNA KILL THIS GUY FOR MONEY. WHITE RABBIT GOT A NEW SWORD AND EVERYTHING.
SWEET TRPSTR, YOU MAKE IT ALL SOUND SO BASE. WE ARE NO MERE HIRED GUNS! WE ARE ARTISANS OF DEATH! MASTER SHOWMEN OF--

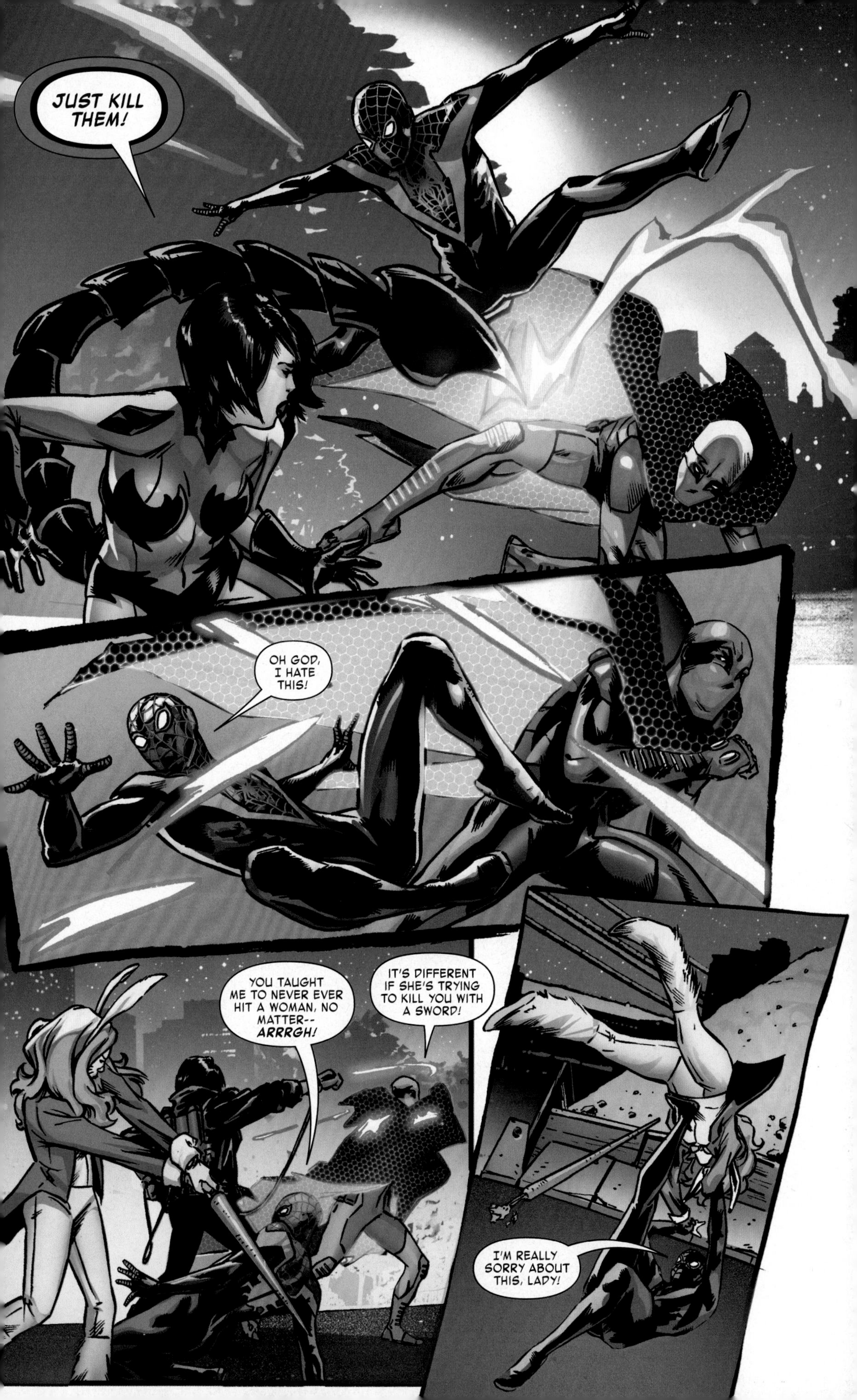
JUST KILL THEM!
OH GOD, I HATE THIS!
YOU TAUGHT ME TO NEVER EVER HIT A WOMAN, NO MATTER-- ARRRGH!
IT'S DIFFERENT IF SHE'S TRYING TO KILL YOU WITH A SWORD!
I'M REALLY SORRY ABOUT THIS, LADY!

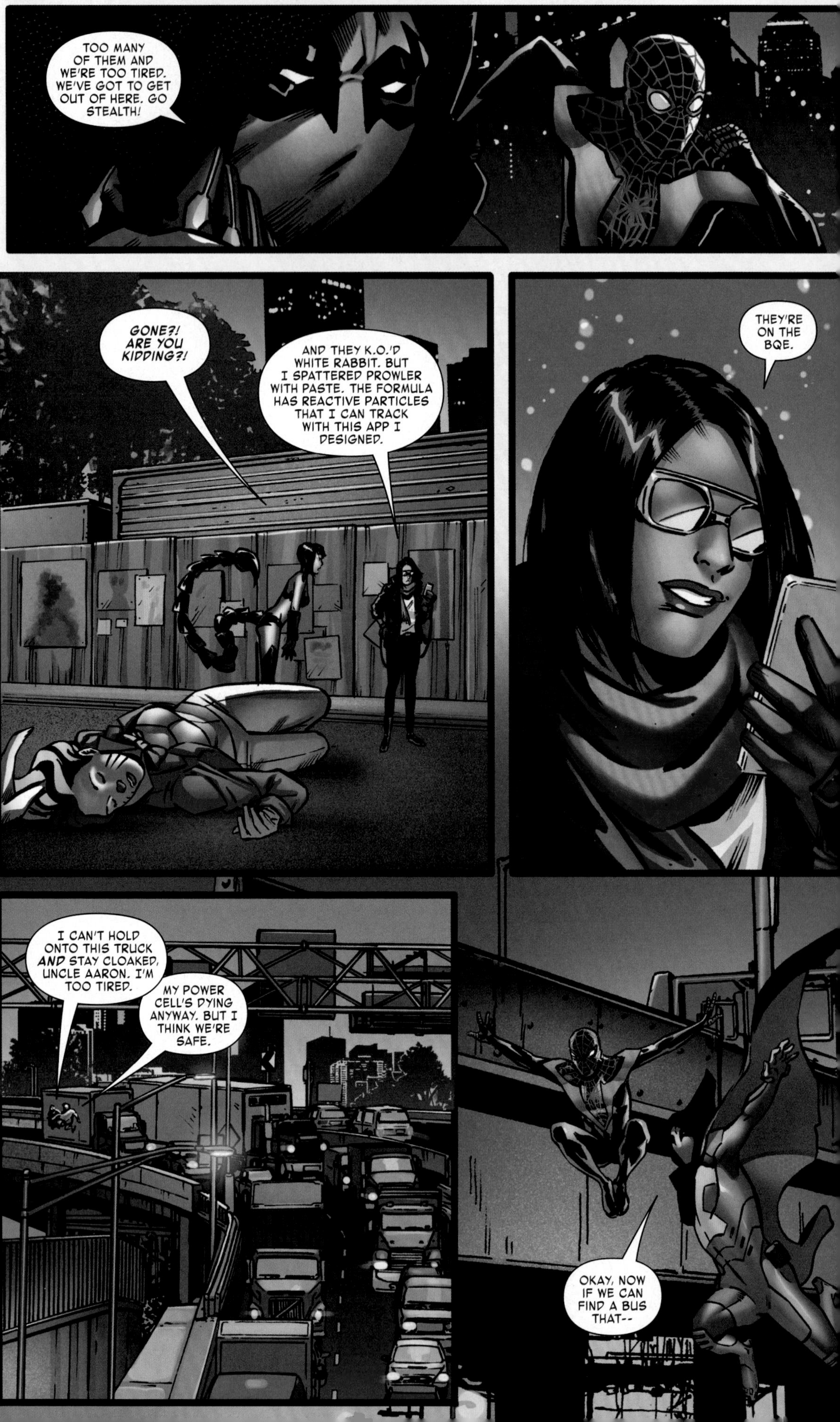
TOO MANY OF THEM AND WE'RE TOO TIRED. WE'VE GOT TO GET OUT OF HERE. GO STEALTH!
GONE?! ARE YOU KIDDING?!
AND THEY K.O.'D WHITE RABBIT. BUT I SPATTERED PROWLER WITH PASTE. THE FORMULA HAS REACTIVE PARTICLES THAT I CAN TRACK WITH THIS APP I DESIGNED.
THEY'RE ON THE BQE.
I CAN'T HOLD ONTO THIS TRUCK AND STAY CLOAKED, UNCLE AARON. I'M TOO TIRED.
MY POWER CELL'S DYING ANYWAY. BUT I THINK WE'RE SAFE.
OKAY, NOW IF WE CAN FIND A BUS THAT--

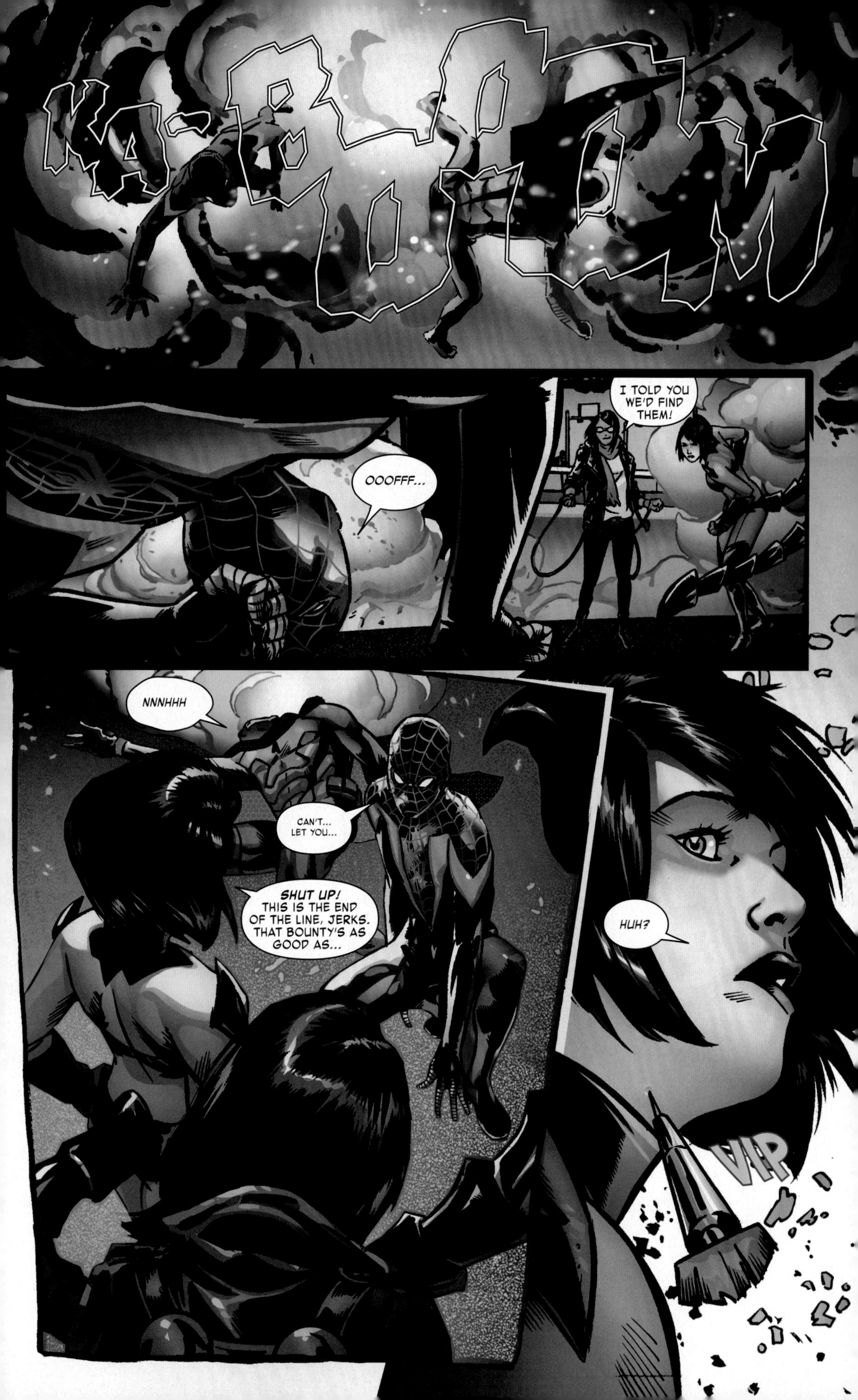
KA-BOOOOM
OOOFFF...
I TOLD YOU WE'D FIND THEM!
NNNHHH
CAN'T... LET YOU...
SHUT UP! THIS IS THE END OF THE LINE, JERKS. THAT BOUNTY'S AS GOOD AS...
HUH?
VIP

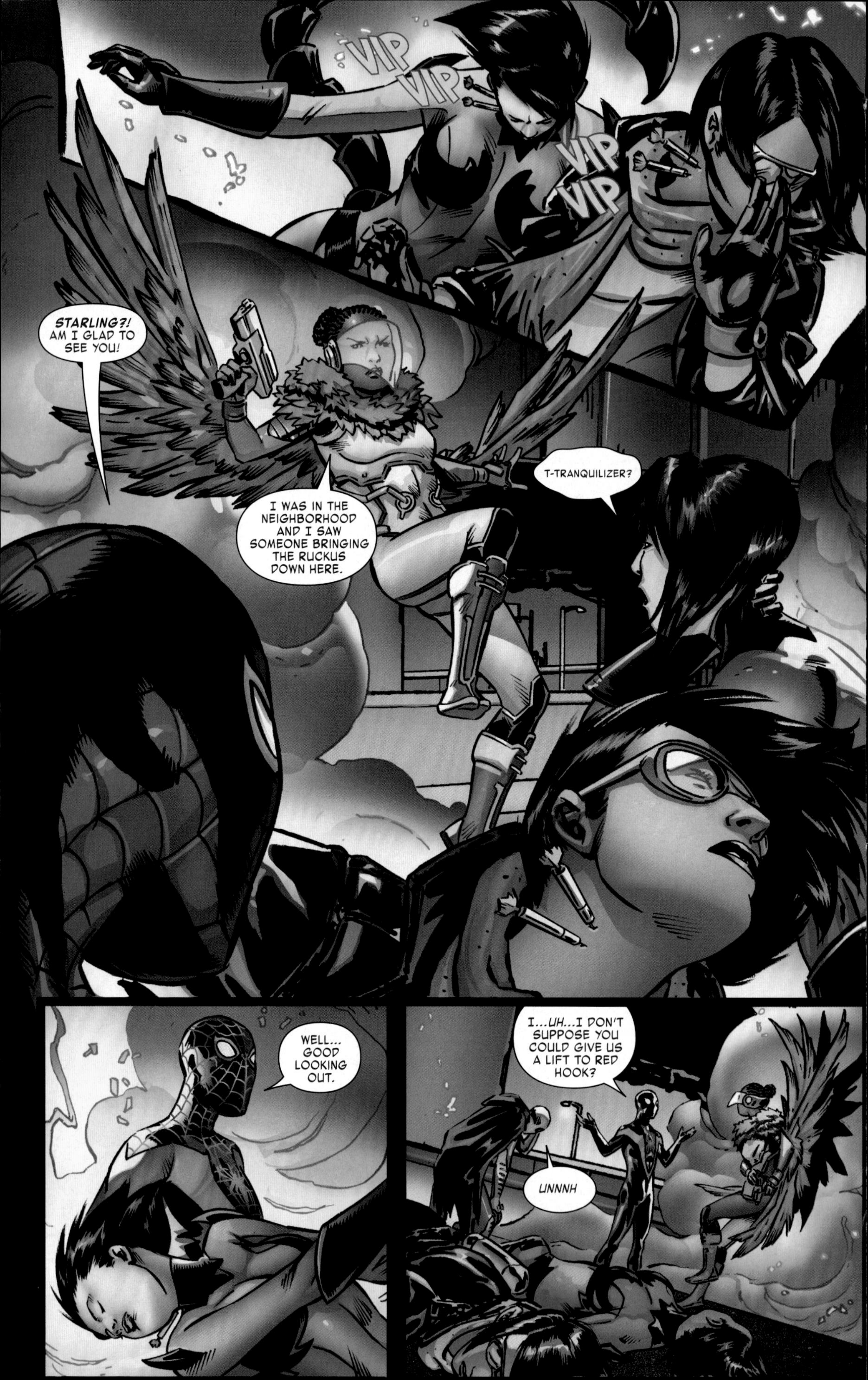
VIP
VIP
VIP
VIP
STARLING?! AM I GLAD TO SEE YOU!
I WAS IN THE NEIGHBORHOOD AND I SAW SOMEONE BRINGING THE RUCKUS DOWN HERE.
T-TRANQUILIZER?
WELL... GOOD LOOKING OUT.
I...UH...I DON'T SUPPOSE YOU COULD GIVE US A LIFT TO RED HOOK?
UNNNH

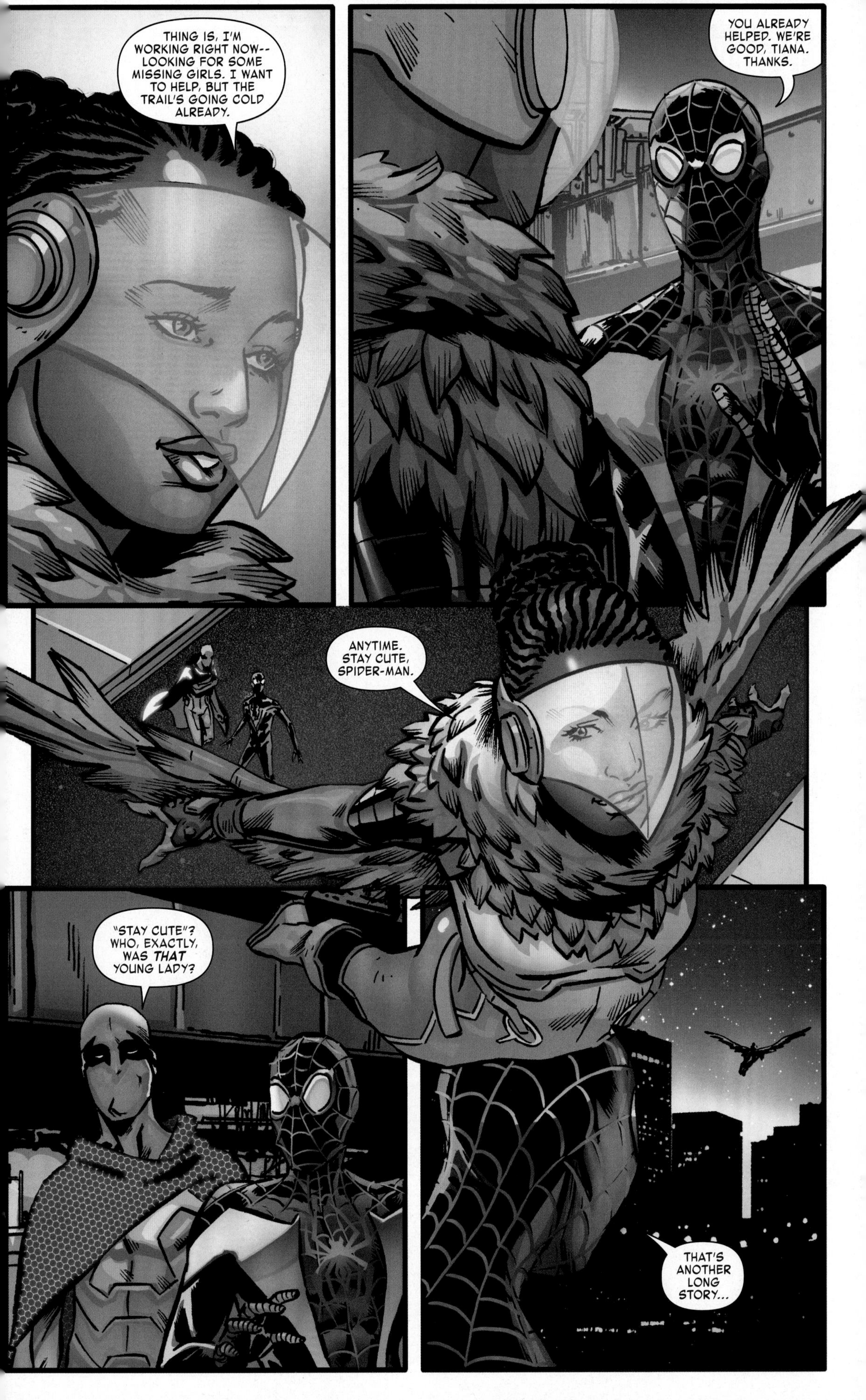
THING IS, I'M WORKING RIGHT NOW-- LOOKING FOR SOME MISSING GIRLS. I WANT TO HELP, BUT THE TRAIL'S GOING COLD ALREADY.
YOU ALREADY HELPED. WE'RE GOOD, TIANA. THANKS.
ANYTIME. STAY CUTE, SPIDER-MAN.
"STAY CUTE"? WHO, EXACTLY, WAS *THAT* YOUNG LADY?
THAT'S ANOTHER LONG STORY...

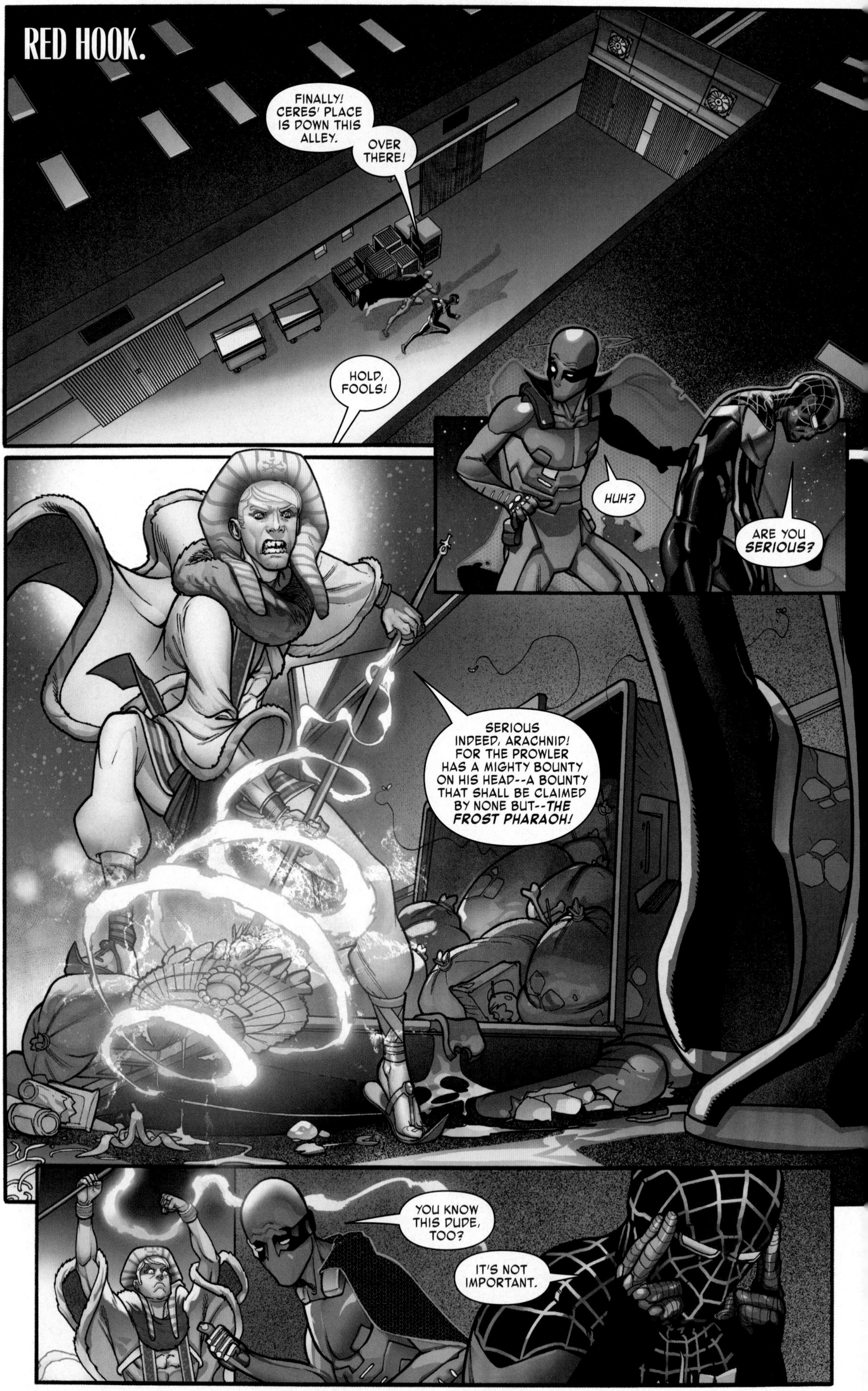
RED HOOK.
FINALLY! CERES' PLACE IS DOWN THIS ALLEY.
OVER THERE!
HOLD, FOOLS!
HUH?
ARE YOU *SERIOUS?*
SERIOUS INDEED, ARACHNID! FOR THE PROWLER HAS A MIGHTY BOUNTY ON HIS HEAD--A BOUNTY THAT SHALL BE CLAIMED BY NONE BUT--*THE FROST PHARAOH!*
YOU KNOW THIS DUDE, TOO?
IT'S NOT IMPORTANT.

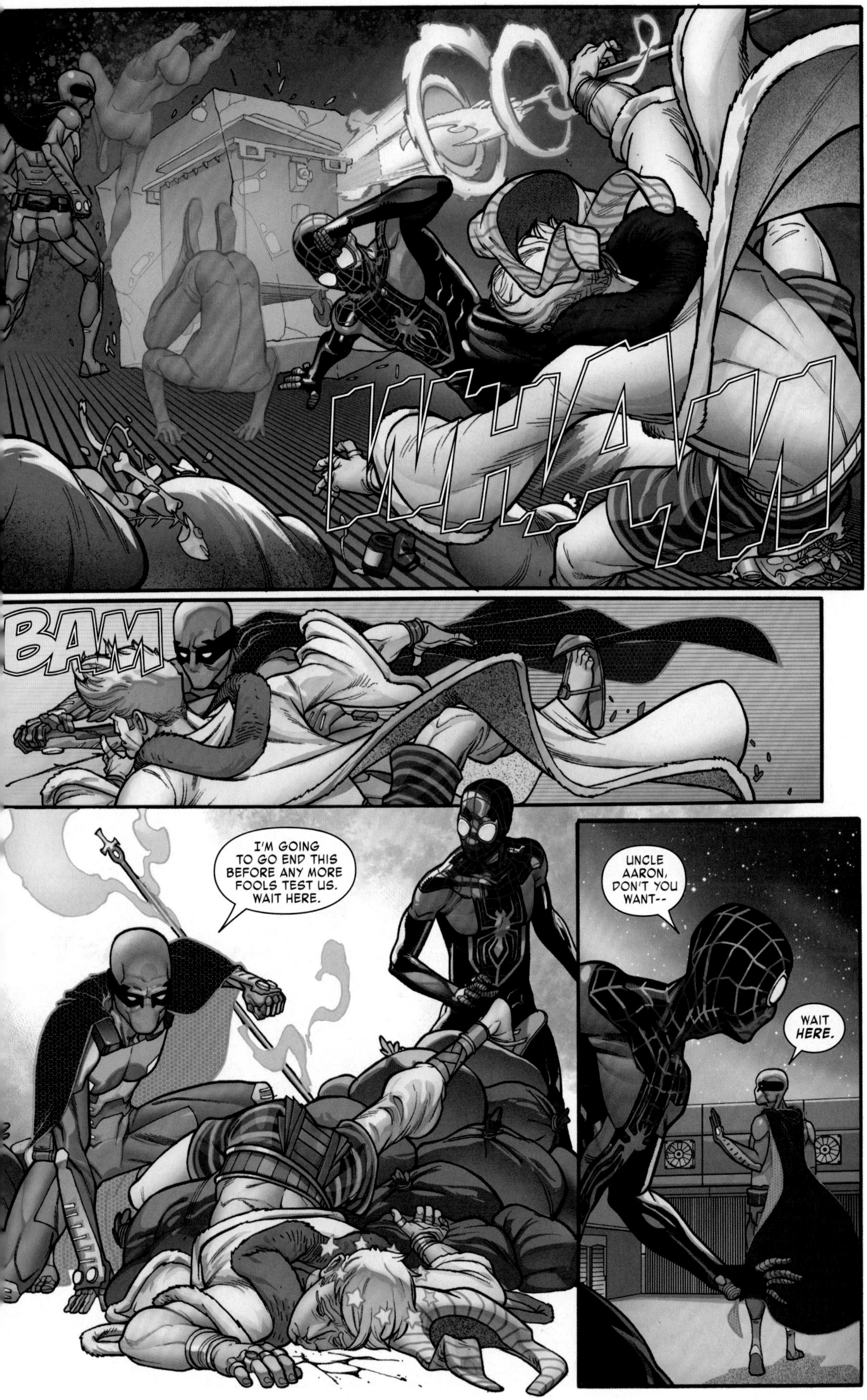
WHAM
BAM
I'M GOING TO GO END THIS BEFORE ANY MORE FOOLS TEST US. WAIT HERE.
UNCLE AARON, DON'T YOU WANT--
WAIT HERE.

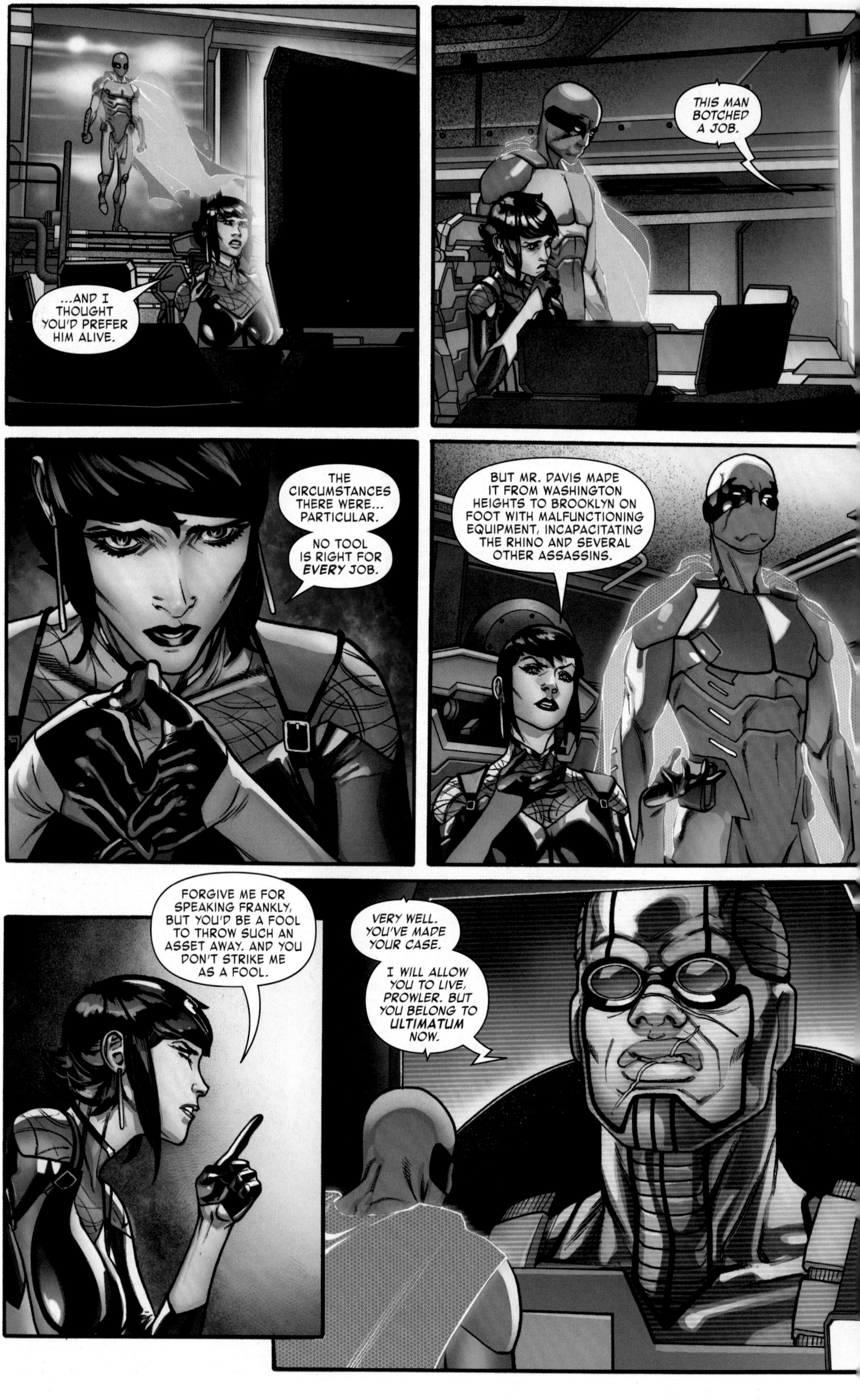
...AND I THOUGHT YOU'D PREFER HIM ALIVE.
THIS MAN BOTCHED A JOB.
THE CIRCUMSTANCES THERE WERE... PARTICULAR.
NO TOOL IS RIGHT FOR EVERY JOB.
BUT MR. DAVIS MADE IT FROM WASHINGTON HEIGHTS TO BROOKLYN ON FOOT WITH MALFUNCTIONING EQUIPMENT, INCAPACITATING THE RHINO AND SEVERAL OTHER ASSASSINS.
FORGIVE ME FOR SPEAKING FRANKLY, BUT YOU'D BE A FOOL TO THROW SUCH AN ASSET AWAY. AND YOU DON'T STRIKE ME AS A FOOL.
VERY WELL. YOU'VE MADE YOUR CASE.
I WILL ALLOW YOU TO LIVE, PROWLER. BUT YOU BELONG TO ULTIMATUM NOW.

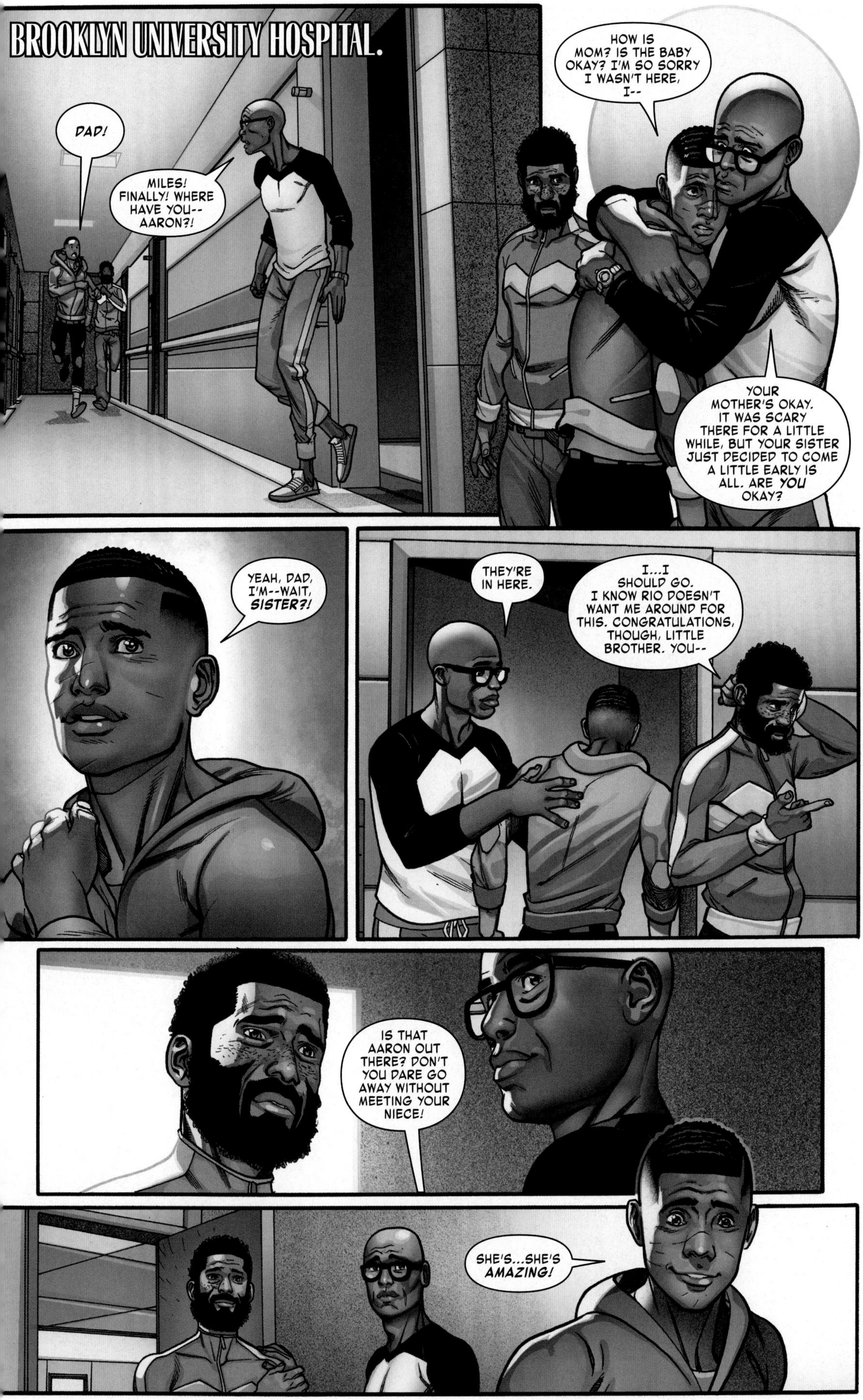
BROOKLYN UNIVERSITY HOSPITAL.
DAD!
MILES! FINALLY! WHERE HAVE YOU-- AARON?!
HOW IS MOM? IS THE BABY OKAY? I'M SO SORRY I WASN'T HERE, I--
YOUR MOTHER'S OKAY. IT WAS SCARY THERE FOR A LITTLE WHILE, BUT YOUR SISTER JUST DECIDED TO COME A LITTLE EARLY IS ALL. ARE *YOU* OKAY?
YEAH, DAD, I'M--WAIT, ***SISTER?!***
THEY'RE IN HERE.
I...I SHOULD GO. I KNOW RIO DOESN'T WANT ME AROUND FOR THIS. CONGRATULATIONS, THOUGH, LITTLE BROTHER. YOU--
IS THAT AARON OUT THERE? DON'T YOU DARE GO AWAY WITHOUT MEETING YOUR NIECE!
SHE'S...SHE'S *AMAZING!*

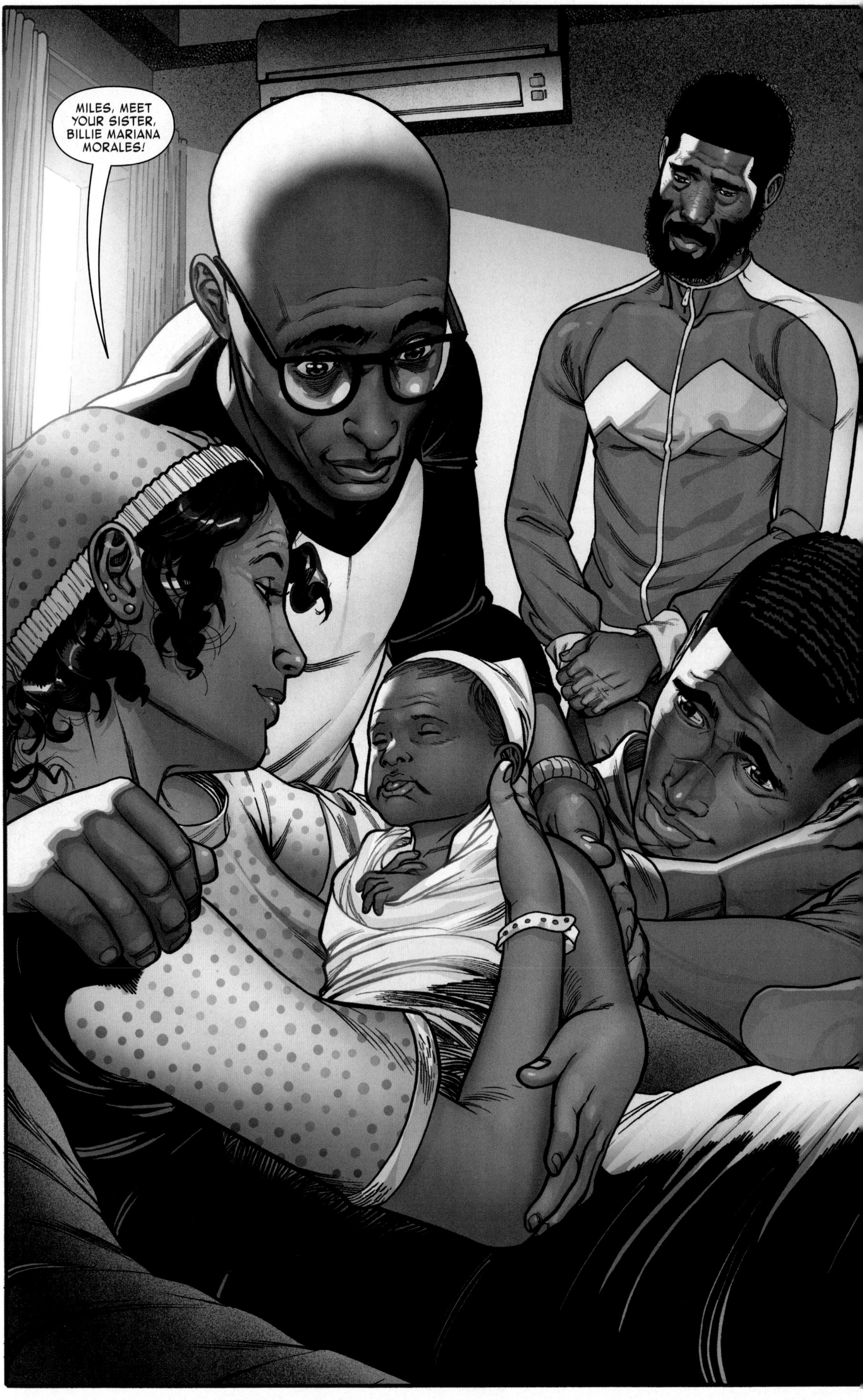
MILES, MEET YOUR SISTER, BILLIE MARIANA MORALES!

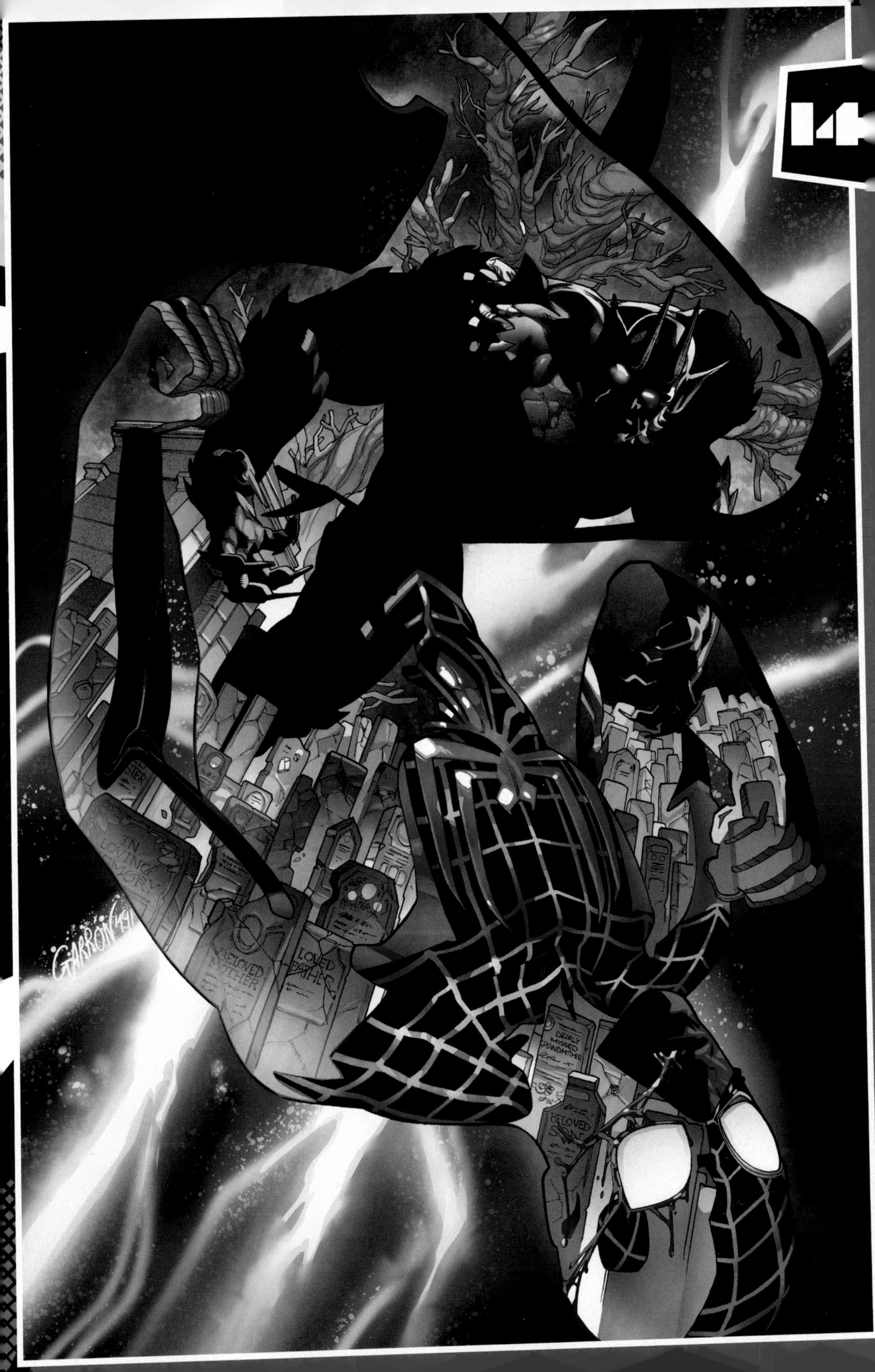
14
IN LOVING MEMORY
BELOVED MOTHER
LOVED FATHER
DEARLY MISSED GRANDMOTHER
BELOVED SON
GARRON '19

I'VE SEEN SOME UGLY THINGS IN THE PAST YEAR, JOURNAL.

HAD SOME HORRIBLE THINGS HAPPEN TO ME.

BUT I'VE ALSO SEEN SOMETHING BEAUTIFUL THAT OUTWEIGHS THE UGLY. HAD SOMETHING AMAZING HAPPEN THAT OUTWEIGHS THE HORROR.

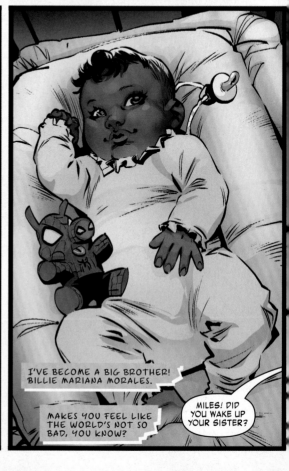

I'VE BECOME A BIG BROTHER! BILLIE MARIANA MORALES.

MAKES YOU FEEL LIKE THE WORLD'S NOT SO BAD, YOU KNOW?

MILES! DID YOU WAKE UP YOUR SISTER?

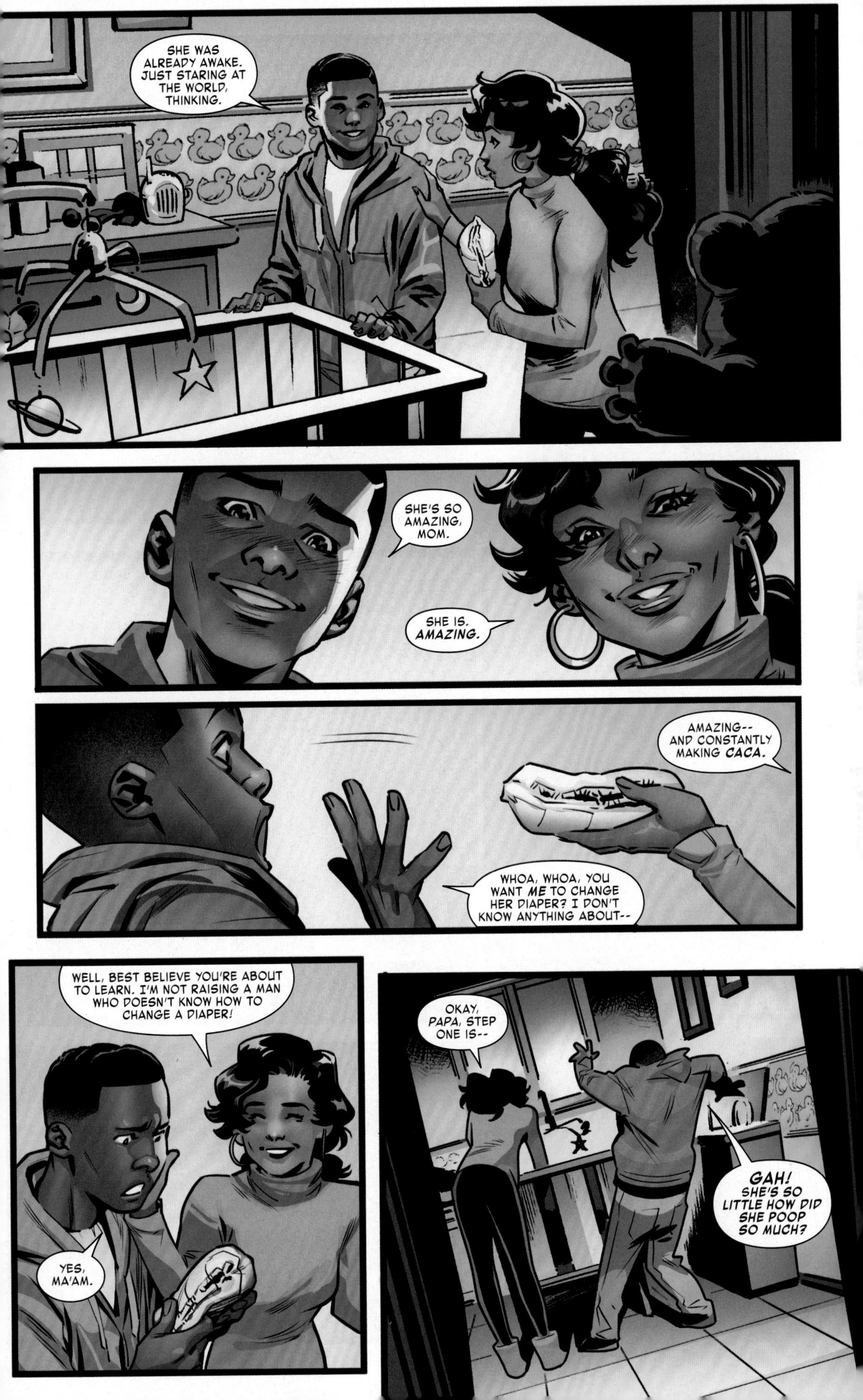
SHE WAS ALREADY AWAKE. JUST STARING AT THE WORLD, THINKING.
SHE'S SO AMAZING, MOM.
SHE IS. *AMAZING.*
AMAZING-- AND CONSTANTLY MAKING *CACA.*
WHOA, WHOA, YOU WANT *ME* TO CHANGE HER DIAPER? I DON'T KNOW ANYTHING ABOUT--
WELL, BEST BELIEVE YOU'RE ABOUT TO LEARN. I'M NOT RAISING A MAN WHO DOESN'T KNOW HOW TO CHANGE A DIAPER!
YES, MA'AM.
OKAY, PAPA, STEP ONE IS--
GAH! SHE'S SO LITTLE HOW DID SHE POOP SO MUCH?

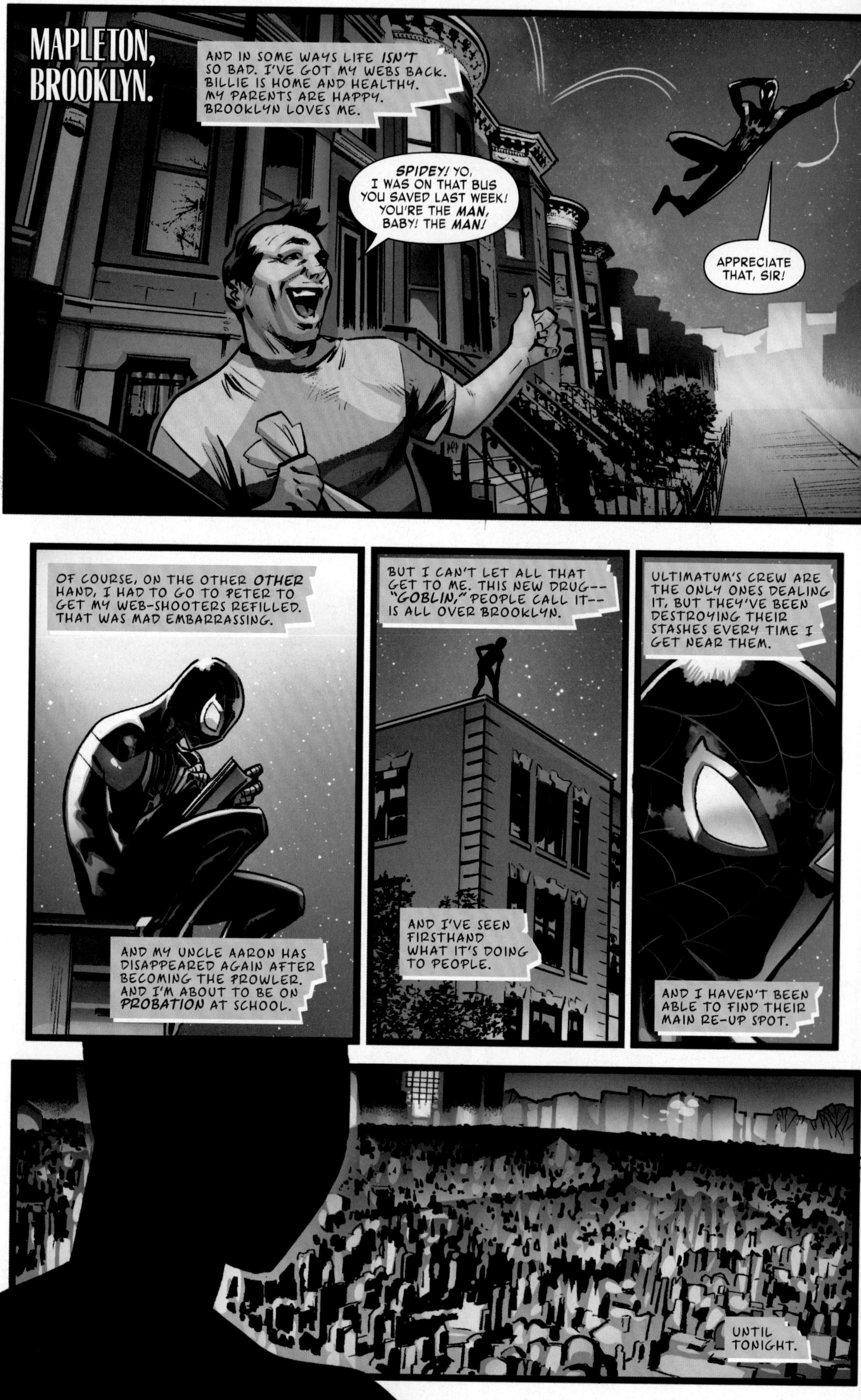
MAPLETON, BROOKLYN.
AND IN SOME WAYS LIFE ISN'T SO BAD. I'VE GOT MY WEBS BACK. BILLIE IS HOME AND HEALTHY. MY PARENTS ARE HAPPY. BROOKLYN LOVES ME.
SPIDEY! YO, I WAS ON THAT BUS YOU SAVED LAST WEEK! YOU'RE THE MAN, BABY! THE MAN!
APPRECIATE THAT, SIR!
OF COURSE, ON THE OTHER OTHER HAND, I HAD TO GO TO PETER TO GET MY WEB-SHOOTERS REFILLED. THAT WAS MAD EMBARRASSING.
AND MY UNCLE AARON HAS DISAPPEARED AGAIN AFTER BECOMING THE PROWLER. AND I'M ABOUT TO BE ON PROBATION AT SCHOOL.
BUT I CAN'T LET ALL THAT GET TO ME. THIS NEW DRUG-- "GOBLIN," PEOPLE CALL IT-- IS ALL OVER BROOKLYN.
AND I'VE SEEN FIRSTHAND WHAT IT'S DOING TO PEOPLE.
ULTIMATUM'S CREW ARE THE ONLY ONES DEALING IT, BUT THEY'VE BEEN DESTROYING THEIR STASHES EVERY TIME I GET NEAR THEM.
AND I HAVEN'T BEEN ABLE TO FIND THEIR MAIN RE-UP SPOT.
UNTIL TONIGHT.

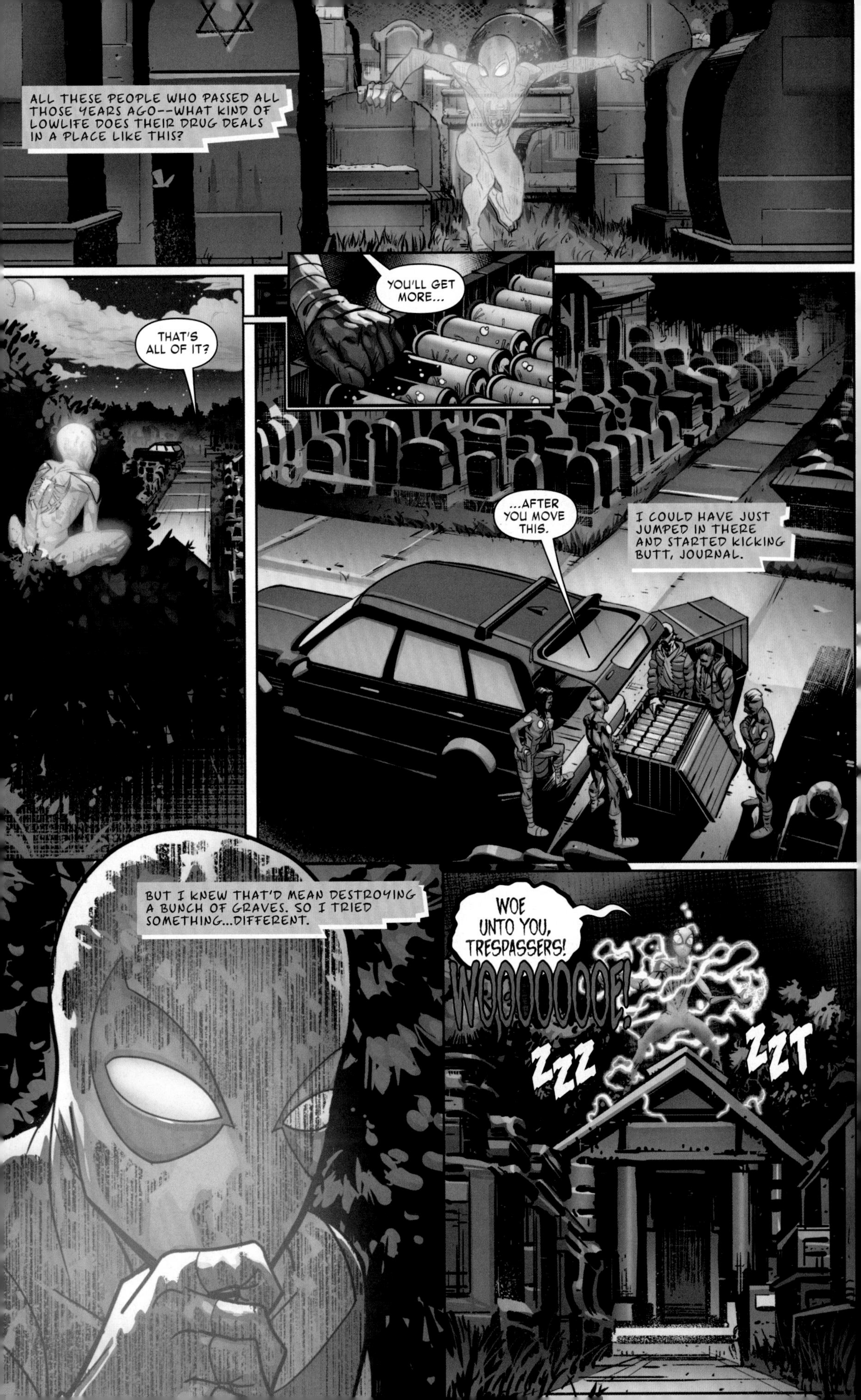
ALL THESE PEOPLE WHO PASSED ALL THOSE YEARS AGO--WHAT KIND OF LOWLIFE DOES THEIR DRUG DEALS IN A PLACE LIKE THIS?
THAT'S ALL OF IT?
YOU'LL GET MORE...
...AFTER YOU MOVE THIS.
I COULD HAVE JUST JUMPED IN THERE AND STARTED KICKING BUTT, JOURNAL.
BUT I KNEW THAT'D MEAN DESTROYING A BUNCH OF GRAVES. SO I TRIED SOMETHING...DIFFERENT.
WOE UNTO YOU, TRESPASSERS!
WOOOOOOOE!
ZZZ
ZZT

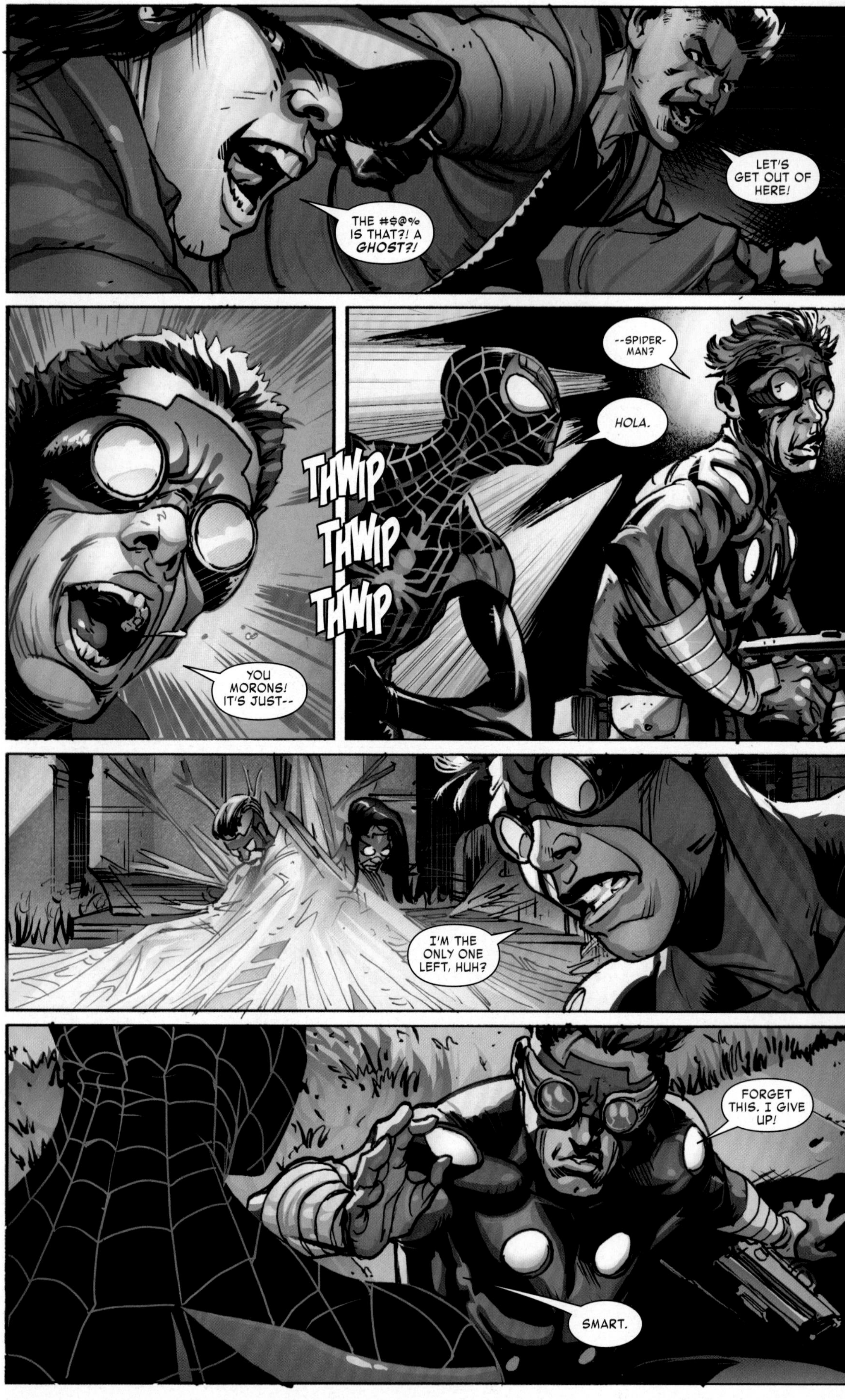
THE #$@% IS THAT?! A GHOST?!
LET'S GET OUT OF HERE!
YOU MORONS! IT'S JUST--
THWIP
THWIP
THWIP
--SPIDER-MAN?
HOLA.
I'M THE ONLY ONE LEFT, HUH?
FORGET THIS. I GIVE UP!
SMART.

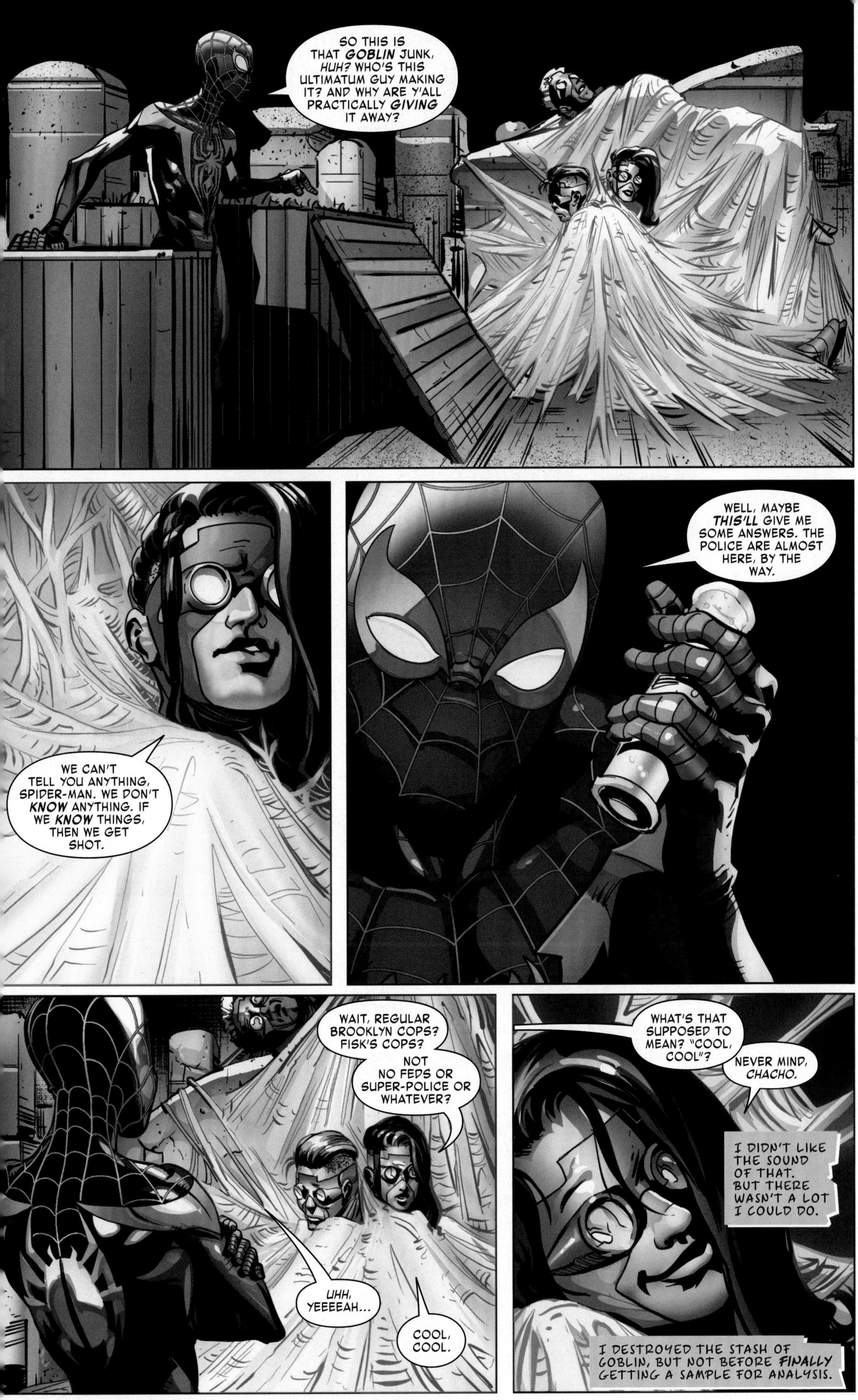
SO THIS IS THAT GOBLIN JUNK, HUH? WHO'S THIS ULTIMATUM GUY MAKING IT? AND WHY ARE Y'ALL PRACTICALLY GIVING IT AWAY?
WE CAN'T TELL YOU ANYTHING, SPIDER-MAN. WE DON'T KNOW ANYTHING. IF WE KNOW THINGS, THEN WE GET SHOT.
WELL, MAYBE THIS'LL GIVE ME SOME ANSWERS. THE POLICE ARE ALMOST HERE, BY THE WAY.
WAIT, REGULAR BROOKLYN COPS? FISK'S COPS?
NOT NO FEDS OR SUPER-POLICE OR WHATEVER?
UHH, YEEEEAH...
COOL, COOL.
WHAT'S THAT SUPPOSED TO MEAN? "COOL, COOL"?
NEVER MIND, CHACHO.
I DIDN'T LIKE THE SOUND OF THAT. BUT THERE WASN'T A LOT I COULD DO.
I DESTROYED THE STASH OF GOBLIN, BUT NOT BEFORE FINALLY GETTING A SAMPLE FOR ANALYSIS.

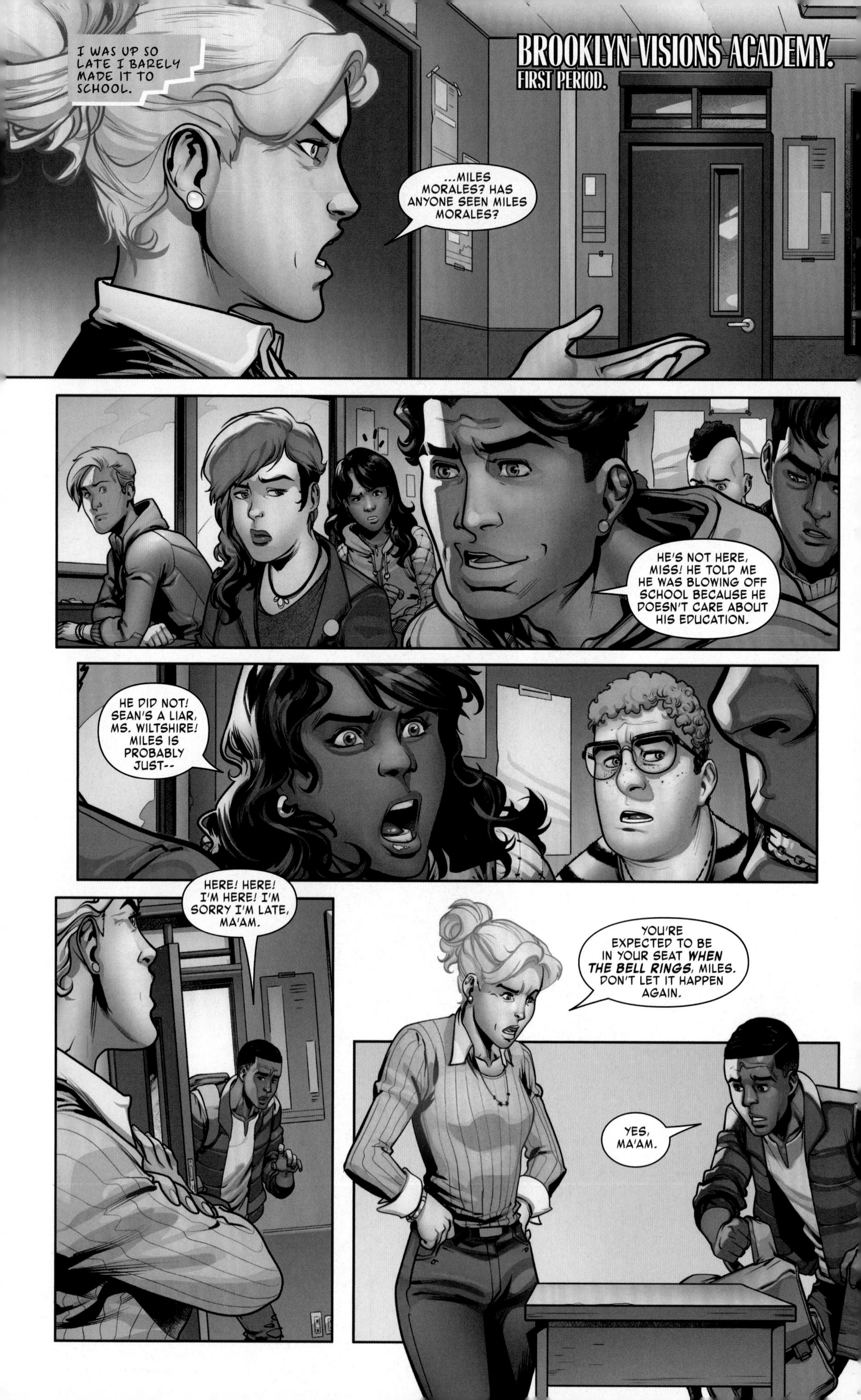

I WAS UP SO LATE I BARELY MADE IT TO SCHOOL.
BROOKLYN VISIONS ACADEMY.
FIRST PERIOD.
...MILES MORALES? HAS ANYONE SEEN MILES MORALES?
HE'S NOT HERE, MISS! HE TOLD ME HE WAS BLOWING OFF SCHOOL BECAUSE HE DOESN'T CARE ABOUT HIS EDUCATION.
HE DID NOT! SEAN'S A LIAR, MS. WILTSHIRE! MILES IS PROBABLY JUST--
HERE! HERE! I'M HERE! I'M SORRY I'M LATE, MA'AM.
YOU'RE EXPECTED TO BE IN YOUR SEAT WHEN THE BELL RINGS, MILES. DON'T LET IT HAPPEN AGAIN.
YES, MA'AM.

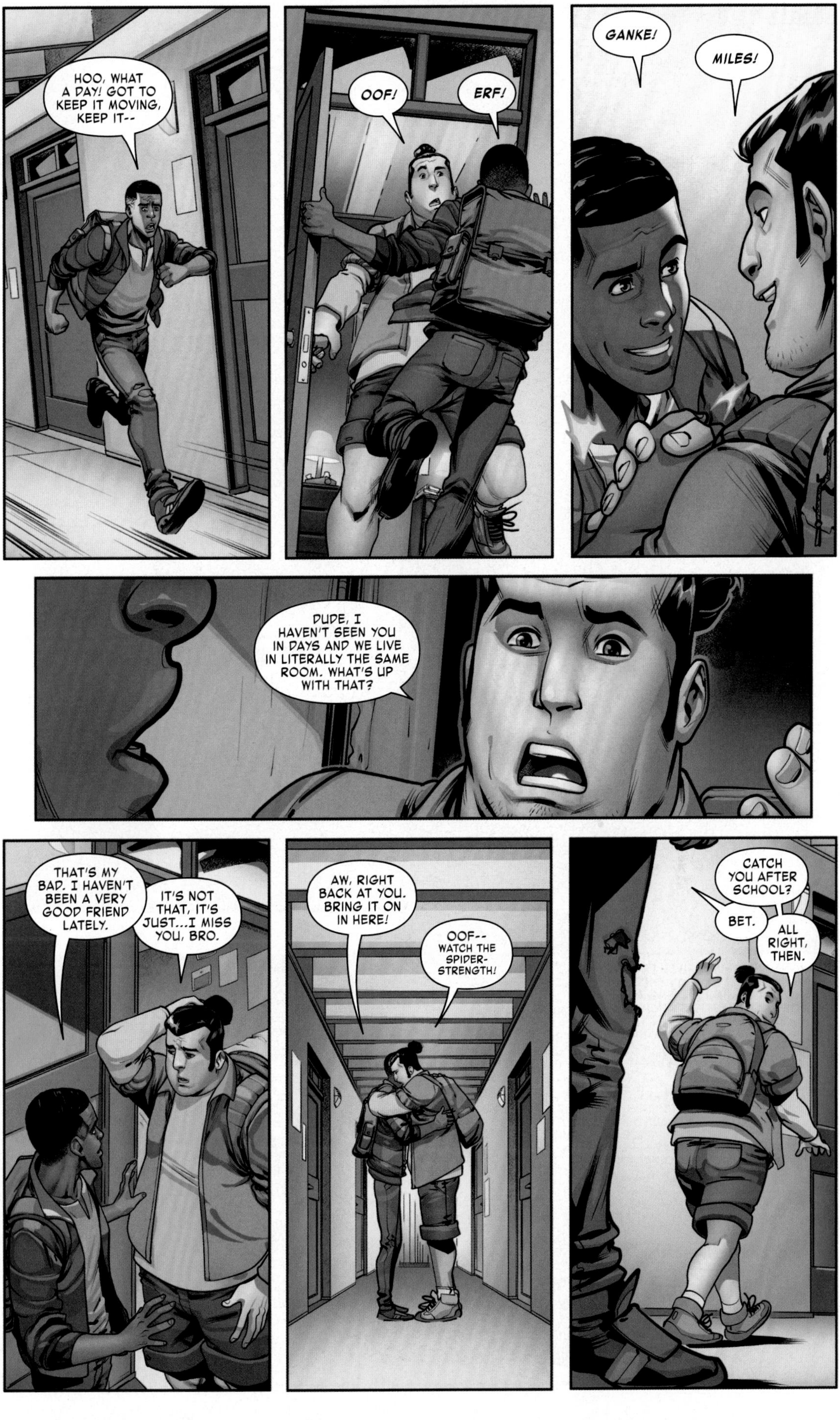
HOO, WHAT A DAY! GOT TO KEEP IT MOVING, KEEP IT--
OOF!
ERF!
GANKE!
MILES!
DUDE, I HAVEN'T SEEN YOU IN DAYS AND WE LIVE IN LITERALLY THE SAME ROOM. WHAT'S UP WITH THAT?
THAT'S MY BAD. I HAVEN'T BEEN A VERY GOOD FRIEND LATELY.
IT'S NOT THAT, IT'S JUST...I MISS YOU, BRO.
AW, RIGHT BACK AT YOU. BRING IT ON IN HERE!
OOF-- WATCH THE SPIDER-STRENGTH!
CATCH YOU AFTER SCHOOL?
BET.
ALL RIGHT, THEN.

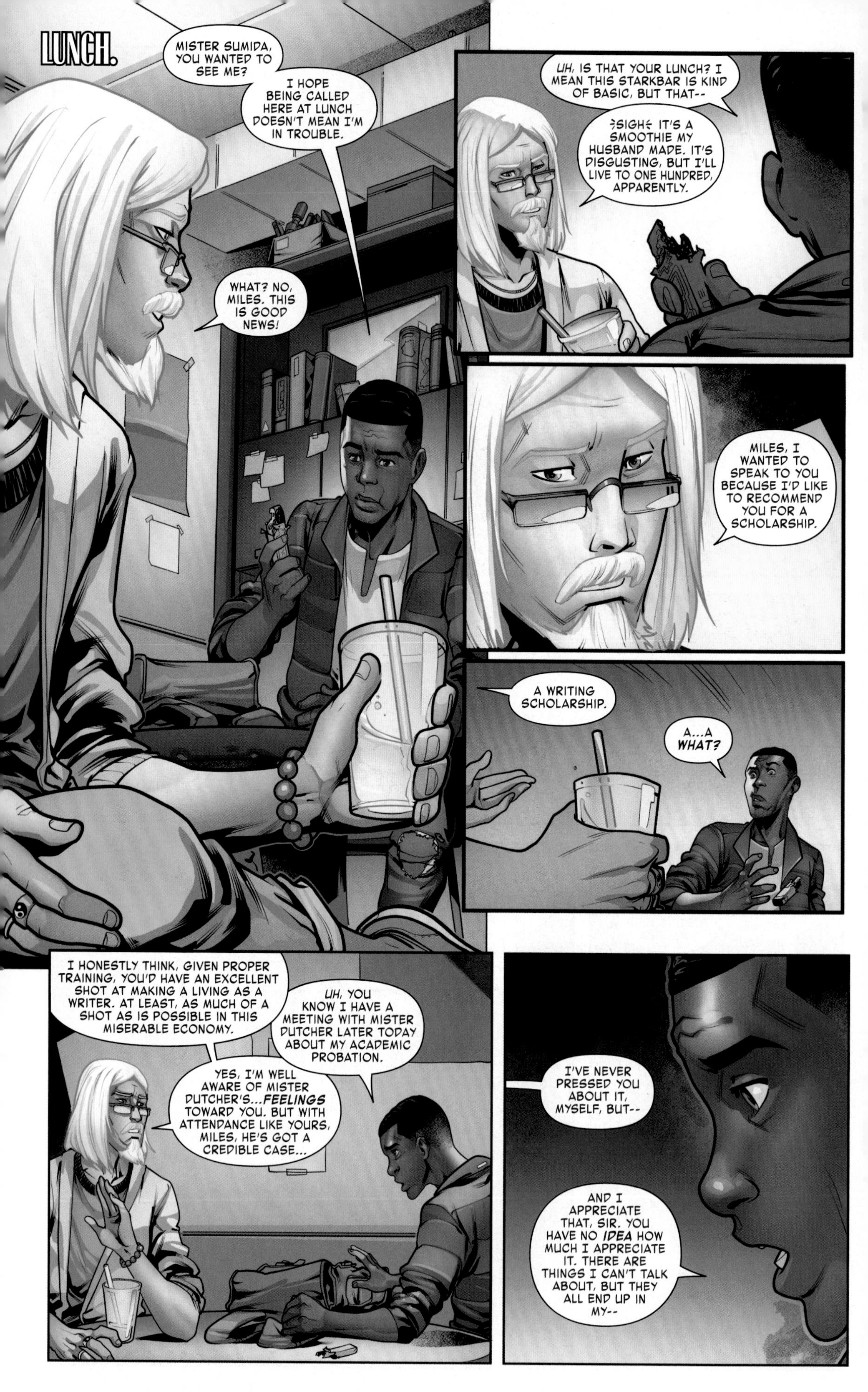
LUNCH.
MISTER SUMIDA, YOU WANTED TO SEE ME?
I HOPE BEING CALLED HERE AT LUNCH DOESN'T MEAN I'M IN TROUBLE.
WHAT? NO, MILES. THIS IS GOOD NEWS!
UH, IS THAT YOUR LUNCH? I MEAN THIS STARKBAR IS KIND OF BASIC, BUT THAT--
⁝SIGH⁝ IT'S A SMOOTHIE MY HUSBAND MADE. IT'S DISGUSTING, BUT I'LL LIVE TO ONE HUNDRED, APPARENTLY.
MILES, I WANTED TO SPEAK TO YOU BECAUSE I'D LIKE TO RECOMMEND YOU FOR A SCHOLARSHIP.
A WRITING SCHOLARSHIP.
A...A WHAT?
I HONESTLY THINK, GIVEN PROPER TRAINING, YOU'D HAVE AN EXCELLENT SHOT AT MAKING A LIVING AS A WRITER. AT LEAST, AS MUCH OF A SHOT AS IS POSSIBLE IN THIS MISERABLE ECONOMY.
UH, YOU KNOW I HAVE A MEETING WITH MISTER DUTCHER LATER TODAY ABOUT MY ACADEMIC PROBATION.
YES, I'M WELL AWARE OF MISTER DUTCHER'S...FEELINGS TOWARD YOU. BUT WITH ATTENDANCE LIKE YOURS, MILES, HE'S GOT A CREDIBLE CASE...
I'VE NEVER PRESSED YOU ABOUT IT, MYSELF, BUT--
AND I APPRECIATE THAT, SIR. YOU HAVE NO IDEA HOW MUCH I APPRECIATE IT. THERE ARE THINGS I CAN'T TALK ABOUT, BUT THEY ALL END UP IN MY--

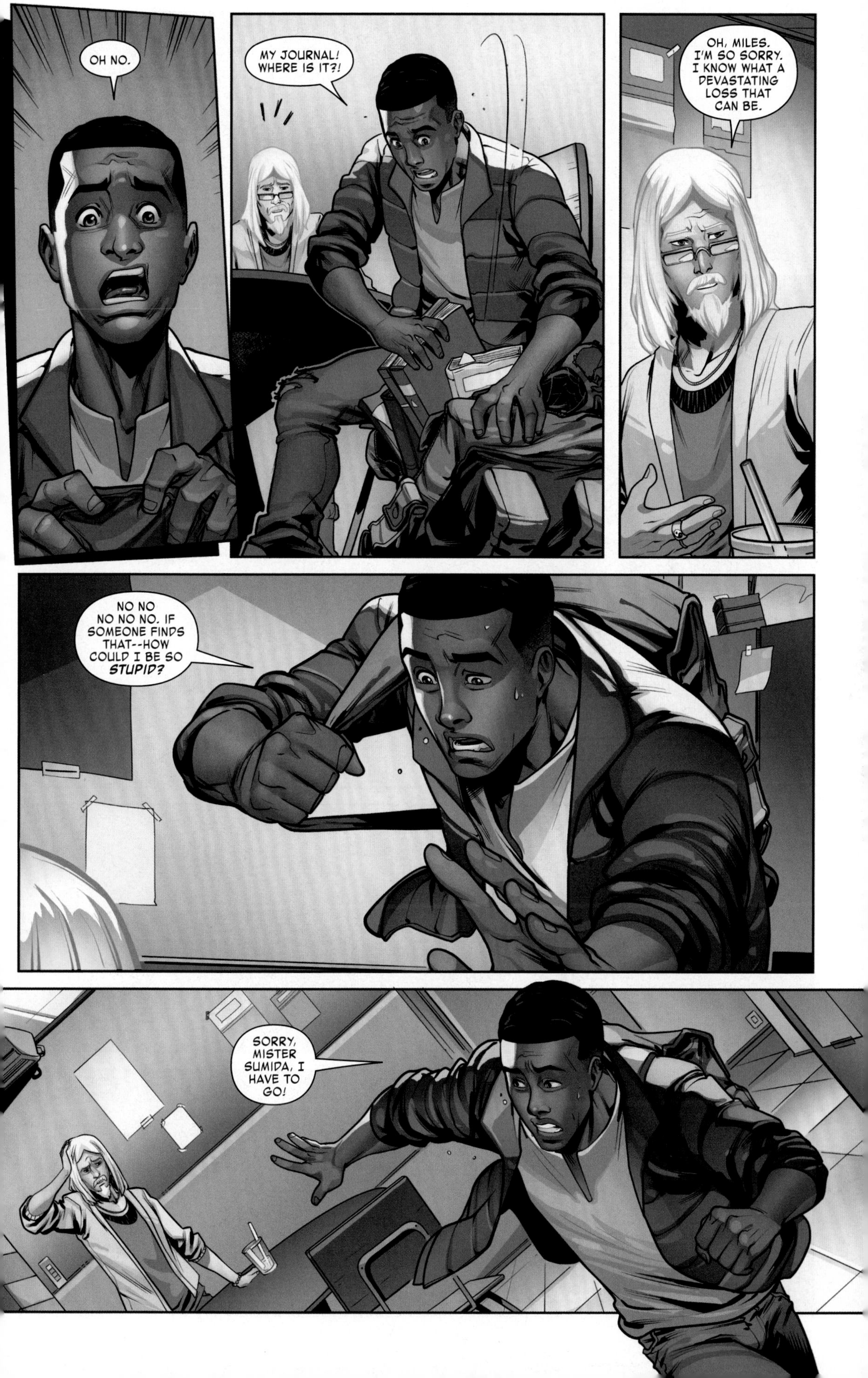
OH NO.
MY JOURNAL! WHERE IS IT?!
OH, MILES. I'M SO SORRY. I KNOW WHAT A DEVASTATING LOSS THAT CAN BE.
NO NO NO NO NO. IF SOMEONE FINDS THAT--HOW COULD I BE SO *STUPID?*
SORRY, MISTER SUMIDA, I HAVE TO GO!

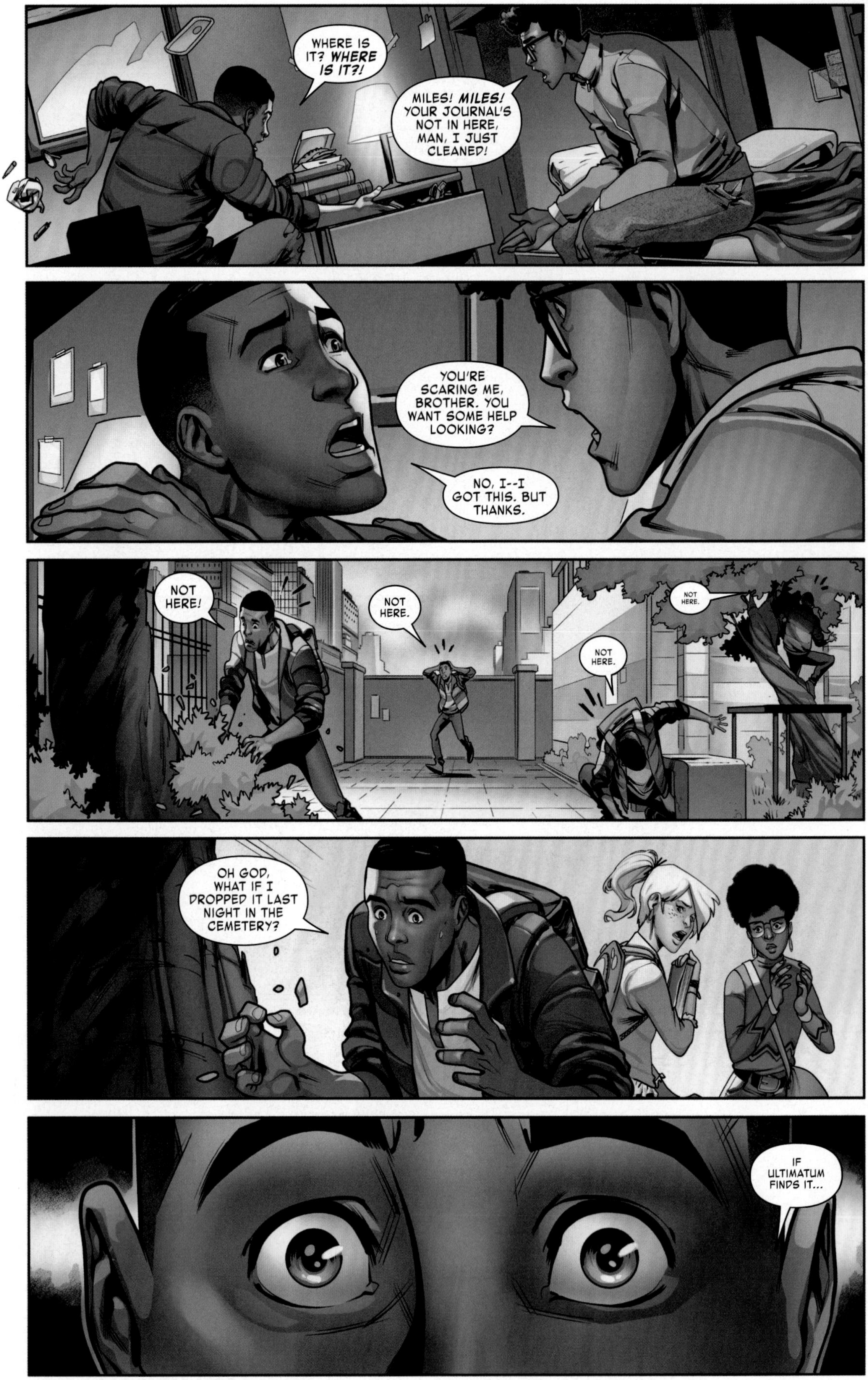
WHERE IS IT? WHERE IS IT?!
MILES! MILES! YOUR JOURNAL'S NOT IN HERE, MAN, I JUST CLEANED!
YOU'RE SCARING ME, BROTHER. YOU WANT SOME HELP LOOKING?
NO, I--I GOT THIS. BUT THANKS.
NOT HERE!
NOT HERE.
NOT HERE.
NOT HERE.
OH GOD, WHAT IF I DROPPED IT LAST NIGHT IN THE CEMETERY?
IF ULTIMATUM FINDS IT...

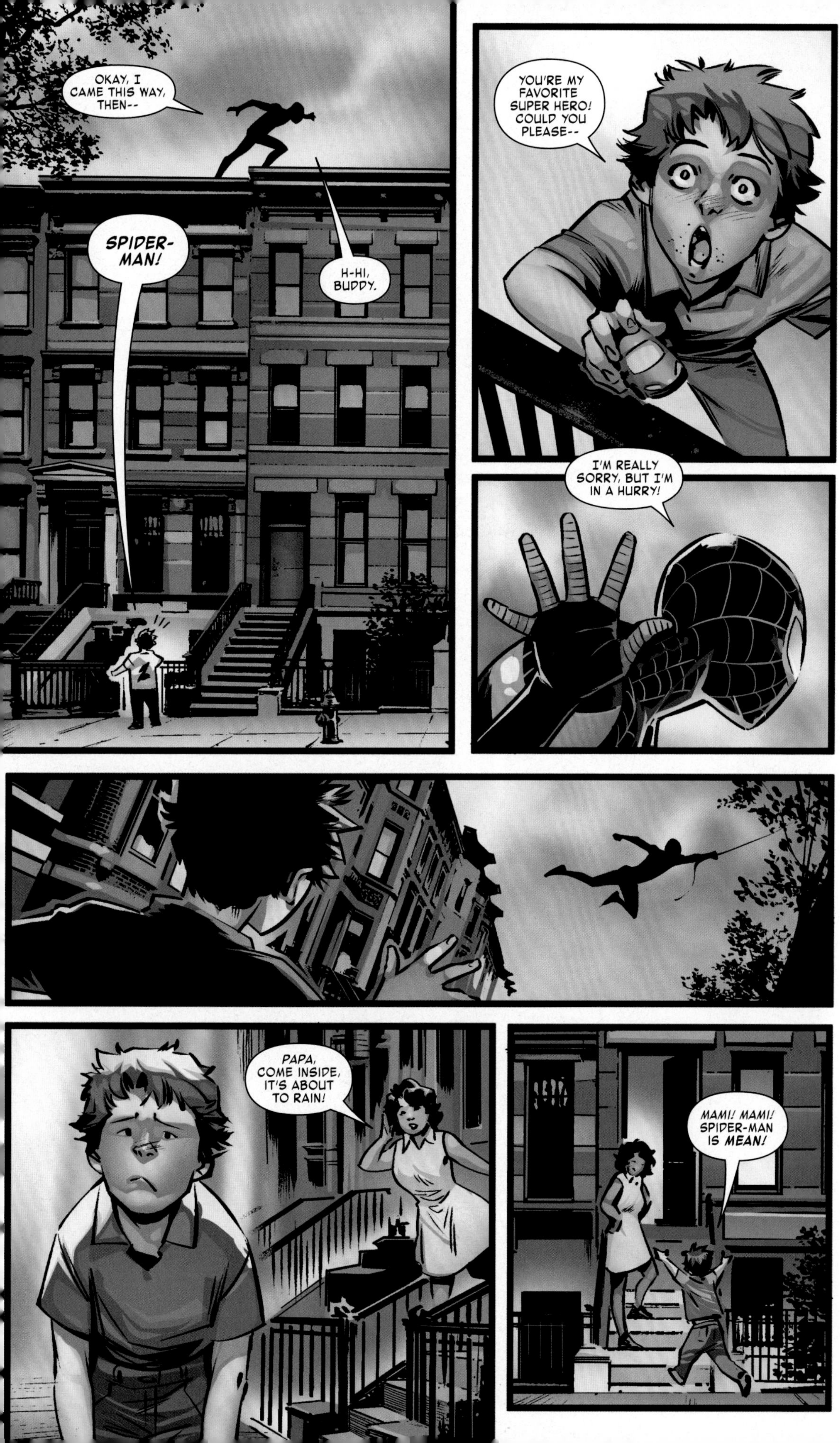
OKAY, I CAME THIS WAY, THEN--
SPIDER-MAN!
H-HI, BUDDY.
YOU'RE MY FAVORITE SUPER HERO! COULD YOU PLEASE--
I'M REALLY SORRY, BUT I'M IN A HURRY!
PAPA, COME INSIDE, IT'S ABOUT TO RAIN!
MAMI! MAMI! SPIDER-MAN IS MEAN!

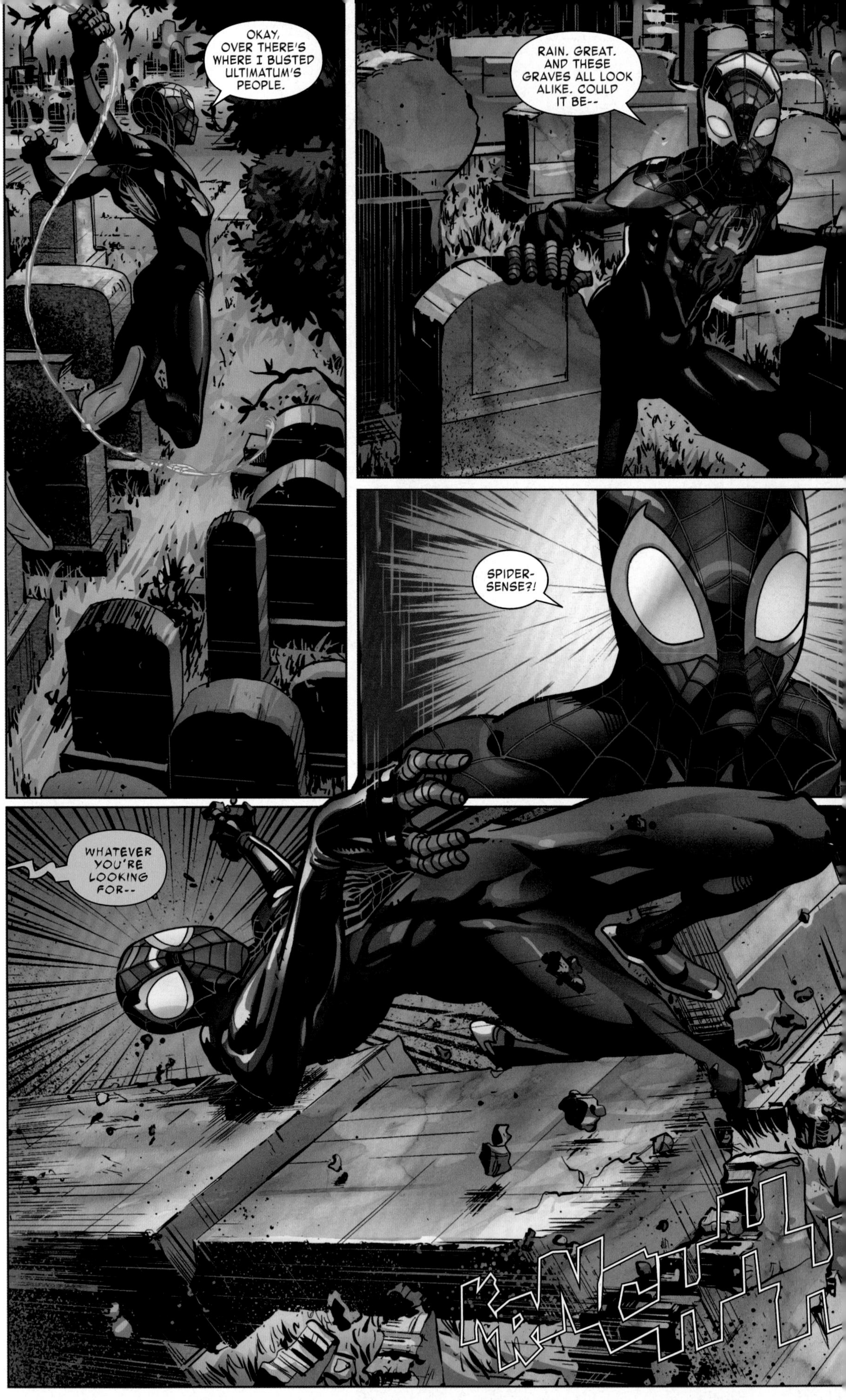
OKAY, OVER THERE'S WHERE I BUSTED ULTIMATUM'S PEOPLE.
RAIN. GREAT. AND THESE GRAVES ALL LOOK ALIKE. COULD IT BE--
SPIDER-SENSE?!
WHATEVER YOU'RE LOOKING FOR--

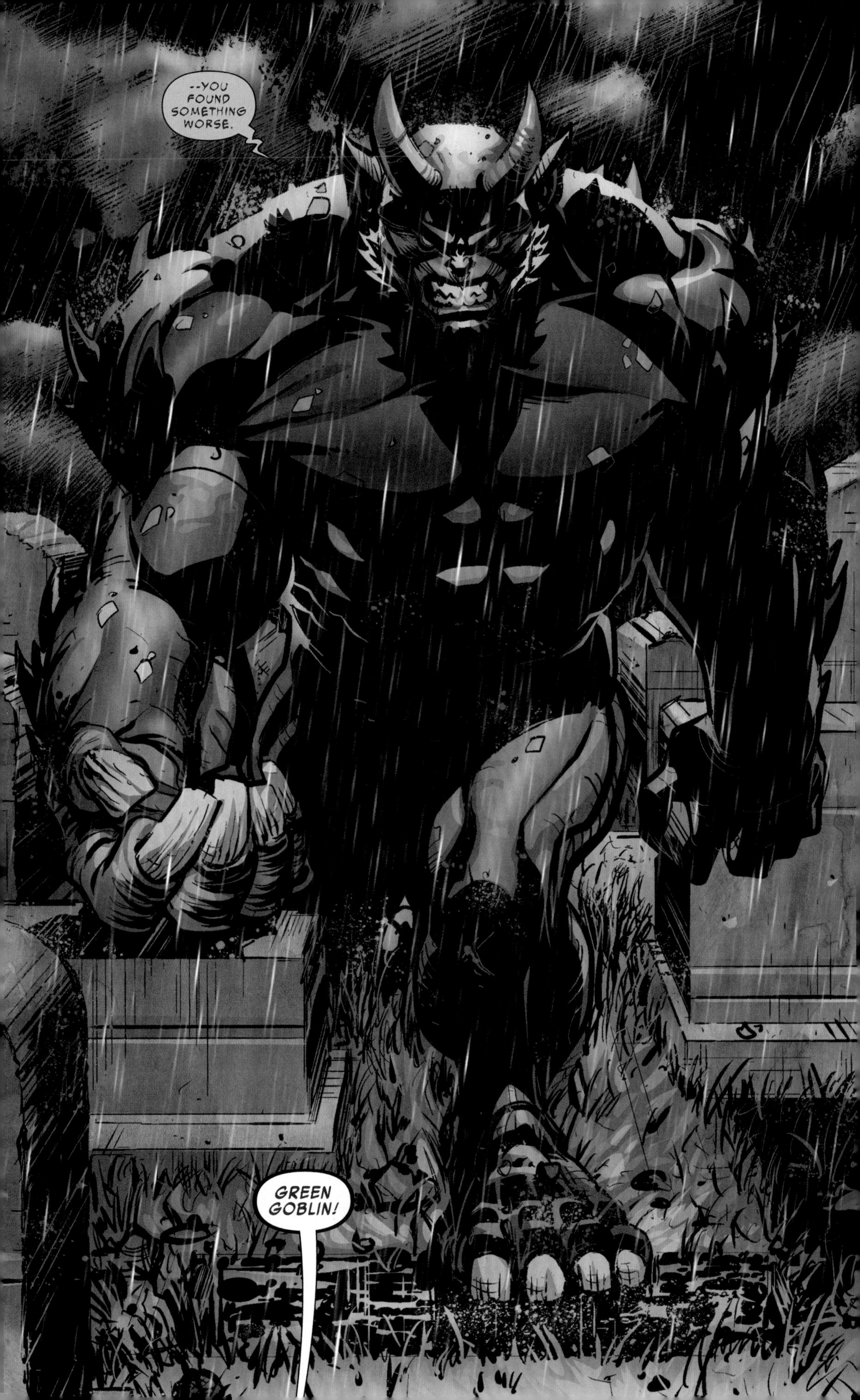
--YOU FOUND SOMETHING WORSE.
GREEN GOBLIN!

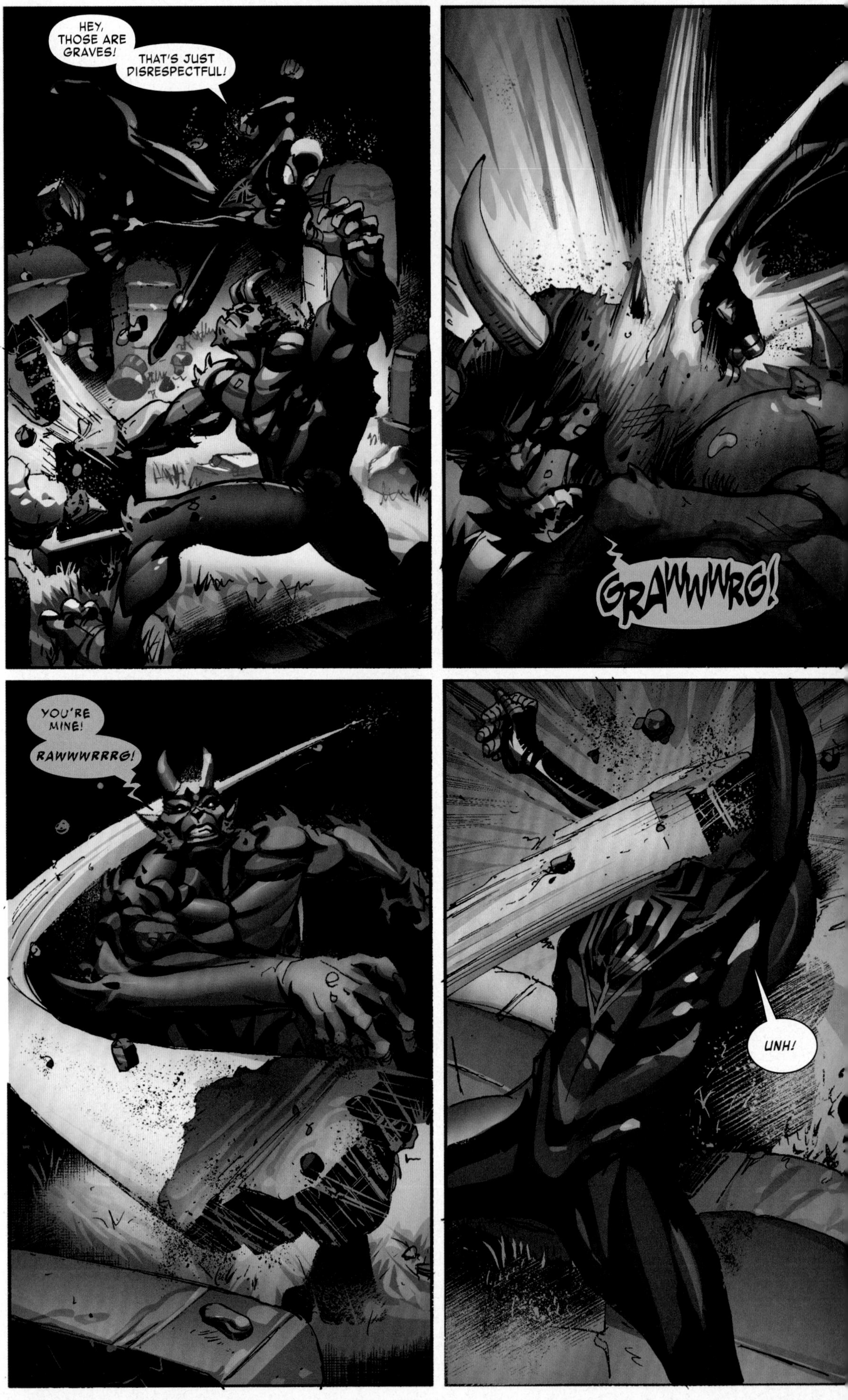
HEY, THOSE ARE GRAVES!
THAT'S JUST DISRESPECTFUL!
GRAWWWRG!
YOU'RE MINE!
RAWWWRRRG!
UNH!

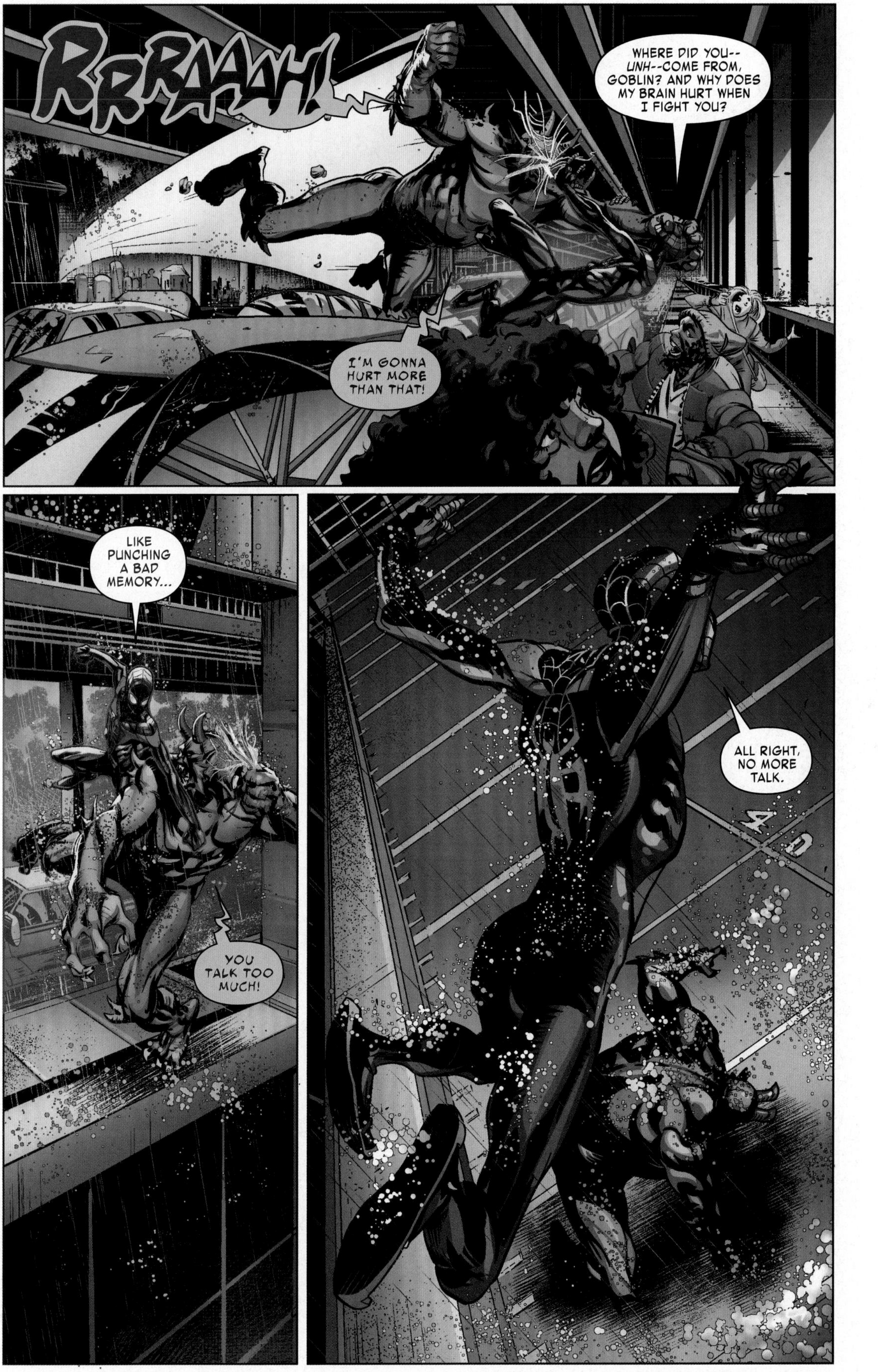
RRRAAAH!
WHERE DID YOU-- UNH--COME FROM, GOBLIN? AND WHY DOES MY BRAIN HURT WHEN I FIGHT YOU?
I'M GONNA HURT MORE THAN THAT!
LIKE PUNCHING A BAD MEMORY...
YOU TALK TOO MUCH!
ALL RIGHT, NO MORE TALK.

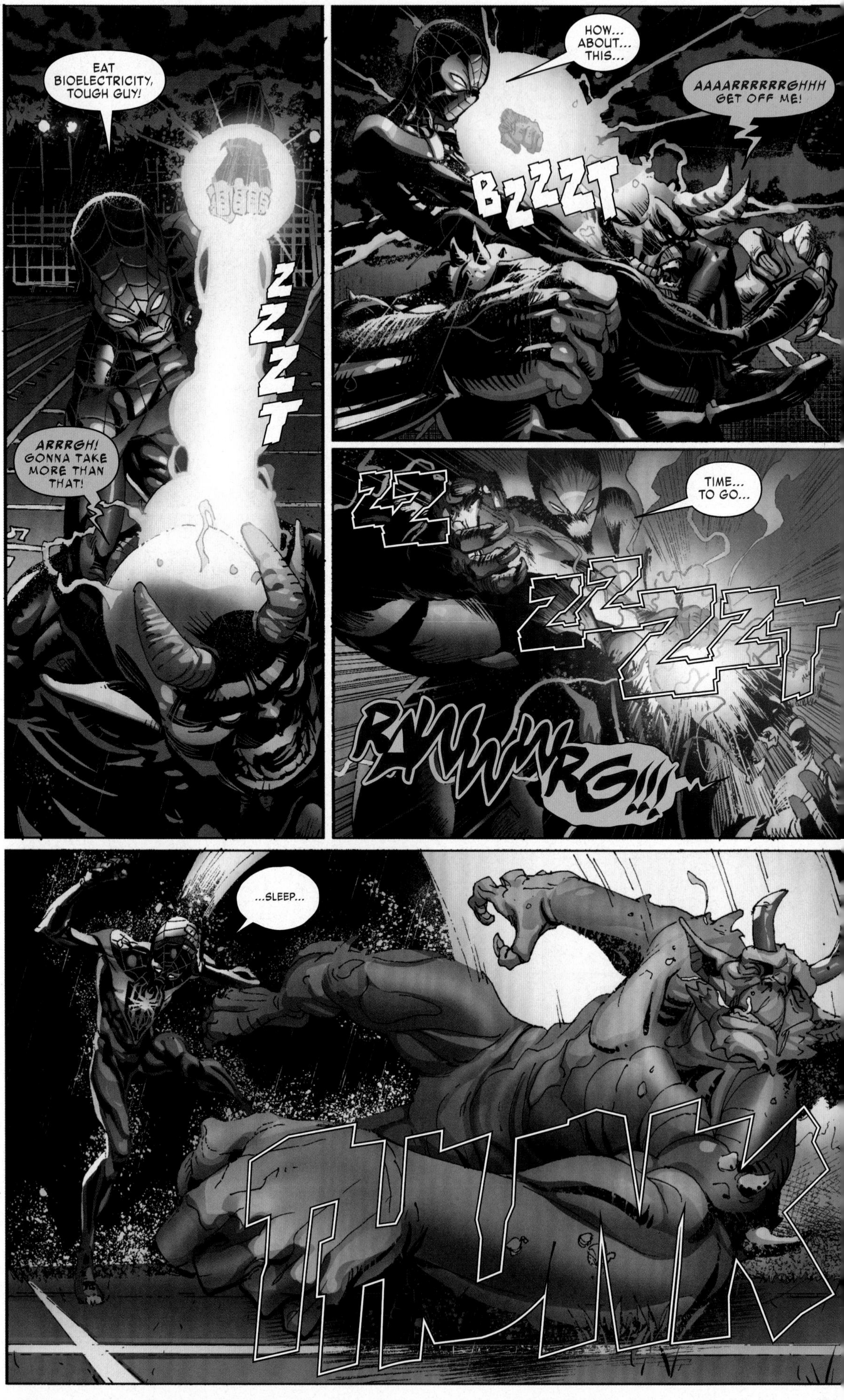

EAT BIOELECTRICITY, TOUGH GUY!
ZZZT
ARRRGH! GONNA TAKE MORE THAN THAT!
HOW... ABOUT... THIS...
AAAARRRRRRGHHH GET OFF ME!
BZZZT
TIME... TO GO...
ZZ
ZZZZZT
RAWWWRG!!!
...SLEEP...
THUNK

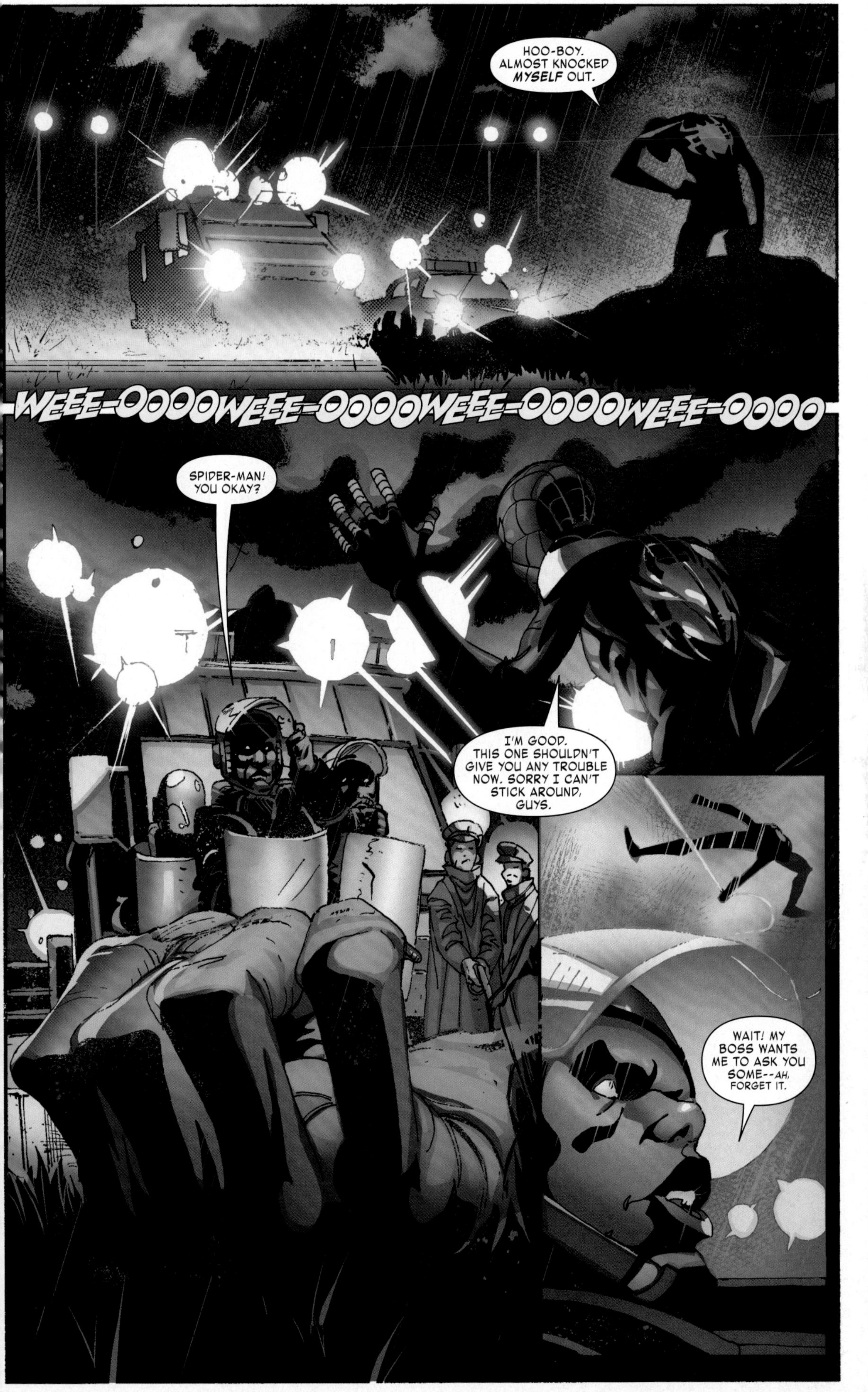
HOO-BOY. ALMOST KNOCKED MYSELF OUT.
WEEE-OOOOWEEE-OOOOWEEE-OOOOWEEE-OOOO
SPIDER-MAN! YOU OKAY?
I'M GOOD. THIS ONE SHOULDN'T GIVE YOU ANY TROUBLE NOW. SORRY I CAN'T STICK AROUND, GUYS.
WAIT! MY BOSS WANTS ME TO ASK YOU SOME--AH, FORGET IT.

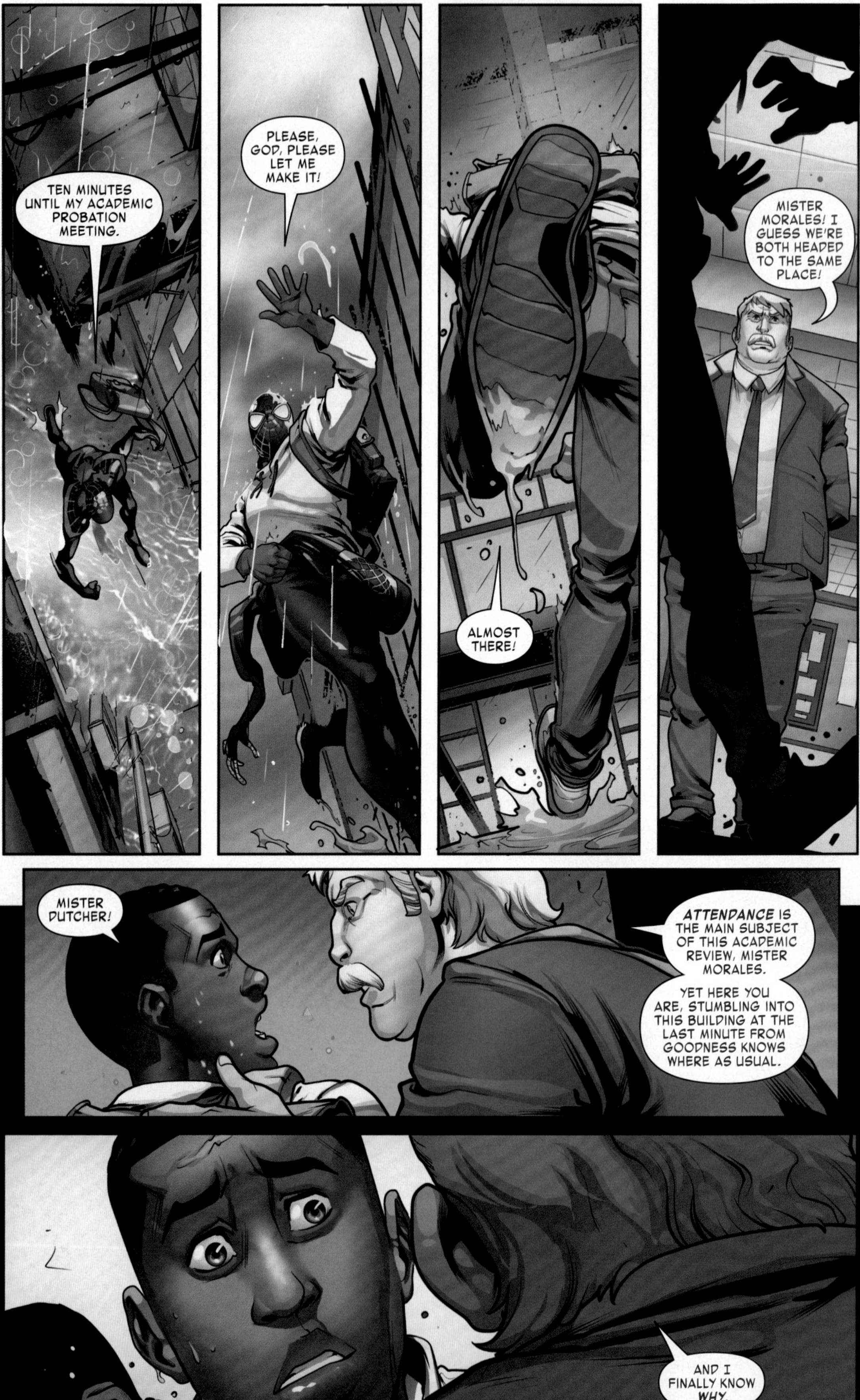
TEN MINUTES UNTIL MY ACADEMIC PROBATION MEETING.
PLEASE, GOD, PLEASE LET ME MAKE IT!
ALMOST THERE!
MISTER MORALES! I GUESS WE'RE BOTH HEADED TO THE SAME PLACE!
MISTER DUTCHER!
ATTENDANCE IS THE MAIN SUBJECT OF THIS ACADEMIC REVIEW, MISTER MORALES.
YET HERE YOU ARE, STUMBLING INTO THIS BUILDING AT THE LAST MINUTE FROM GOODNESS KNOWS WHERE AS USUAL.
AND I FINALLY KNOW *WHY*.

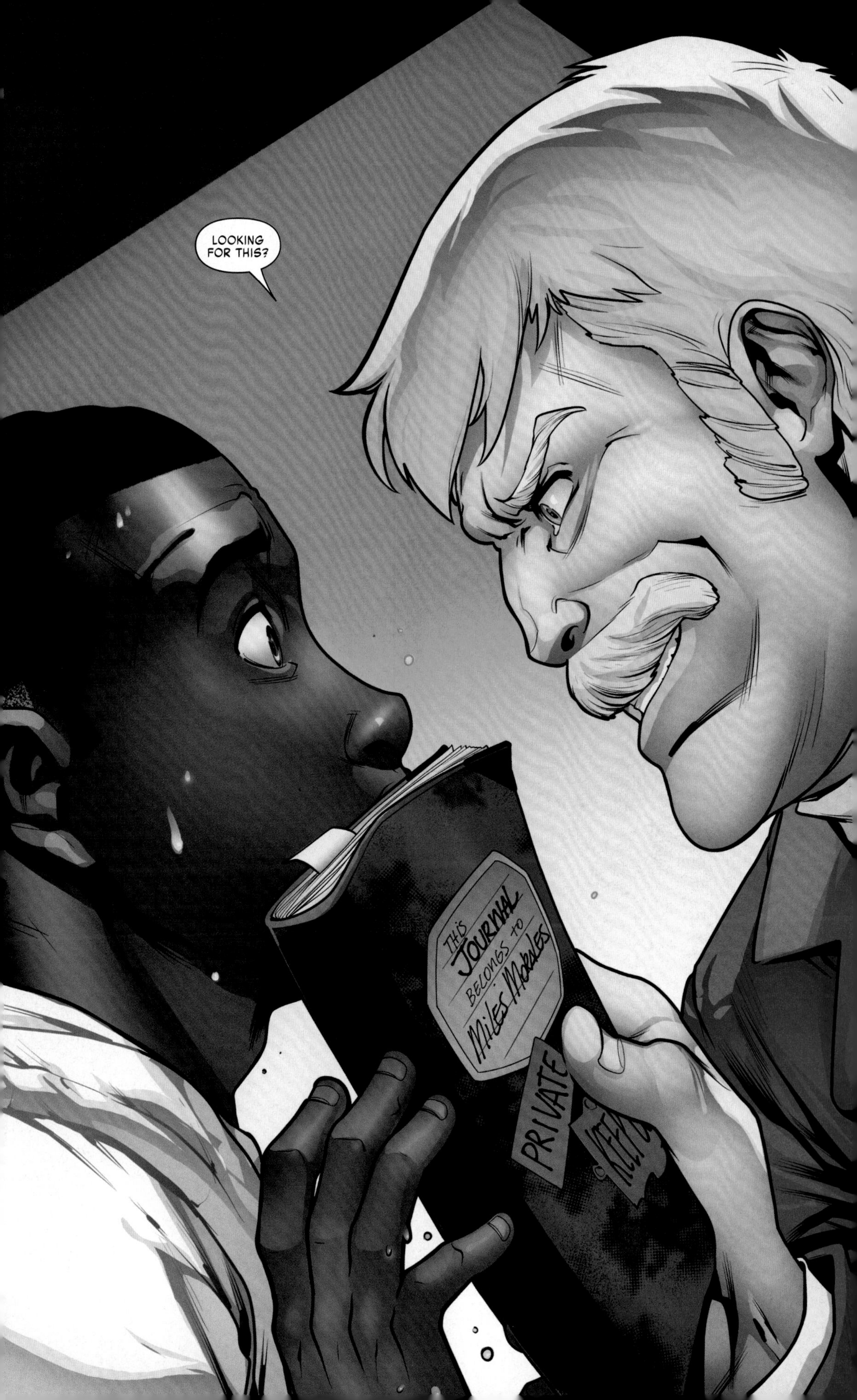
LOOKING FOR THIS?
THIS JOURNAL BELONGS TO Miles Morales
PRIVATE

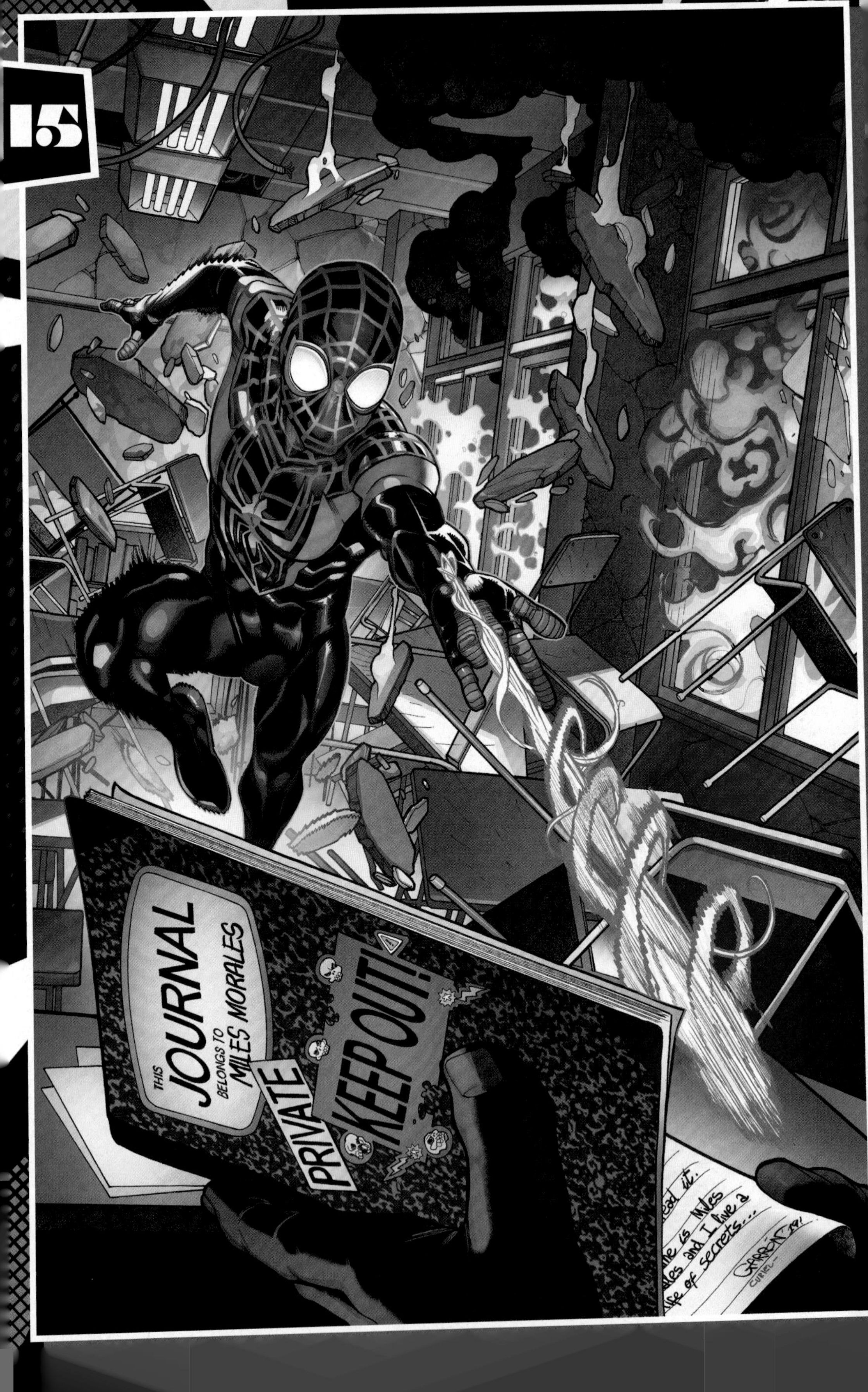
15
THIS JOURNAL BELONGS TO MILES MORALES
PRIVATE
KEEP OUT!
GARRON '19
CURIEL

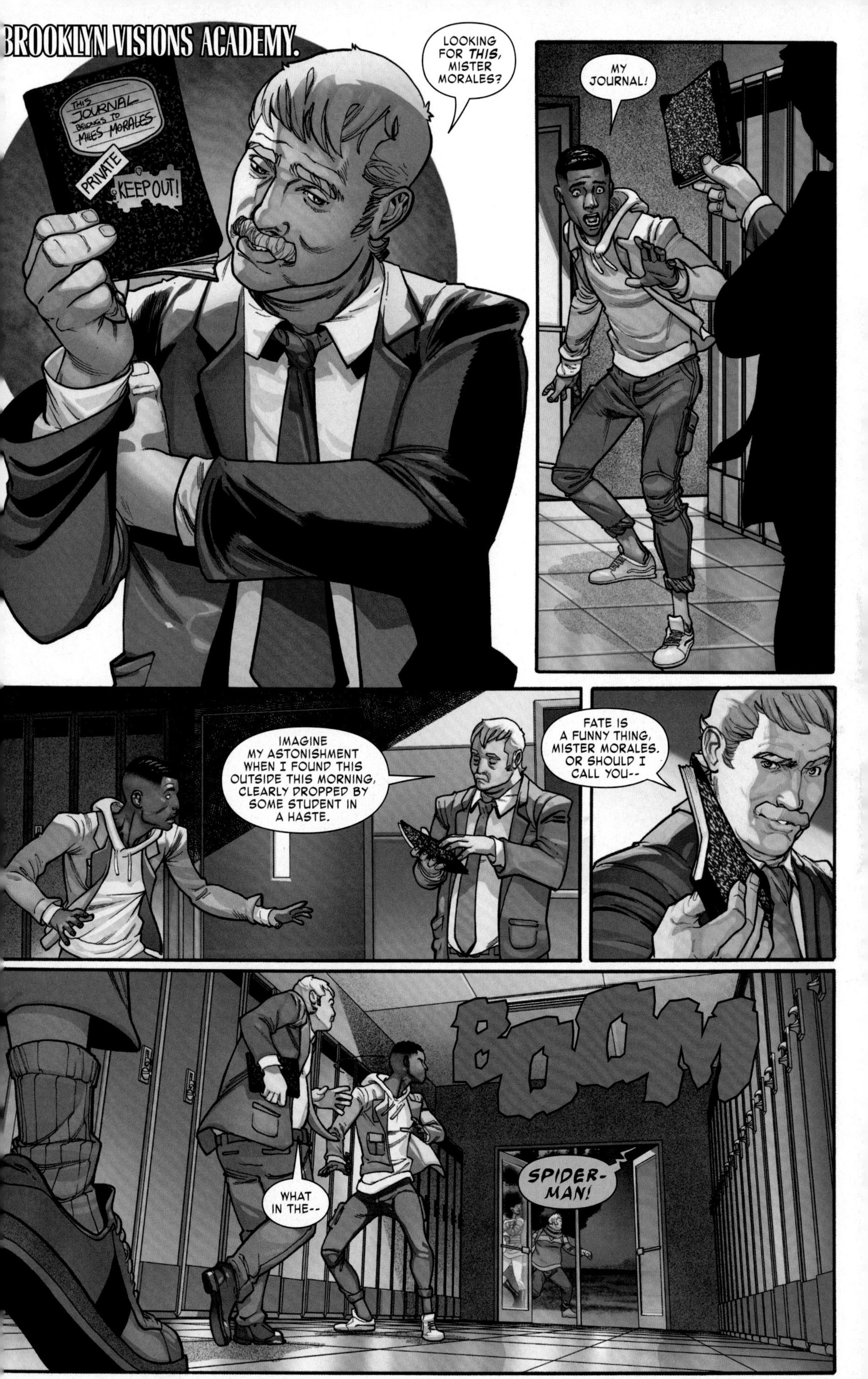
BROOKLYN VISIONS ACADEMY.
THIS JOURNAL BELONGS TO MILES MORALES
PRIVATE
KEEP OUT!
LOOKING FOR THIS, MISTER MORALES?
MY JOURNAL!
IMAGINE MY ASTONISHMENT WHEN I FOUND THIS OUTSIDE THIS MORNING, CLEARLY DROPPED BY SOME STUDENT IN A HASTE.
FATE IS A FUNNY THING, MISTER MORALES. OR SHOULD I CALL YOU--
BOOM
WHAT IN THE--
SPIDER-MAN!

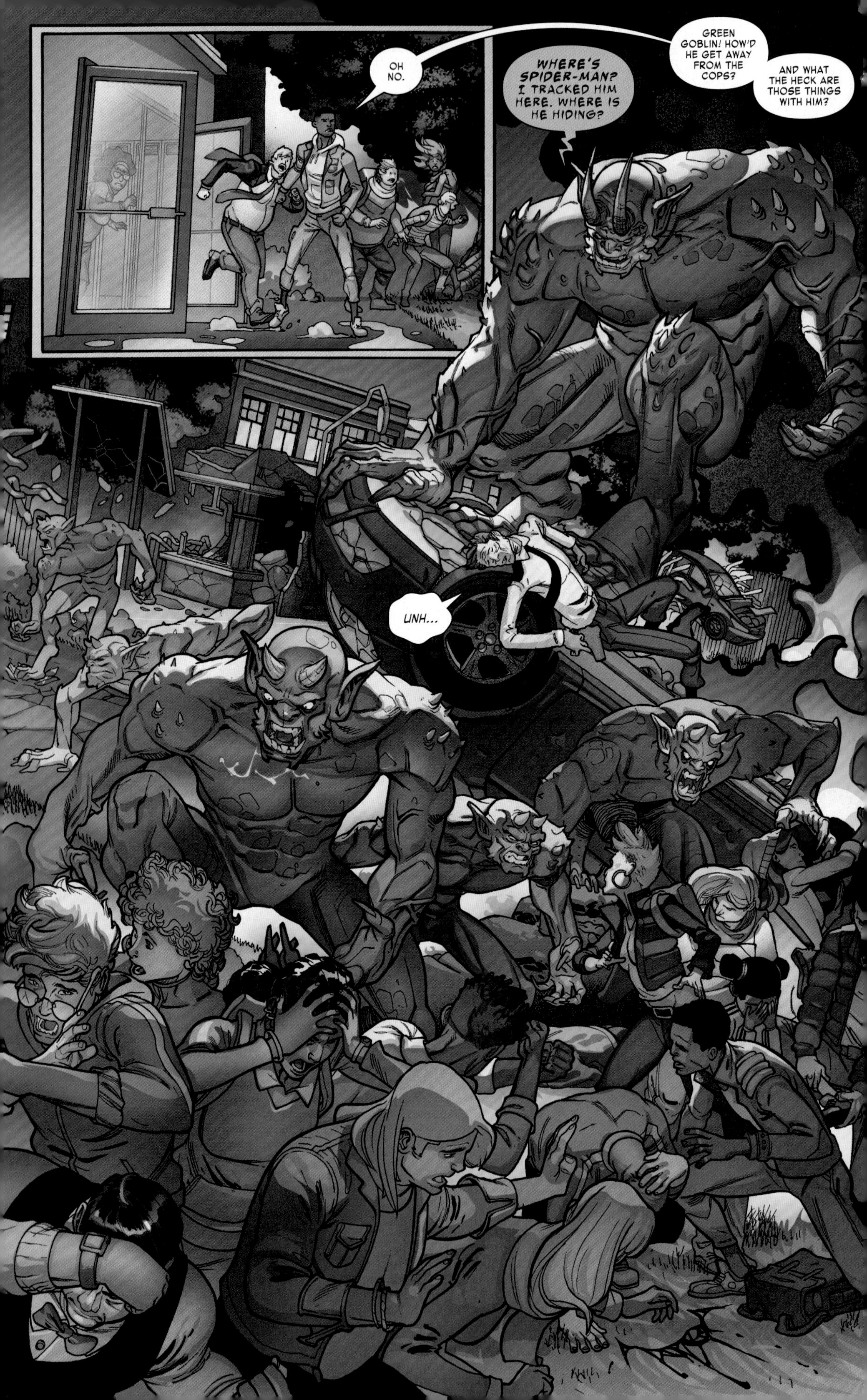
OH NO.
WHERE'S SPIDER-MAN? I TRACKED HIM HERE. WHERE IS HE HIDING?
GREEN GOBLIN! HOW'D HE GET AWAY FROM THE COPS?
AND WHAT THE HECK ARE THOSE THINGS WITH HIM?
UNH...

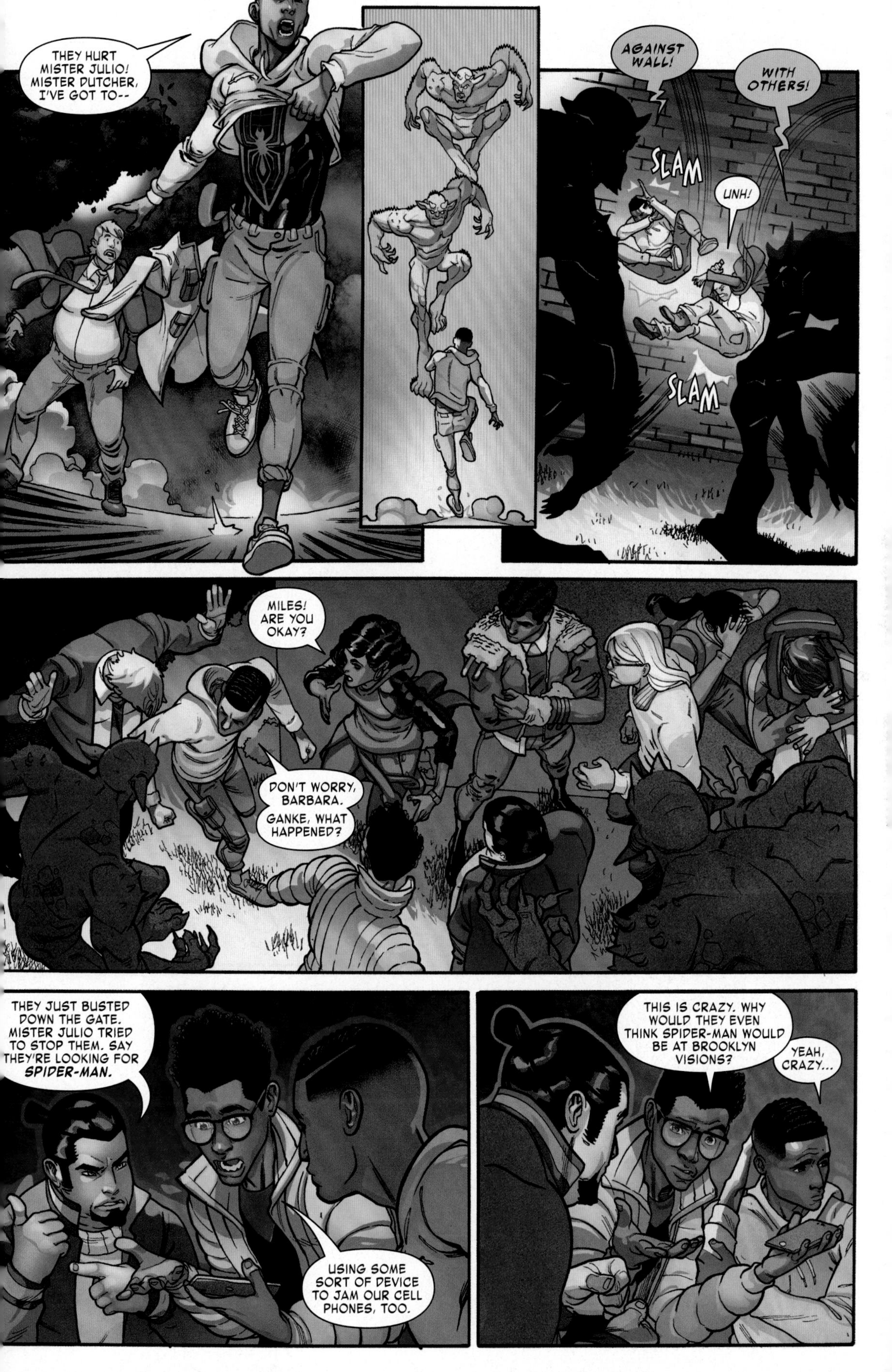
THEY HURT MISTER JULIO! MISTER DUTCHER, I'VE GOT TO--
AGAINST WALL!
WITH OTHERS!
SLAM
UNH!
SLAM
MILES! ARE YOU OKAY?
DON'T WORRY, BARBARA.
GANKE, WHAT HAPPENED?
THEY JUST BUSTED DOWN THE GATE. MISTER JULIO TRIED TO STOP THEM. SAY THEY'RE LOOKING FOR SPIDER-MAN.
USING SOME SORT OF DEVICE TO JAM OUR CELL PHONES, TOO.
THIS IS CRAZY. WHY WOULD THEY EVEN THINK SPIDER-MAN WOULD BE AT BROOKLYN VISIONS?
YEAH, CRAZY...

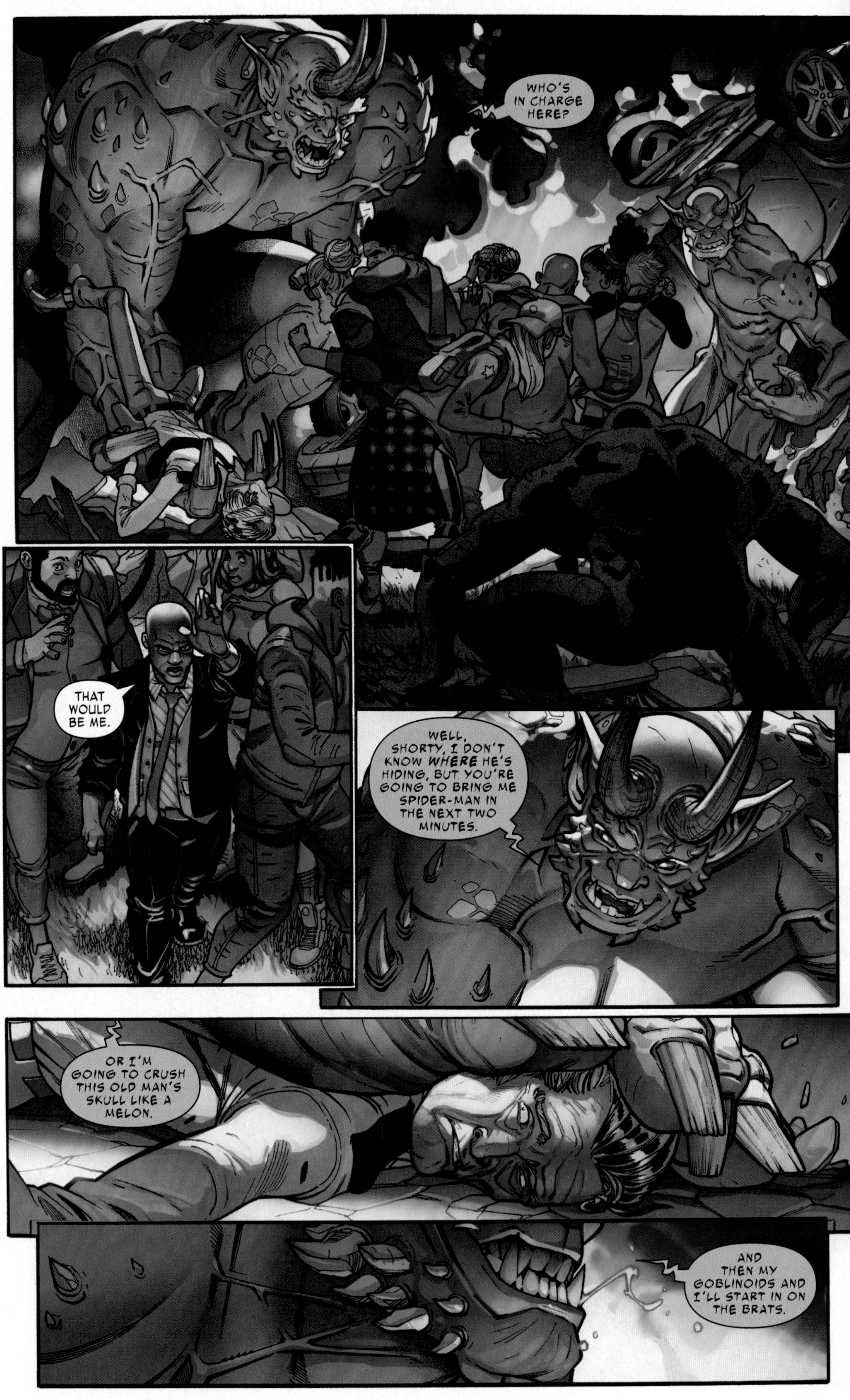
WHO'S IN CHARGE HERE?
THAT WOULD BE ME.
WELL, SHORTY, I DON'T KNOW *WHERE* HE'S HIDING, BUT YOU'RE GOING TO BRING ME SPIDER-MAN IN THE NEXT TWO MINUTES.
OR I'M GOING TO CRUSH THIS OLD MAN'S SKULL LIKE A MELON.
AND THEN MY GOBLINOIDS AND I'LL START IN ON THE BRATS.

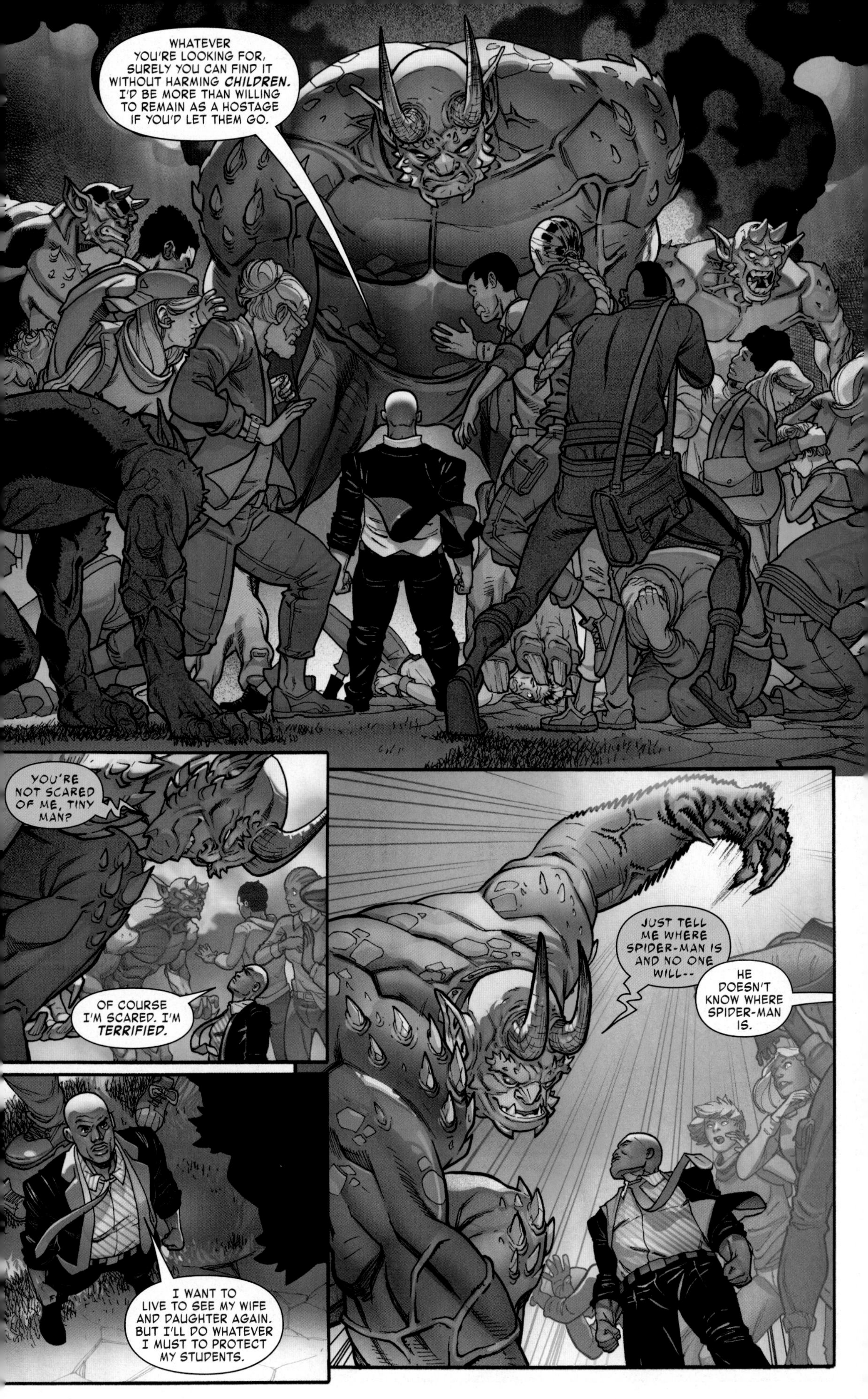
WHATEVER YOU'RE LOOKING FOR, SURELY YOU CAN FIND IT WITHOUT HARMING *CHILDREN.* I'D BE MORE THAN WILLING TO REMAIN AS A HOSTAGE IF YOU'D LET THEM GO.
YOU'RE NOT SCARED OF ME, TINY MAN?
OF COURSE I'M SCARED. I'M *TERRIFIED.*
I WANT TO LIVE TO SEE MY WIFE AND DAUGHTER AGAIN. BUT I'LL DO WHATEVER I MUST TO PROTECT MY STUDENTS.
JUST TELL ME WHERE SPIDER-MAN IS AND NO ONE WILL--
HE DOESN'T KNOW WHERE SPIDER-MAN IS.

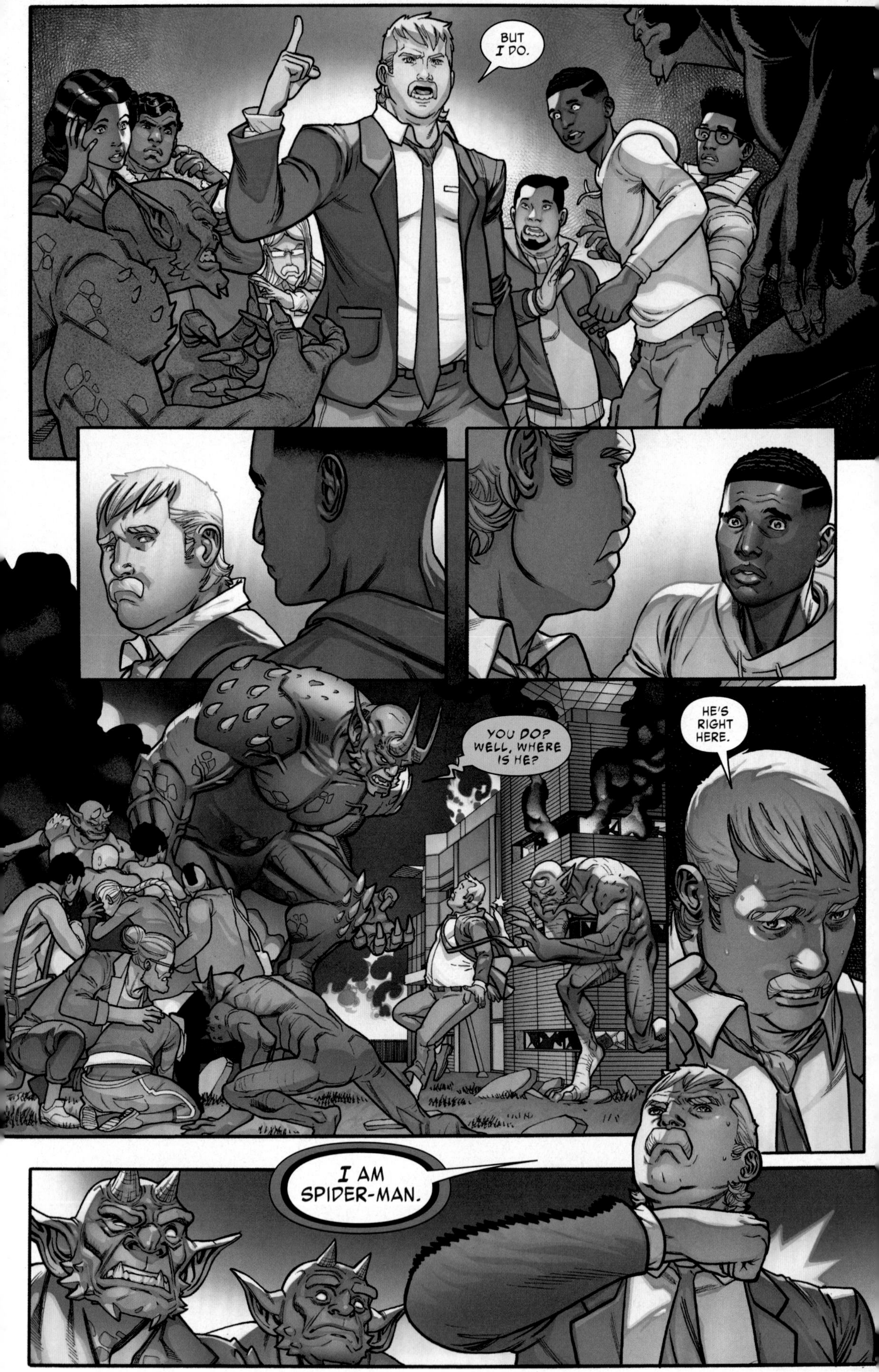
BUT I DO.
YOU DO? WELL, WHERE IS HE?
HE'S RIGHT HERE.
I AM SPIDER-MAN.

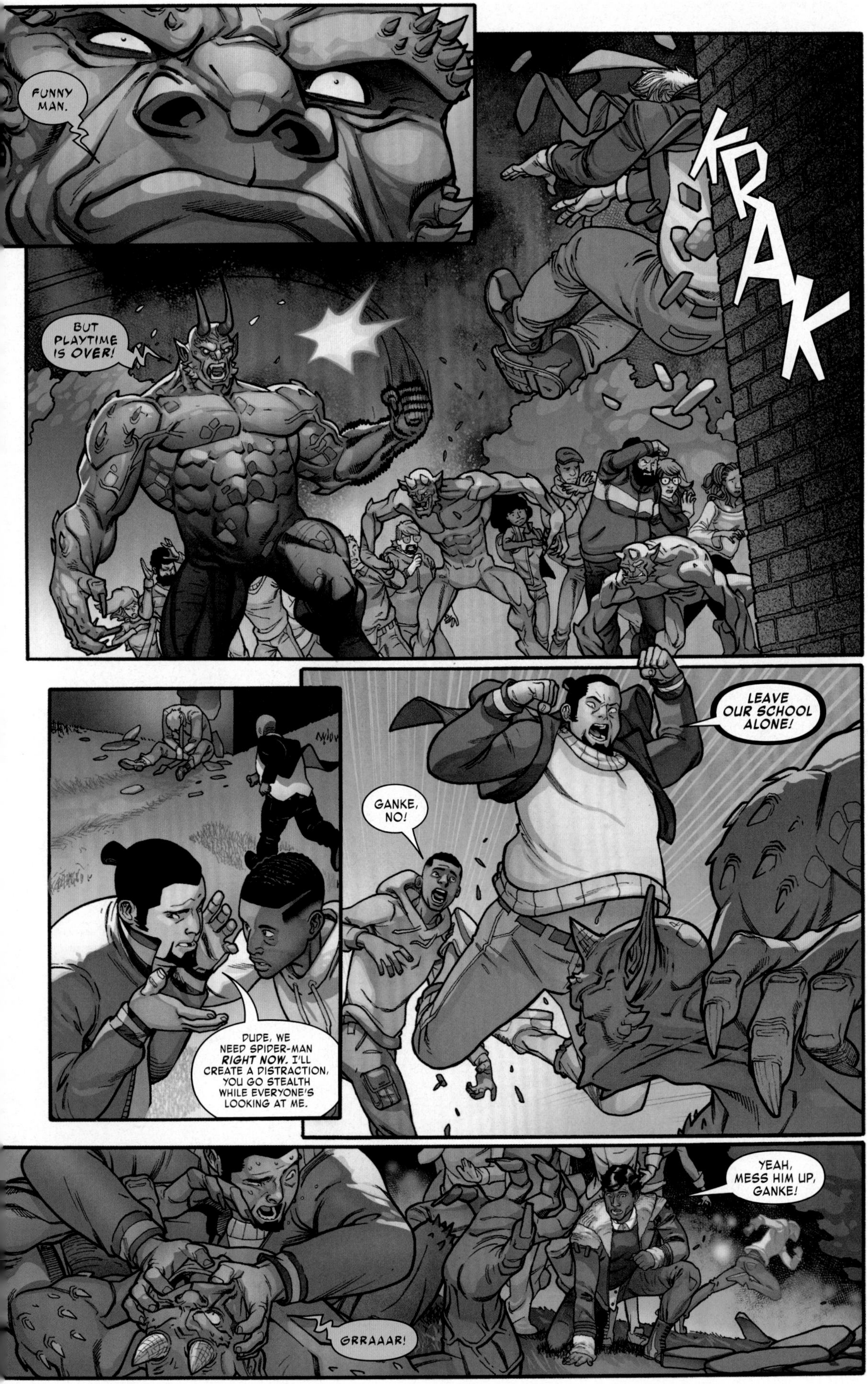
FUNNY MAN.
KRAK
BUT PLAYTIME IS OVER!
DUDE, WE NEED SPIDER-MAN RIGHT NOW. I'LL CREATE A DISTRACTION, YOU GO STEALTH WHILE EVERYONE'S LOOKING AT ME.
LEAVE OUR SCHOOL ALONE!
GANKE, NO!
YEAH, MESS HIM UP, GANKE!
GRRAAAR!

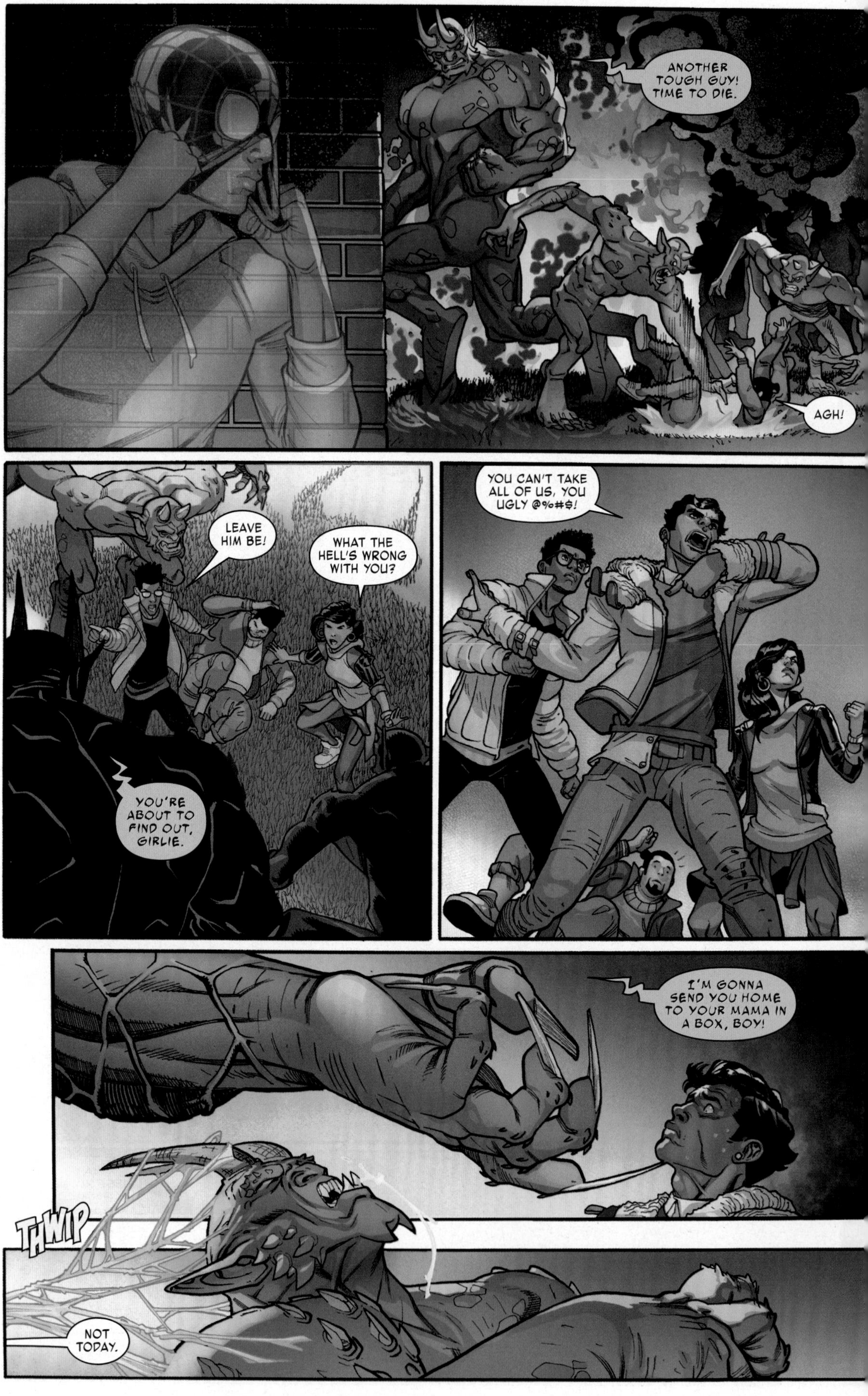
ANOTHER TOUGH GUY! TIME TO DIE.
AGH!
LEAVE HIM BE!
WHAT THE HELL'S WRONG WITH YOU?
YOU'RE ABOUT TO FIND OUT, GIRLIE.
YOU CAN'T TAKE ALL OF US, YOU UGLY @%#$!
I'M GONNA SEND YOU HOME TO YOUR MAMA IN A BOX, BOY!
THWIP
NOT TODAY.

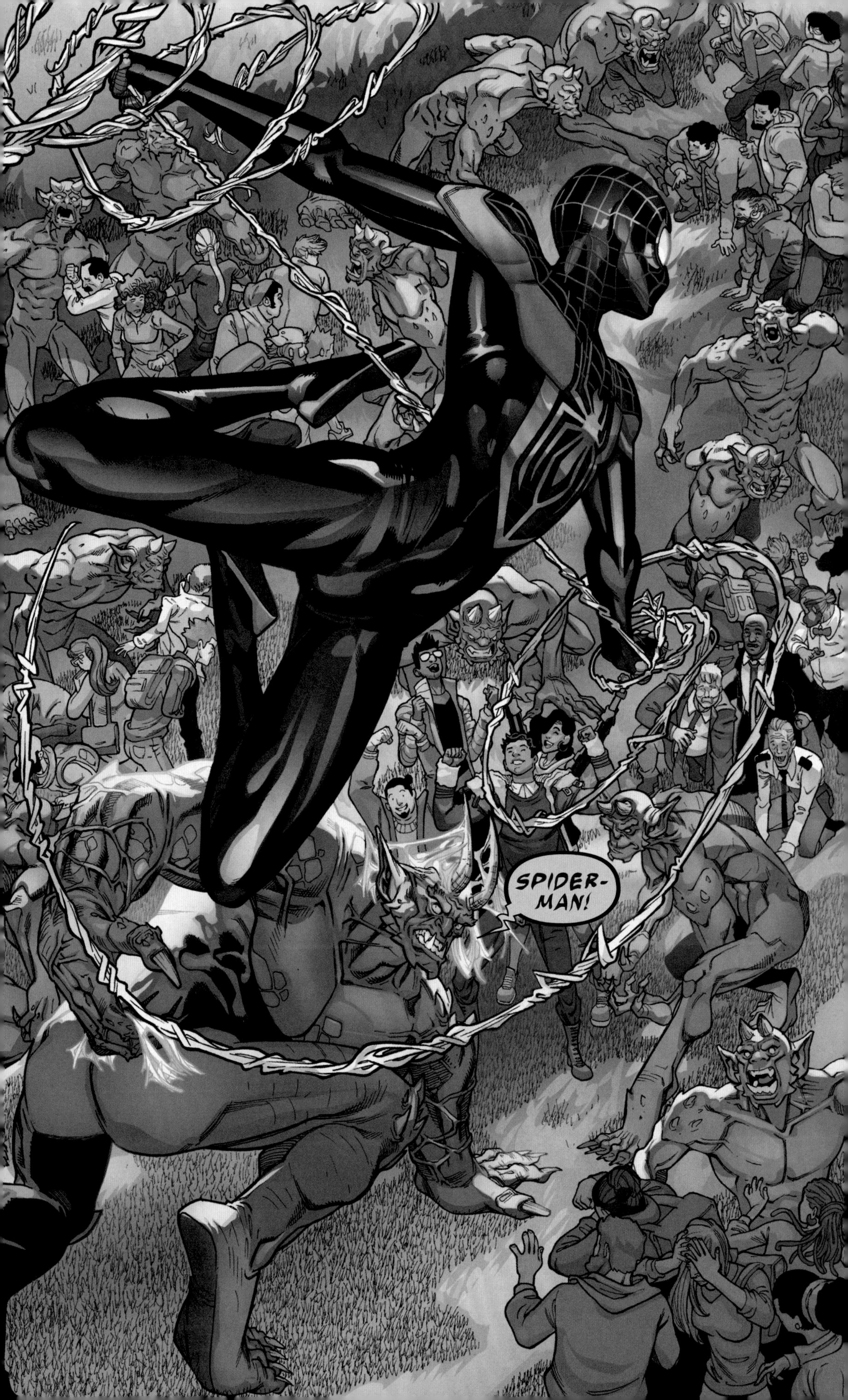
SPIDER-MAN!

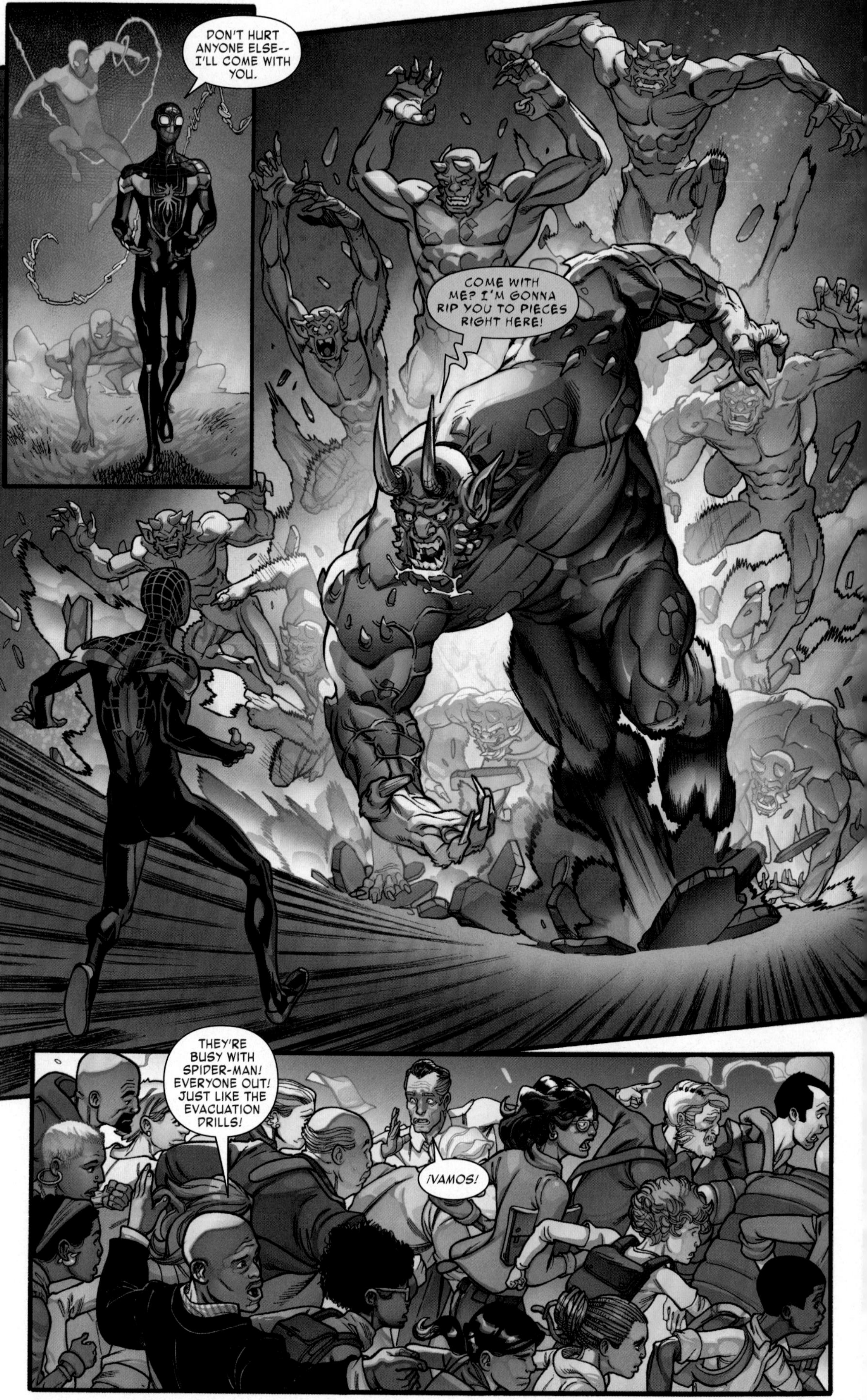
DON'T HURT ANYONE ELSE-- I'LL COME WITH YOU.
COME WITH ME? I'M GONNA RIP YOU TO PIECES RIGHT HERE!
THEY'RE BUSY WITH SPIDER-MAN! EVERYONE OUT! JUST LIKE THE EVACUATION DRILLS!
¡VAMOS!

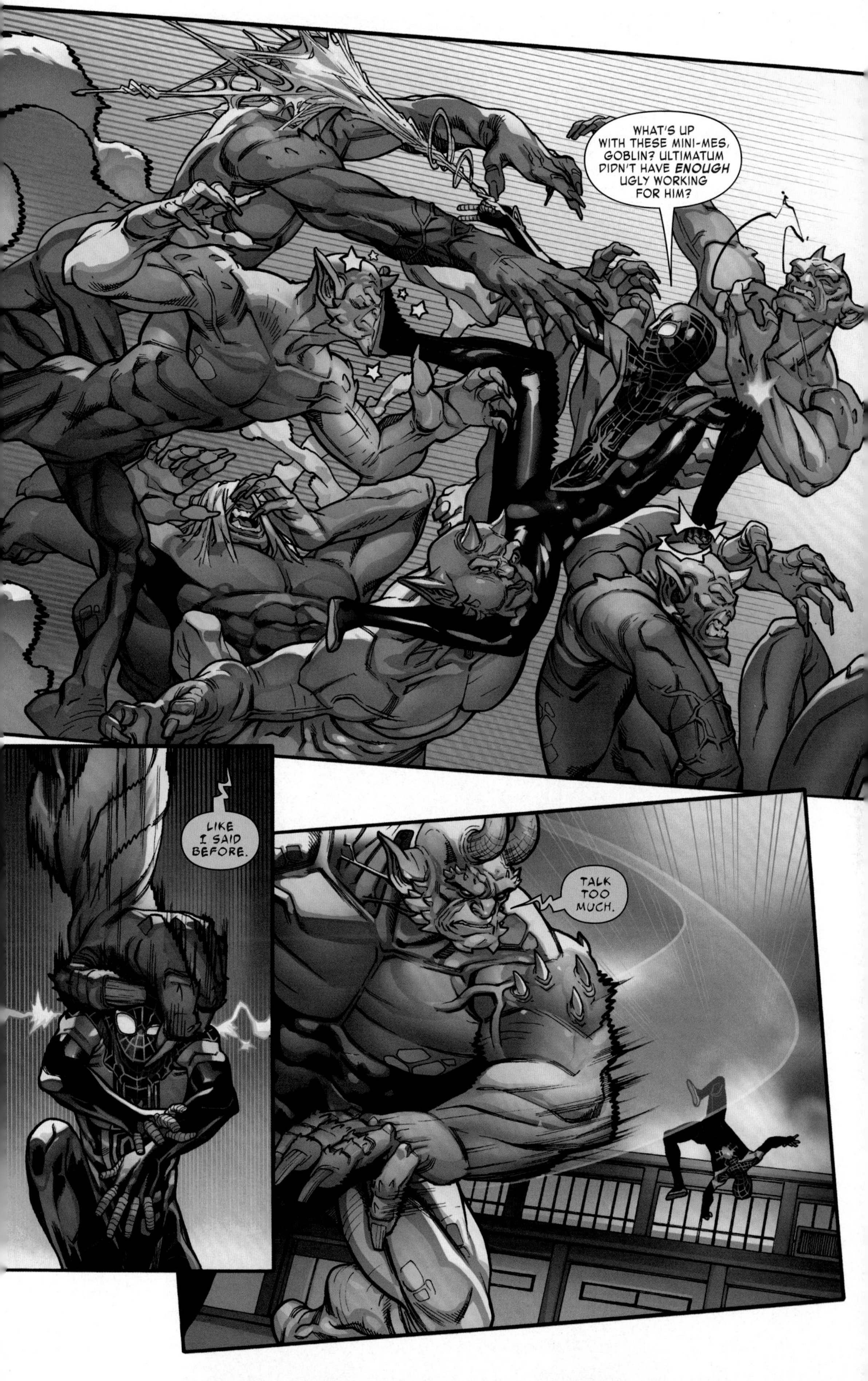
WHAT'S UP WITH THESE MINI-MES, GOBLIN? ULTIMATUM DIDN'T HAVE ENOUGH UGLY WORKING FOR HIM?
LIKE I SAID BEFORE.
TALK TOO MUCH.

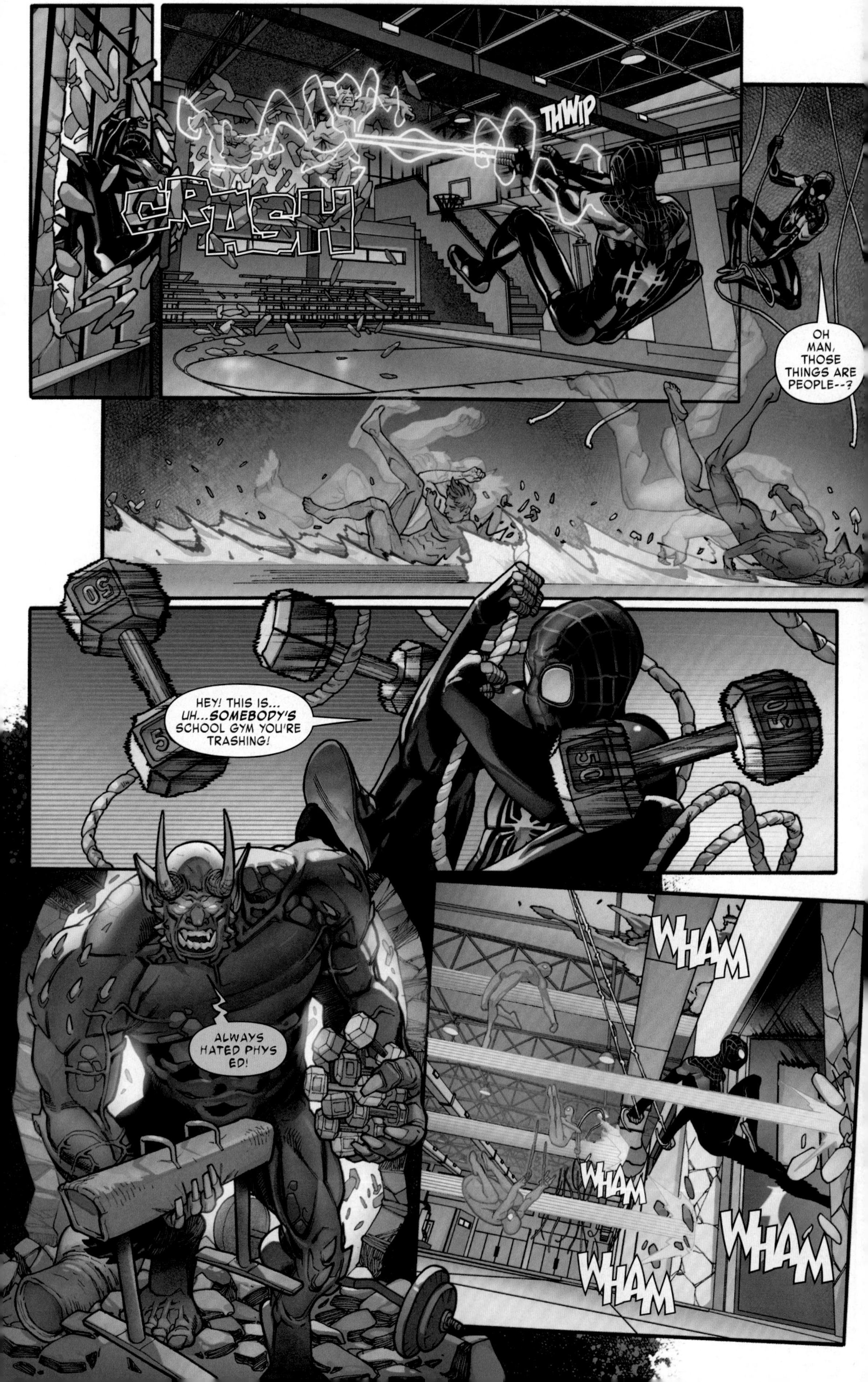
THWIP
CRASH
OH MAN, THOSE THINGS ARE PEOPLE--?
HEY! THIS IS... UH...SOMEBODY'S SCHOOL GYM YOU'RE TRASHING!
ALWAYS HATED PHYS ED!
WHAM
WHAM
WHAM
WHAM

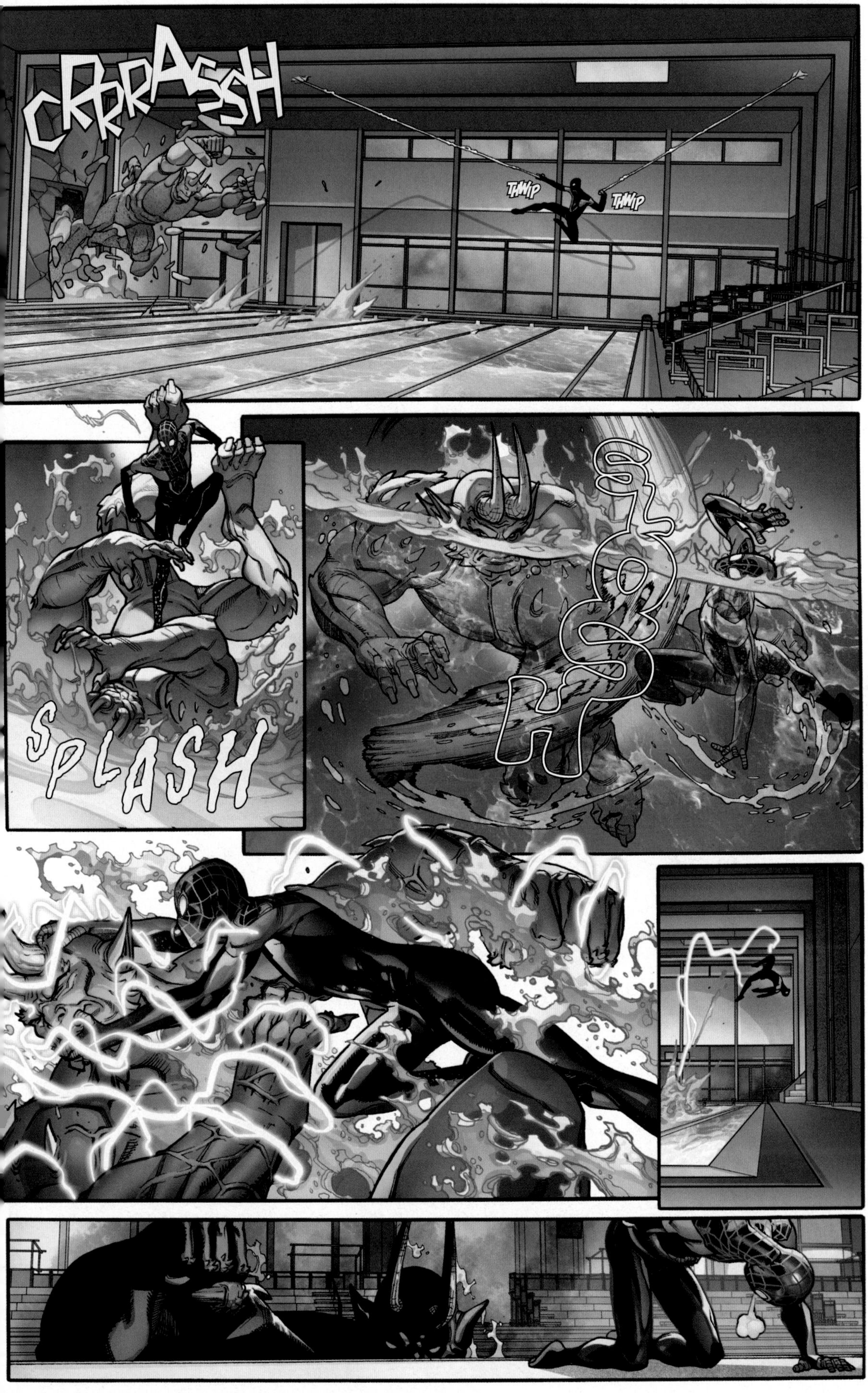
CRRRASSH
THWIP
THWIP
SPLASH
SPLOOSH

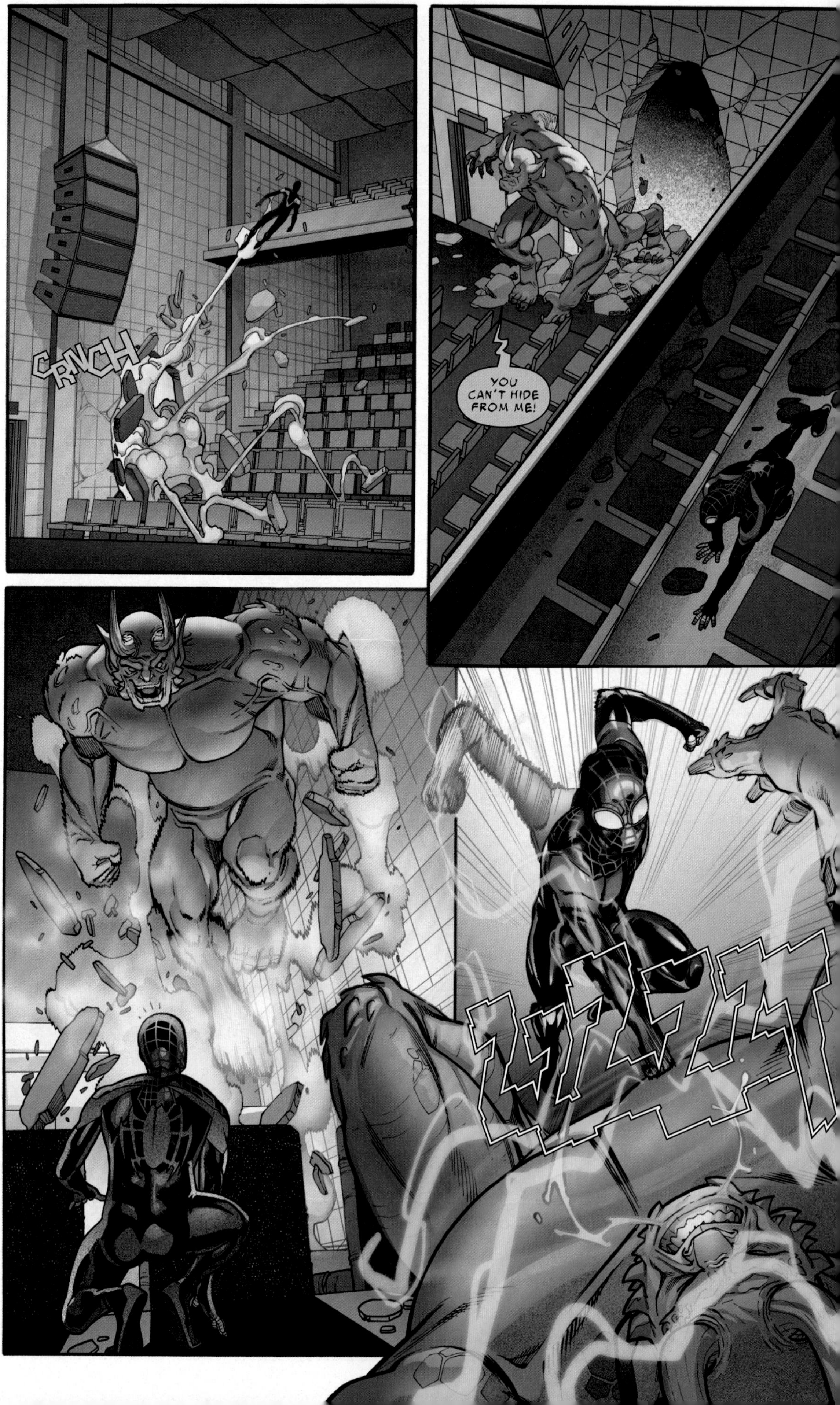
CRNCH
YOU CAN'T HIDE FROM ME!

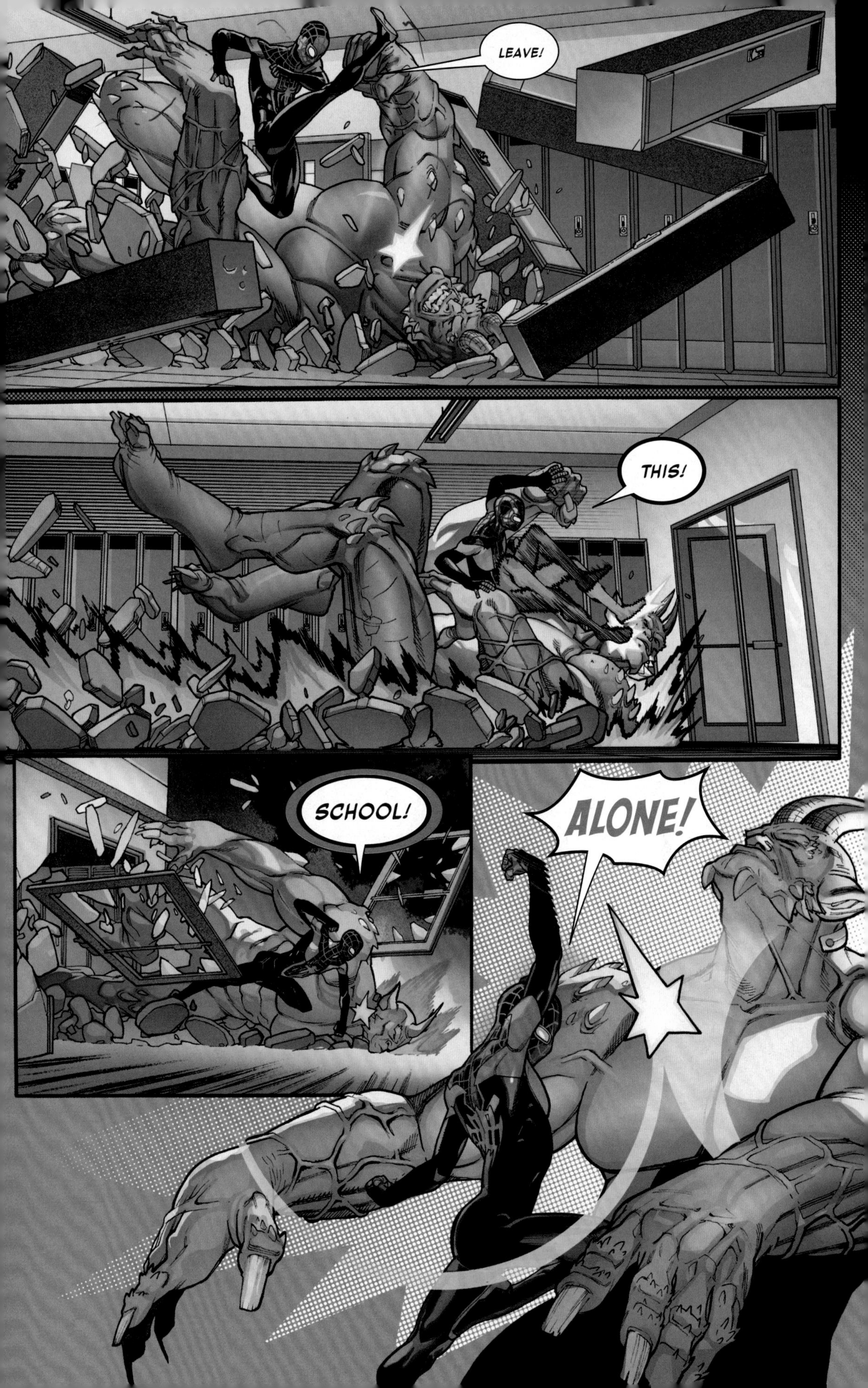
LEAVE!
THIS!
SCHOOL!
ALONE!

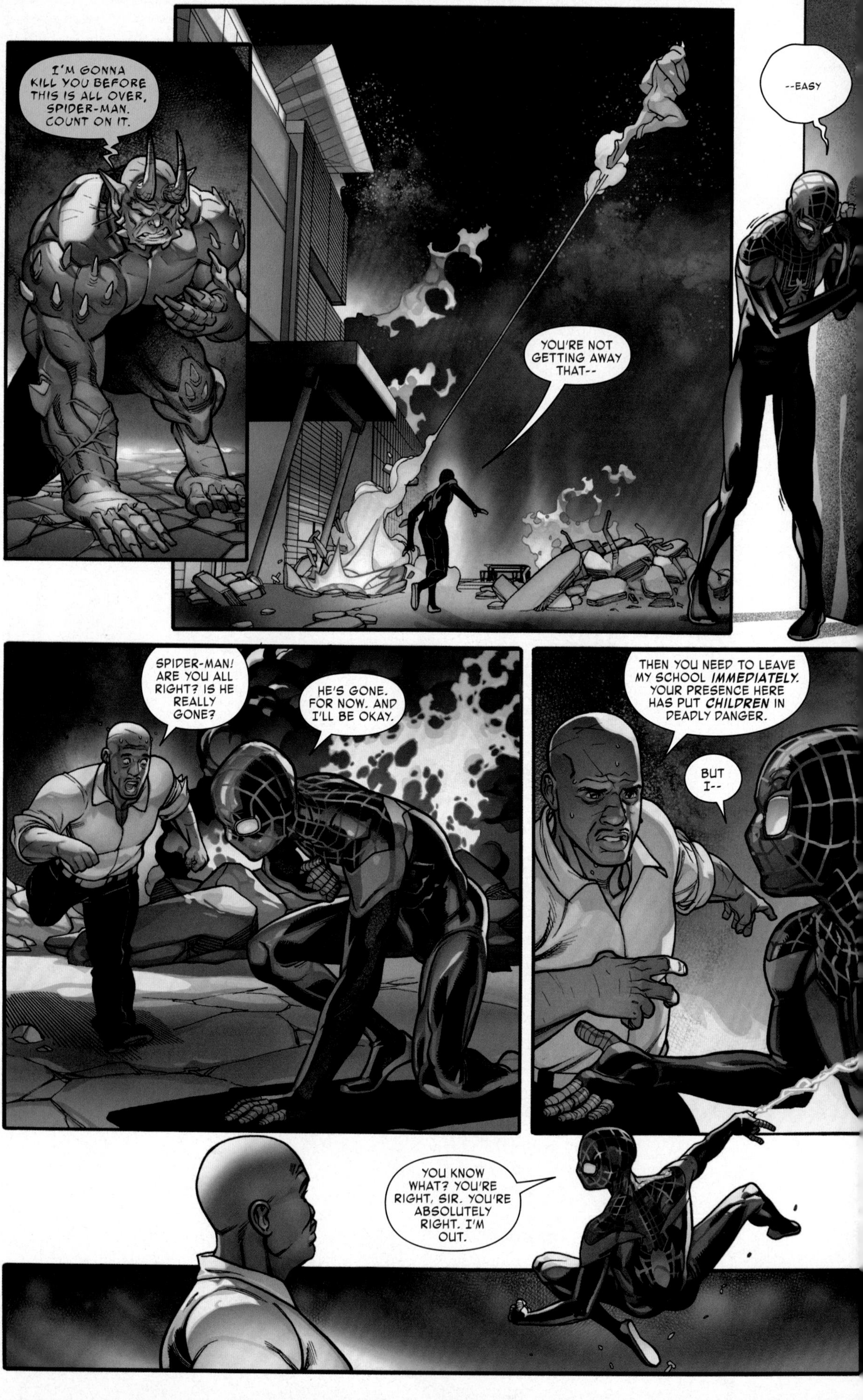

I'M GONNA KILL YOU BEFORE THIS IS ALL OVER, SPIDER-MAN. COUNT ON IT.
YOU'RE NOT GETTING AWAY THAT--
--EASY
SPIDER-MAN! ARE YOU ALL RIGHT? IS HE REALLY GONE?
HE'S GONE. FOR NOW. AND I'LL BE OKAY.
THEN YOU NEED TO LEAVE MY SCHOOL IMMEDIATELY. YOUR PRESENCE HERE HAS PUT CHILDREN IN DEADLY DANGER.
BUT I--
YOU KNOW WHAT? YOU'RE RIGHT, SIR. YOU'RE ABSOLUTELY RIGHT. I'M OUT.

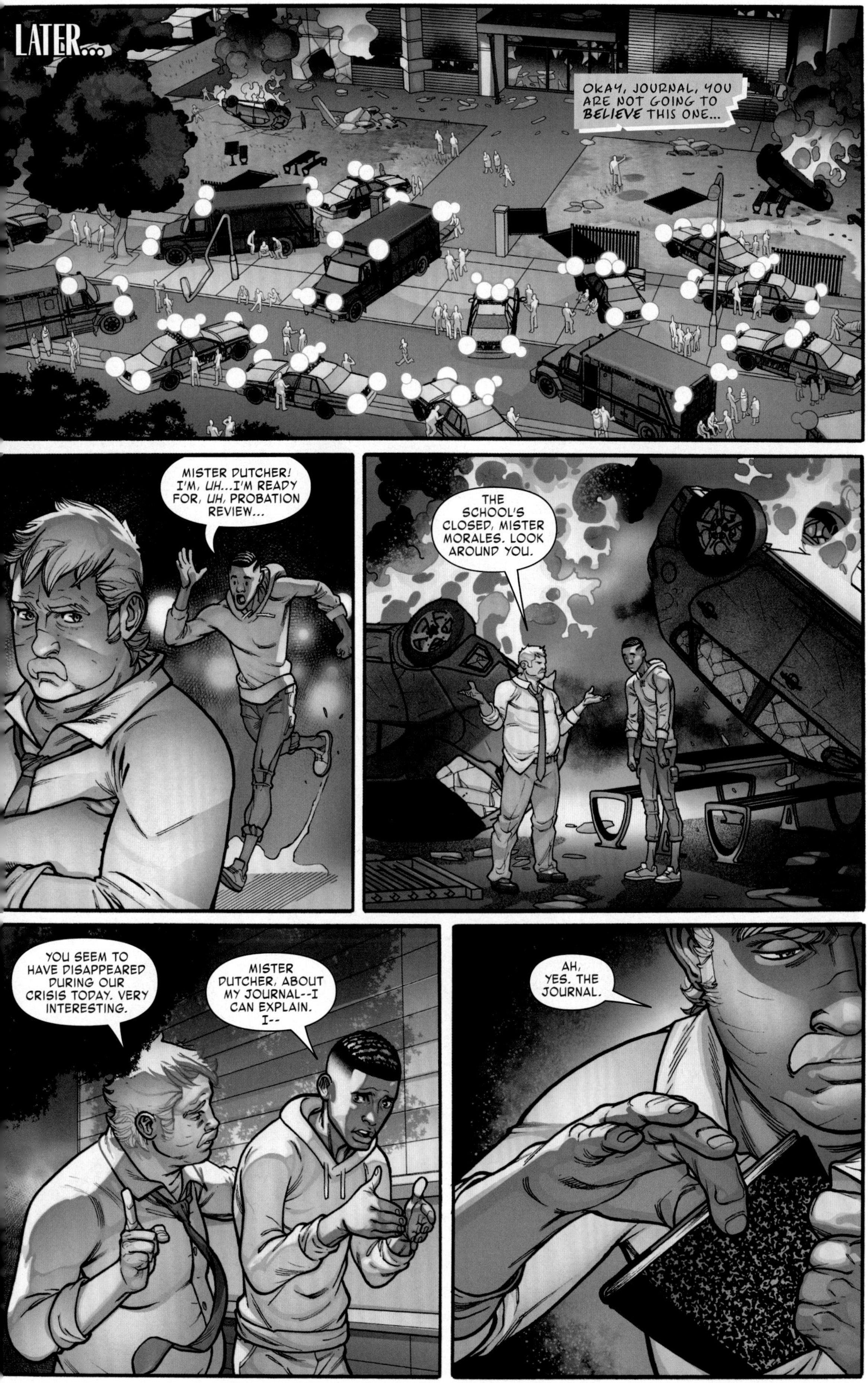
LATER...
OKAY, JOURNAL, YOU ARE NOT GOING TO BELIEVE THIS ONE...
MISTER DUTCHER! I'M, UH...I'M READY FOR, UH, PROBATION REVIEW...
THE SCHOOL'S CLOSED, MISTER MORALES. LOOK AROUND YOU.
YOU SEEM TO HAVE DISAPPEARED DURING OUR CRISIS TODAY. VERY INTERESTING.
MISTER DUTCHER, ABOUT MY JOURNAL--I CAN EXPLAIN. I--
AH, YES. THE JOURNAL.

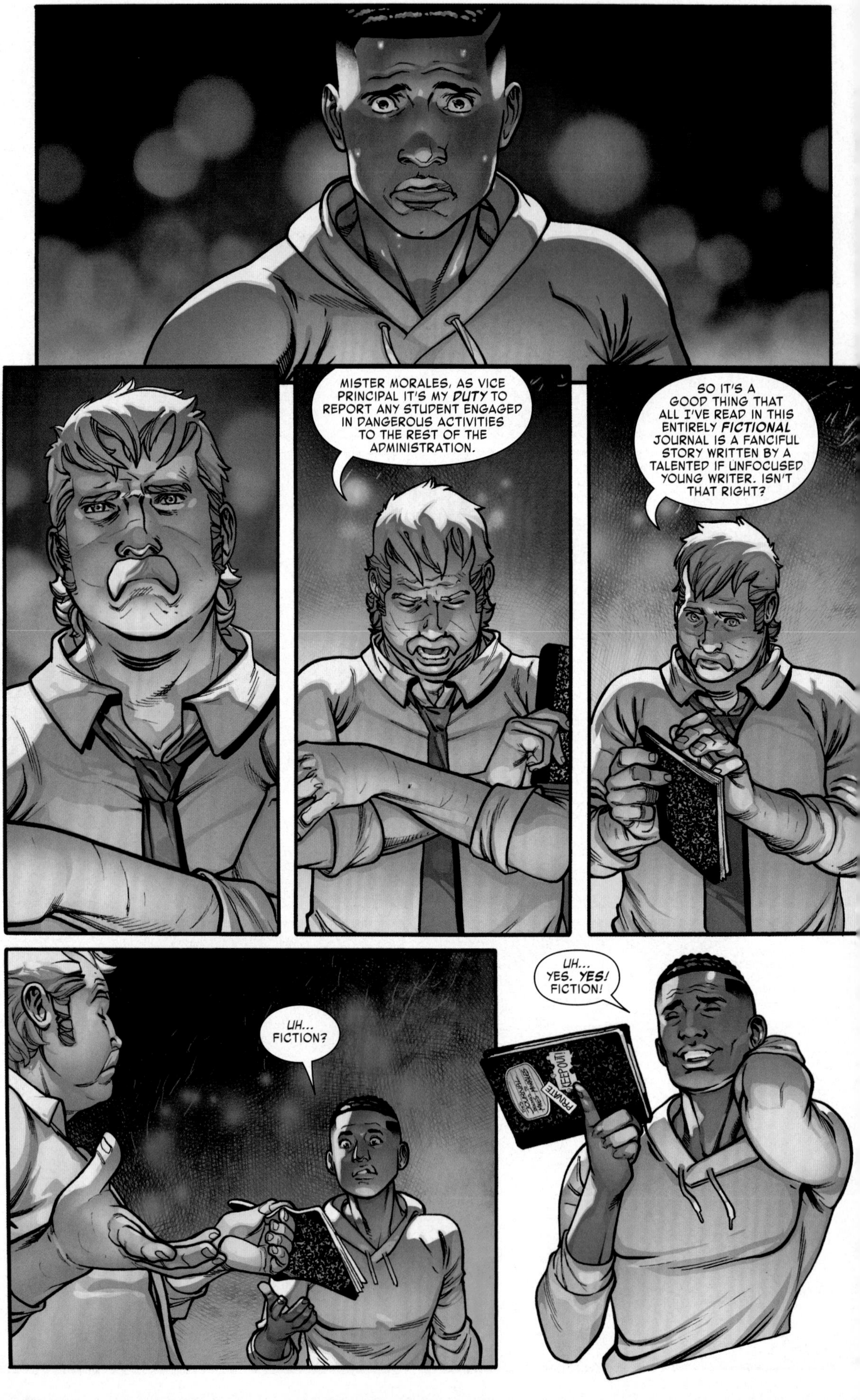
MISTER MORALES, AS VICE PRINCIPAL IT'S MY *DUTY* TO REPORT ANY STUDENT ENGAGED IN DANGEROUS ACTIVITIES TO THE REST OF THE ADMINISTRATION.
SO IT'S A GOOD THING THAT ALL I'VE READ IN THIS ENTIRELY *FICTIONAL* JOURNAL IS A FANCIFUL STORY WRITTEN BY A TALENTED IF UNFOCUSED YOUNG WRITER. ISN'T THAT RIGHT?
UH... FICTION?
UH... YES. *YES!* FICTION!
KEEP OUT!
PRIVATE

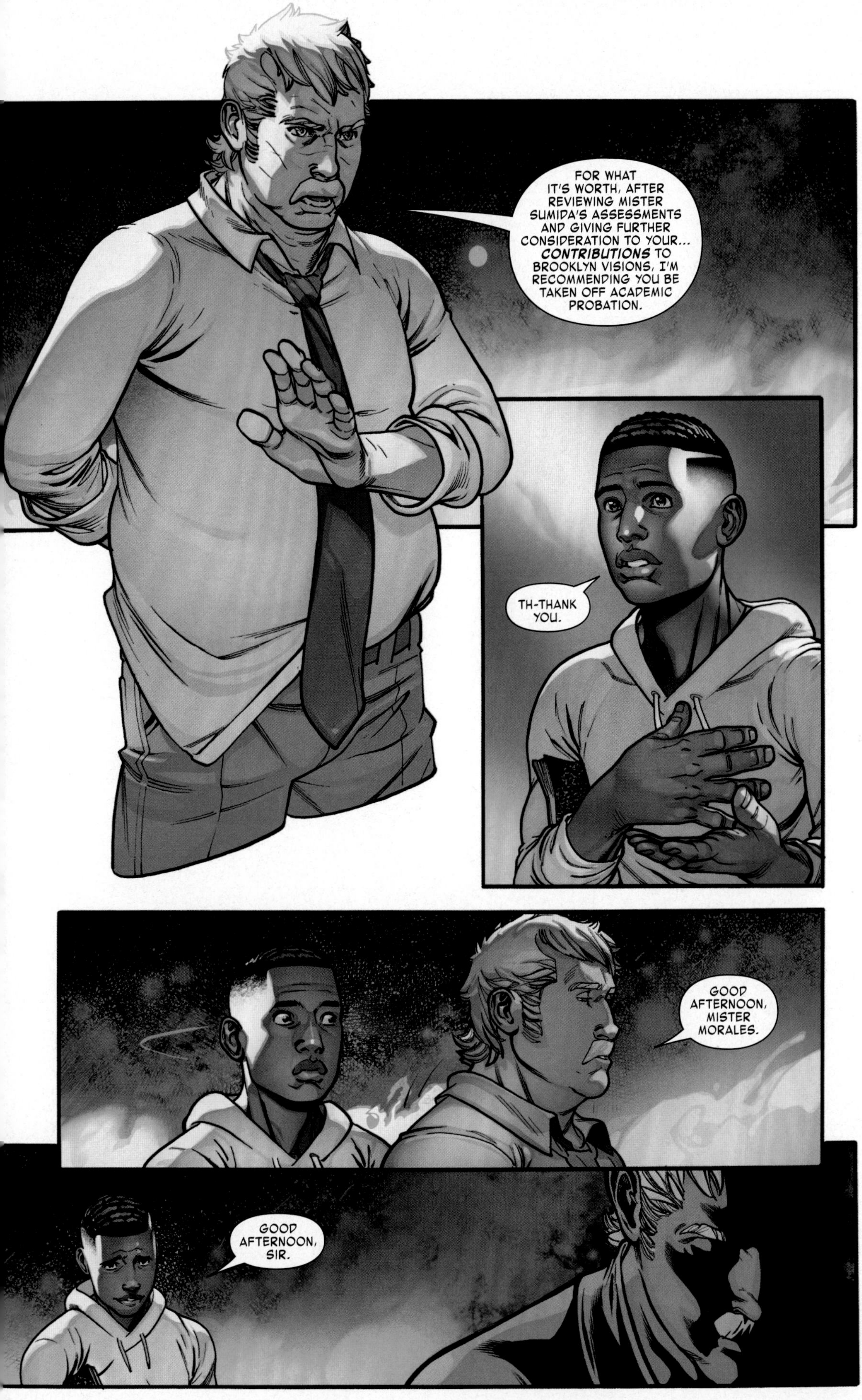
FOR WHAT IT'S WORTH, AFTER REVIEWING MISTER SUMIDA'S ASSESSMENTS AND GIVING FURTHER CONSIDERATION TO YOUR... *CONTRIBUTIONS* TO BROOKLYN VISIONS, I'M RECOMMENDING YOU BE TAKEN OFF ACADEMIC PROBATION.
TH-THANK YOU.
GOOD AFTERNOON, MISTER MORALES.
GOOD AFTERNOON, SIR.

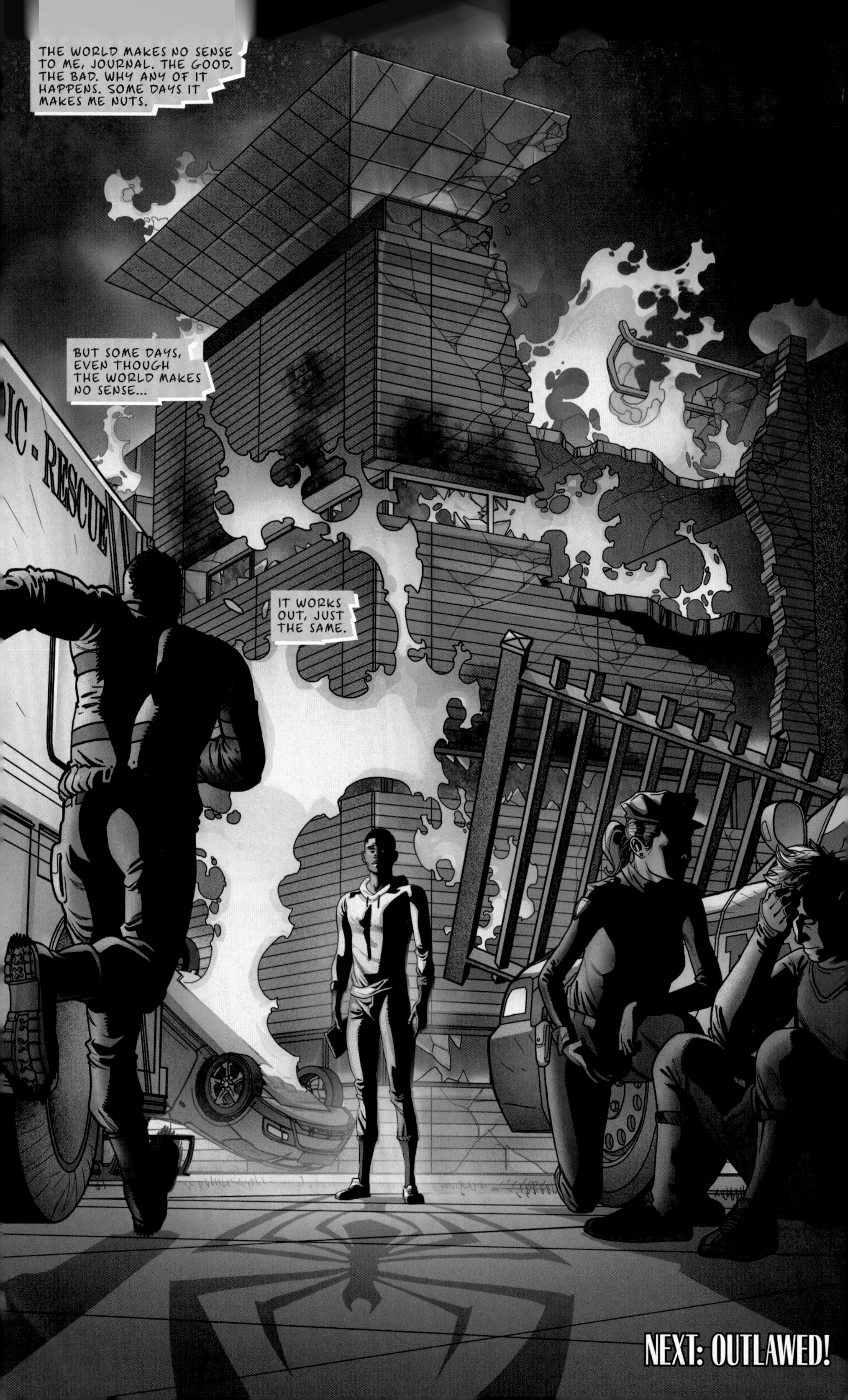
THE WORLD MAKES NO SENSE TO ME, JOURNAL. THE GOOD. THE BAD. WHY ANY OF IT HAPPENS. SOME DAYS IT MAKES ME NUTS.
BUT SOME DAYS, EVEN THOUGH THE WORLD MAKES NO SENSE...
IT WORKS OUT, JUST THE SAME.
IC - RESCUE
NEXT: OUTLAWED!

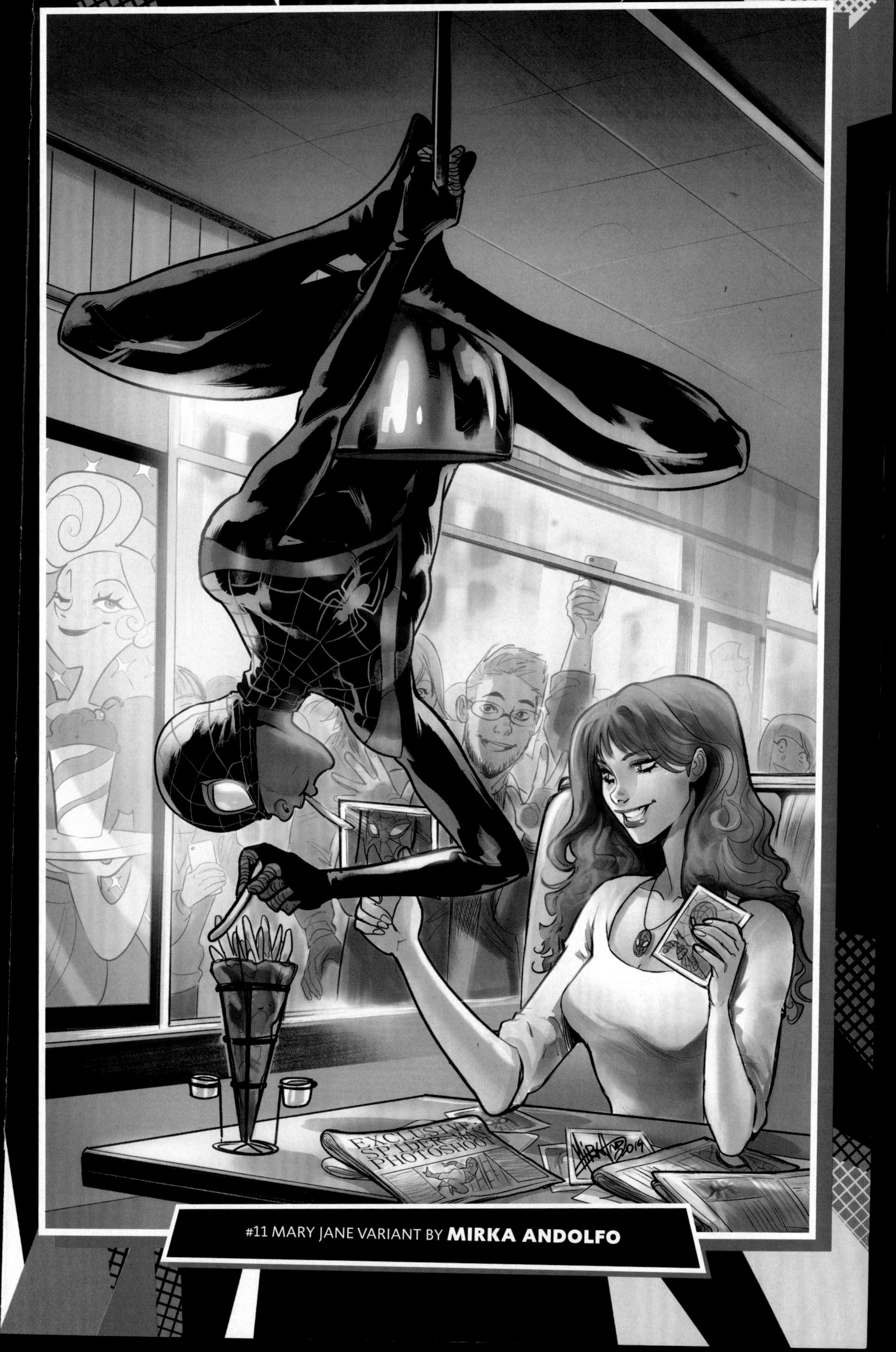
EXCLUSIVE
PHOTOSHOOT

#11 MARY JANE VARIANT BY **MIRKA ANDOLFO**

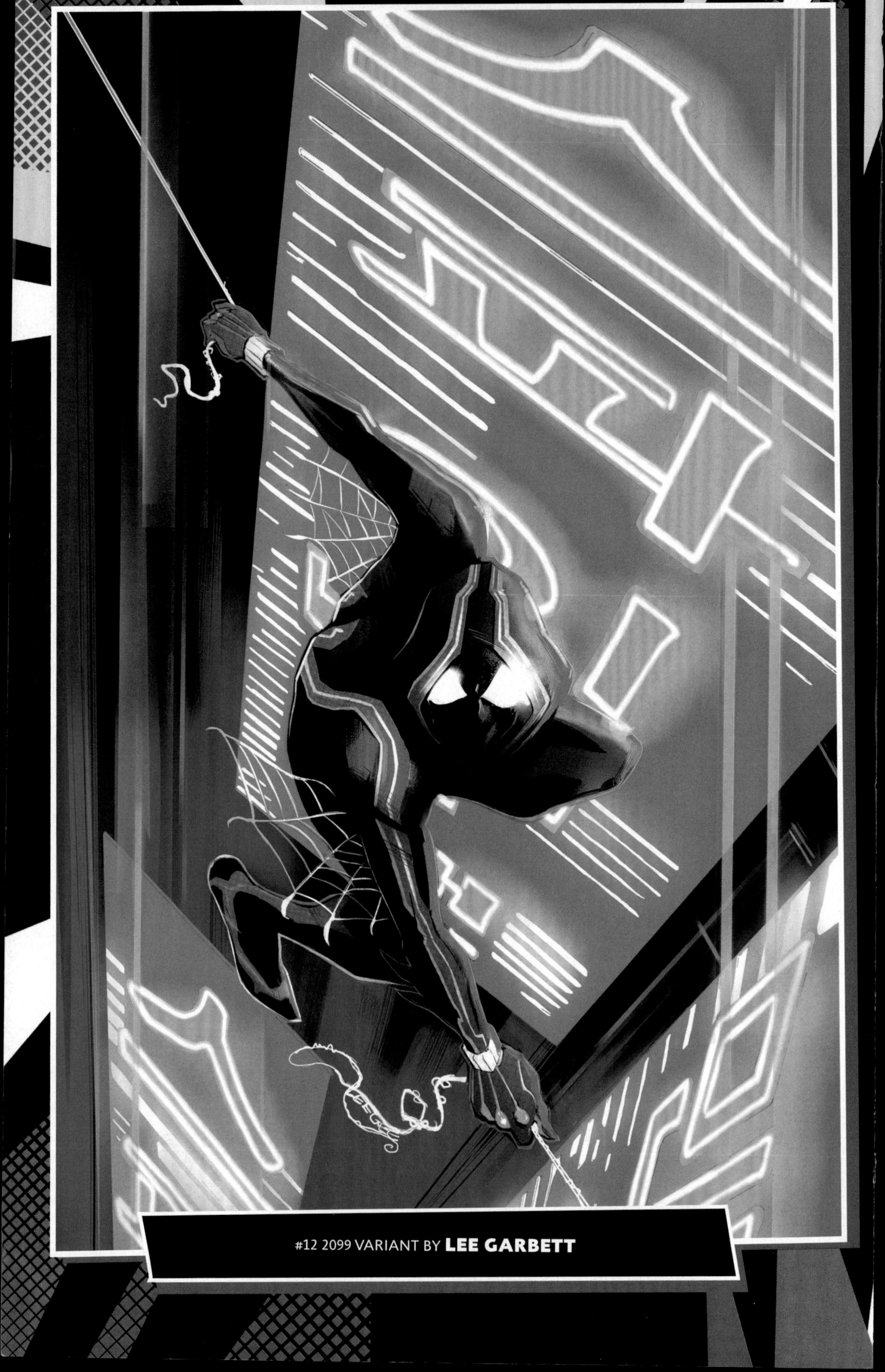

#12 2099 VARIANT BY **LEE GARBETT**

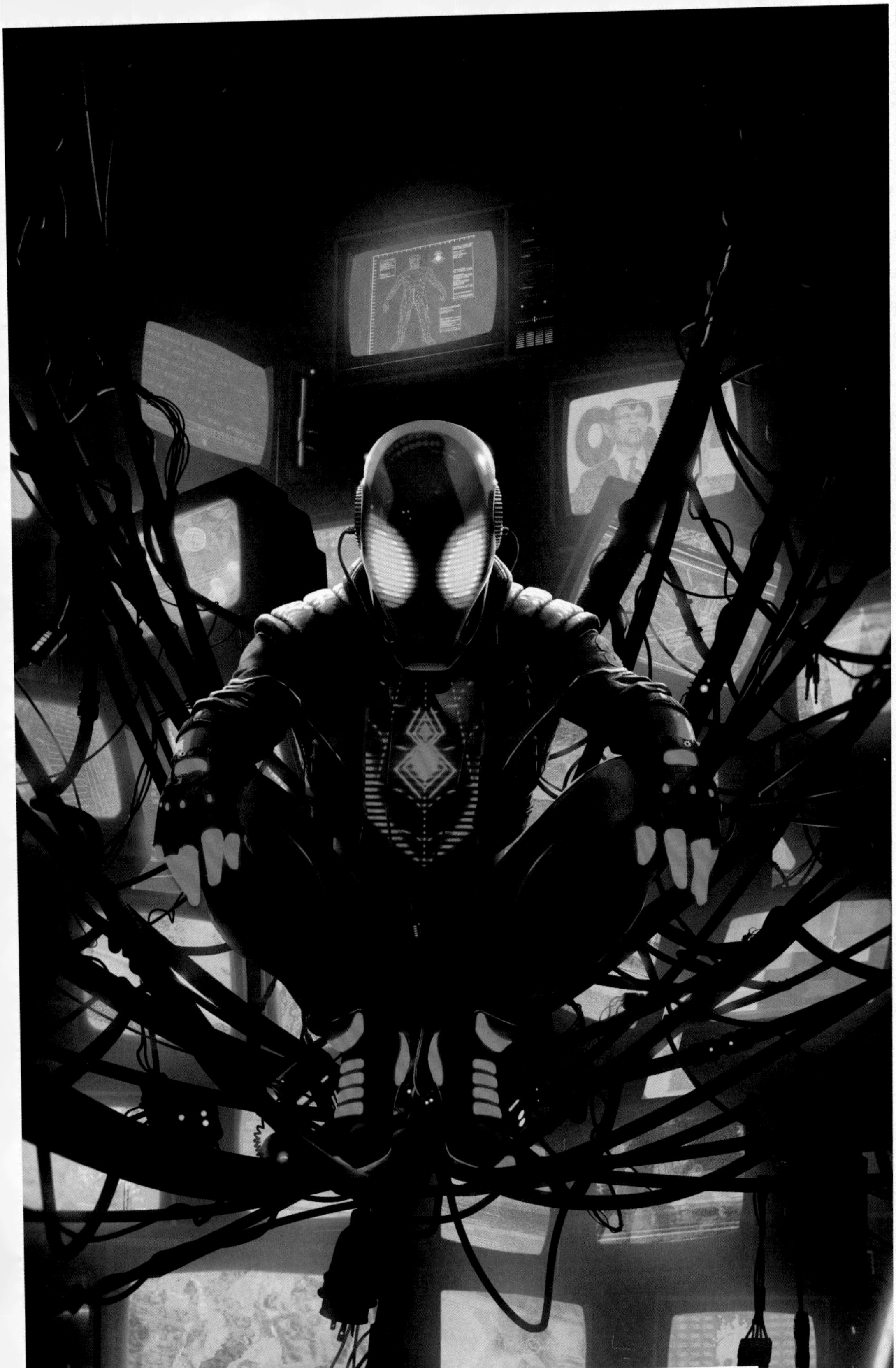

#13 2020 VARIANT BY **RAHZZAH**

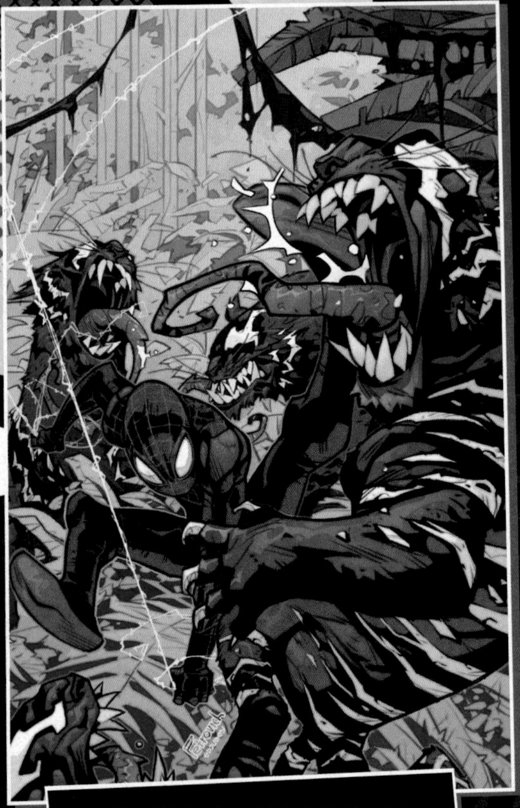

#13 VENOM ISLAND VARIANT BY
EDUARD PETROVICH

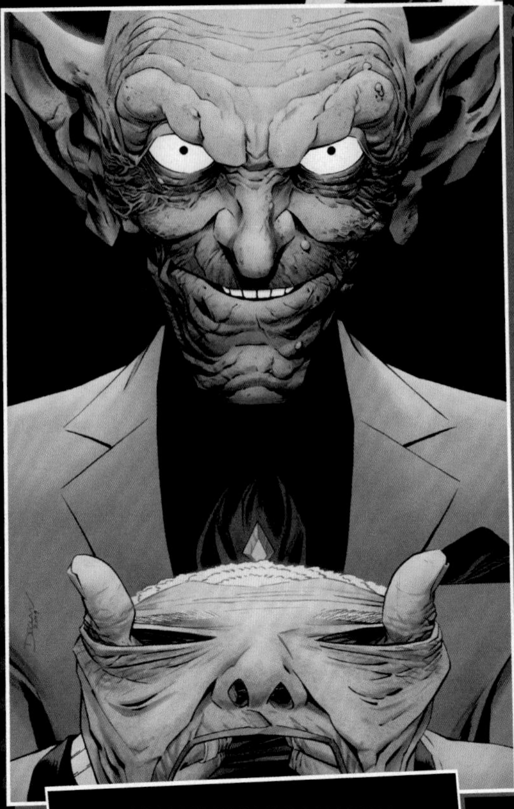

#14 MARVELS X VARIANT BY
DECLAN SHALVEY

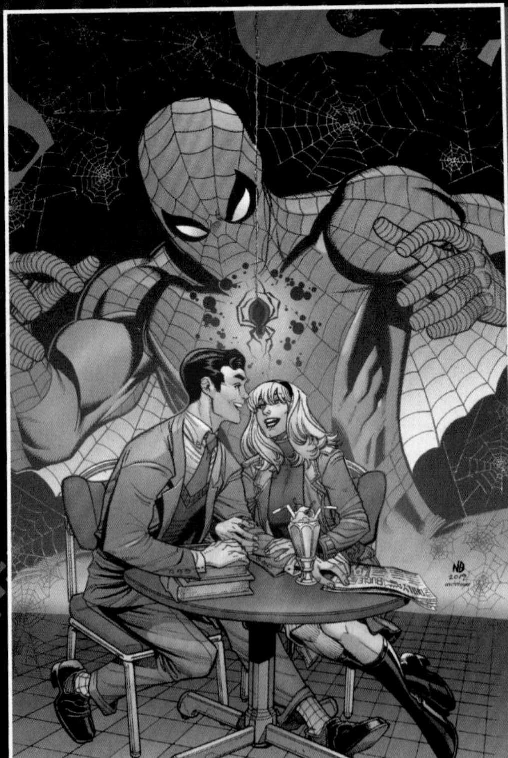

#15 GWEN STACY VARIANT BY
NICK BRADSHAW & **ERICK ARCINIEGA**